To John,

With love
from Claire x
in a post-Brexit
Britain!

CK

Sex & Power

A Manual on Male-Female Relations

Simon Sheppard

There are two kinds of people in this world – those who separate people into two kinds of people, and those who don't.

First published in Great Britain 2013

Second printing 2015. Some chapters
have been moved and revised for greater
clarity. Pages 68 and 128 are new.

Cover design by Charles Krafft
featuring a portrait by Walter Klett.

ISBN 978 1 901240 24 5

The Heretical Press
PO Box 301, Carshalton, Surrey SM5 4QW

Contents

'Leslie' was an English 33-year-old who had undergone a sex-change from male to female. Once there had been an altercation in a traffic jam with a male car driver. He had rudely interrupted Leslie's course and then asked 'Are you a woman or what?' This had so incensed Leslie that she had picked up her racing bike and wiped it all over the bonnet of the man's car, heavily scratching it. Her display of extreme male aggression would probably have been sufficient to discourage retaliation.

Another time someone was visiting Leslie's North London council flat, bragging that through his contacts he could get anything. Leslie left the room and returned a few moments later with several hundred pounds, the proceeds of the recent sale of some item of audio equipment or other, and laid it on the table. 'Get me a shooter' she said, 'I want a sub-machine gun.'

Relations between Leslie and I had soured since she had taken away a Uher tape recorder, promising to buy it for £50, but never paid for it. A mutual friend warned me that if I called on her to collect the debt I risked being beaten up.

A year or two later I was conducting a survey at the side of a road in North London and Leslie came walking along. She invited me round the corner for a fight.

Blue-shaded boxes contain original material, yellow denotes material from other sources.

1 Sex Differences

Why can't a woman be more like a man?

The most important sex organ in humans is not the genitals, but the brain. Mating in animals follows automatically from simple cues, such as the scent emitted by a female in season, but human sexual activity involves both lower and higher functions of the brain.

Sexual arousal from photographs

We can find photographs of naked bodies are arousing, when we know it is not an actual object we can touch and engage with. This is our lower brain speaking to us with messages that have impelled our behaviour for the millions of years of our evolutionary history – our *phylogeny*, the entire evolutionary development of the human species.

Differences in male and female brains

Male and female brains differ greatly, because the male brain is modified a few weeks after conception. The Y chromosome is responsible for creating a pair of testes and these send a sequence of testosterone pulses to condition the developing male brain. The quantities of testosterone involved are minute: millionths of a gramme. No such sequence takes place for females – for mammals the default state is to be female. Sexualization follows an uninterrupted course. For birds it is the opposite way round: the default state is to be male.

Some of this is covered in the book *BrainSex* by Anne Moir and David Jessel, but since these sex differences are neglected in modern politically correct discourse, this chapter will summarise the current knowledge and get it out of the way.

The corpus collosum links the two halves of the brain

One physical, readily measurable difference in male and female brains is the width of the corpus collosum. This structure links the two cerebral hemispheres, the left and right halves of the brain. Broadly speaking, logical and speech functions are situated in the left hemisphere, with artistic and emotional processes in the right. In females the corpus collosum is wide and in males it is narrow, and this accounts for the great capacity females have for sensing and expressing emotions. Typically, males are confused about their emotions and might only discuss them in the early hours of the morning after too many drinks. In contrast a favourite female occupation is to sit around thinking about and discussing her feelings, particularly with other females.

Logic is mixed with emotion

This difference between the sexes stems directly from the width of the corpus collosum. With around four times the neural pathways in females it forms a sort of super-highway for processing emotions, plus a tendency to mix

For both sexes, the left cerebral hemisphere is dominant for language, logic, analytical thought and complex motor behaviour, while the right hemisphere is engaged with non-linguistic functions such as recognition of faces, music and intuition.

logic and emotion together. In males the narrowness of the corpus collosum results in feelings quite literally being bottled up.

Speech problems usually afflict men

In general, the more feminine the brain, the more diffuse is its organisation. Aphasias – language problems – are rare in females, with men being nearly four times more likely to stammer than women. Prosopagnosia, the inability to recognise faces, like autism, appears similarly to be a disorder mainly affecting males (the author being among them).

Effects of pre-natal stress

While most people are right-handed, some are 'mixed-handed.' They might favour writing with one hand but catching a ball with the other. Several studies have linked mixed-handedness with mothers having endured stress during pregnancy, and this suggests that the location of many brain functions is fluid. The early formation of a wide corpus collosum will lead to a general diffusion of functions in the female brain subsequently.

Hormonal influence during gestation and puberty

Sexualization is a two-stage process: firstly in the foetus, then at puberty when a second surge of hormones causes the testes to descend or menstruation to begin (menarche). Hormones affect us throughout our life but their influence is never so strong as during brain formation of the unborn baby. This formation phase defines male sexuality, including homosexuality.

How a process works is often revealed by the manner in which it fails. Ruthlessly simplifying, we can use male homosexuality to illustrate how the male brain is formed.

Perhaps as early as six weeks after conception a sequence of testosterone pulses takes place which fix several features. Two will be used to illustrate. The first is 'mating object' and the second is denoted, vaguely but meaningfully, 'sexual identity.'

Why can't a woman be more like a man?
Men are so decent, such regular chaps;
Ready to help you through any mishaps;
Ready to buck you up whenever you're glum.
Why can't a woman be a chum?

Why is thinking something women never do?
And why is logic never even tried?
Straightening up their hair is all they ever do.
Why don't they straighten up the mess that's inside?

My Fair Lady (1964)

A sequence of testosterone pulses produces different outcomes of 'sexual identity' and 'mating object'

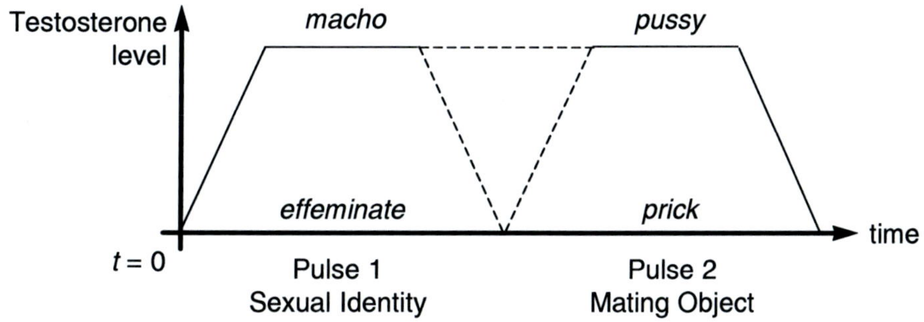

Male and female mating objects

The normal male mating object is the vagina, sight of which he finds fascinating and arousing, while the male homosexual and female mating object is the penis.

Sexual arousal on two levels

The proper fixing of mating object in the developing male brain is essential for procreation and species survival; it is a vital evolutionary requirement and operates at the basic biological level. However we do not attempt to mate every time we are aroused and this involves higher brain functions and conscious control.

A masculine sexual identity is associated with vigour and assertiveness, while the female expectation is of sensitivity and passivity. Four combinations of mating object and sexual identity can follow from high or low testosterone pulses, as shown in the diagram.

Different types of male homosexual

With two high testosterone pulses a normal male brain results – a masculine heterosexual. If the first pulse is low we get an effeminate heterosexual (low then high testosterone); with an interruption in the second pulse we get a macho homosexual (high then low); with both pulses absent we get an effeminate homosexual.

The HPA axis

Of course 'sexual identity' is a glaring over-simplification. Various conditioning stages have been proposed and it is easy to envisage a dozen or more. Other features could include the width of the corpus collosum, as already mentioned, and the operation of the hypothalamus (or more correctly, the hypothalamic region, the HPA axis). It is conceivable – if not likely – that the width of the corpus collosum and the functions of the hypothalamus are modified by testosterone pulses in exactly the same way.

Confirmation of the scheme

A great deal of evidence, from both animals and humans, has accumulated to confirm this scheme. In humans, to quote just two findings, the administration of hormones (e.g. to prevent miscarriage) has been shown to alter the function of the hypothalamus, and male babies were affected when an oestrogen-like substance, diethylstilbesterol, was given to diabetic mothers in the 1950s and 60s.

Functions of the hypothalamus

In females the hypothalamus acts like an oscillator, modulating hormones according to the time of the month. The female hormone progesterone gradually builds up to a peak, then falls back to zero, and this pattern repeats every menstrual cycle. In the male the hypothalamus acts as a stabiliser, smoothing out hormonal variations.

Hormonal modulation in the female. Function of the hypothalamus

Male homosexuals can be separated into two groups according to the type of hypothalamus they have. After being experimentally injected with a small amount of hormone some individuals respond with a female-type hypothalamus, increasing the change, while others have a male-type one which attempts to suppress the change and stabilise it.

This is not the end of the matter regarding hormones of course. Testosterone (or its more potent form, dihydroxytestosterone, DHT) produces the obvious physical changes in the genitalia which cause the midwife to exclaim 'It's a boy!' or 'It's a girl!' as a new person emerges. Under the influence of DHT what would be the ovaries become testes, the clitoris becomes a penis, the labia major becomes a scrotum and the labia minora becomes a urethra.

A female goes on to become male

Extra sexes

This process is so complex it's remarkable that it doesn't go wrong more often. Usually the ovaries produce small amounts of testosterone, but in females with Turner's syndrome the influence of testosterone is completely absent. As girls they get lost coming home from school and sometimes even inside their own house. They dream of romance and having children, and baby-sit at every available opportunity. As adults however, they are often barren. These 'super-females' represent an extreme form of femininity, either entirely devoid of testosterone or insensitive to it.

Turner's syndrome and other sexes

In practice there are more than just two sexes. One practically invisible extra sex is XYY males, while yet another variant, XXY males, are often confused about their sexual identity. Numerous other conditions exist.

Sex distributions

The complex male conditioning process accounts in part for the greater variation we see in males. While females do not deviate much from the average, males vary much more. An individual who is exceptionally dull-witted or intelligent will almost always be male. Although the average intelligence of males and females is similar, the distributions are different (Graph 1).

Males vary more than females

Graph 1. Coincident bell curves of male and female intelligence

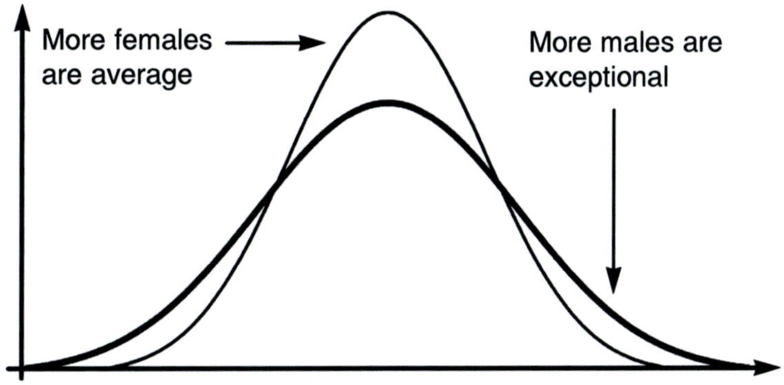

Sensitivity to touch at birth

For a few traits there are extreme differences between the sexes, some apparent just a few hours after birth. One is sensitivity to touch: in some tests even the most insensitive female baby is still more sensitive than the most sensitive male baby. There is no overlap at all (Graph 2).

Graph 2. Non-overlapping bell curves of male and female sensitivity to touch

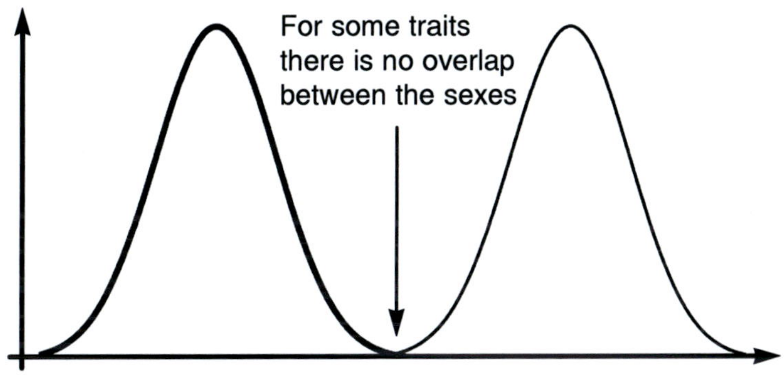

Mostly there is overlap

For many traits however, there is overlap. The most obvious example is height: males are generally taller than females, but there are tall females and short males. Most traits probably follow this pattern (Graph 3).

Graph 3. Overlapping bell curves of male and female height

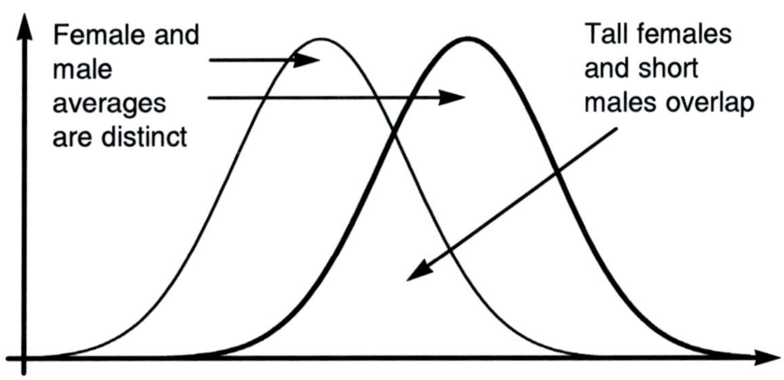

Males expressing female traits

Many males express female characteristics, because generations of females have been selecting males with feminine traits as husbands (e.g. monogamous males). However, the converse does not hold: females expressing masculine traits are rare because they are less likely to have children, and over evolutionary time their genes tend to disappear from the population.

More males express female traits than females express male ones

It follows that when a male expresses a female trait, because males vary more, the female trait can be expressed more strongly than in females themselves. This explains why top chefs are almost invariably male. Females have a superior sense of taste and smell (in fact taste and smell are intimately entwined), but when a male exhibits this feminine trait his senses can be exceptionally acute.

Males can express female traits very strongly

This pattern is not limited to taste and smell; any female trait can be expressed by a male in exaggerated form. This accounts for exceptionally loquacious males and, perhaps, the outrageously camp homosexual. Males can express feminine characteristics with masculine force.

Female acquire male adaptations

An important component in the evolutionary process is a law Darwin called 'the equal transmission of characters,' which applies to all mammals. Back in the jungles, plains, prairies and small settlements of 50-150 people in which we have spent most of our past, male traits developed chiefly from hunting prowess and contests for females. Before very long, characters thus acquired by the male appear in the female. If not for the equal transmission of characters, Darwin said, women would be as unintelligent in comparison to men as the peahen is drab compared to the peacock. The human female would just be a dim-witted, though perhaps pretty, breeding machine.

Darwin's 'equal transmission of characters'

Probably the equal transmission of characters is the engine which has impelled the extraordinary speed of human evolution. As male adaptations (such as intelligence) are acquired by the female, effectively the male has to compete with a copy of himself. He must constantly innovate, fuelling an

A 2005 paper by Haier et al., 'The neuroanatomy of general intelligence: sex matters,' reproduced magnetic resonance images of actual activity in male and female brains. Women show many more white matter areas (associated with neural communication) and far fewer gray matter areas (related to processing) than men. The authors concluded that men and women achieve similar IQ results using different regions of the brain.

> It is indeed fortunate that the law of equal transmission of characters to both sexes prevails with mammals; otherwise it is probable that man would have become as superior in mental endowment to woman, as the peacock is in ornamental plumage to the peahen.
>
> Darwin, *The Descent of Man*

Humans' rapid evolutionary progress

evolutionary advance which has been practically exponential. Humans have progressed enormously in a relatively short time span, developing behaviours and intricate social structures which have taken other social animals, notably ants, many hundreds of millions of years to achieve.

Dominance by divergence – the origin of sex

Notwithstanding, male variability is the ultimate assurance of male predominance. A uniform system (or population) will be vulnerable in some way, and variation in its competitor guarantees that its weak spot will eventually be struck upon. I call this *dominance by divergence*. Sooner or later from the diverse system will emerge an individual, strategy or genetic mutation which is capable of overcoming the more uniform system. Its very uniformity renders it vulnerable. The capacity sex provides for variation and mutation within a species is the reason sex exists. Were sex not evolutionarily advantageous, many more species would be hermaphrodite.

Some introductory notes

Reducing the number of variables by largely neglecting other cultures

This approach is from an unapologetically Occidental (i.e. Western) perspective, for good scientific reasons. A telling example will be given. When people in European societies join a bus, or enter a waiting room, they will evenly distribute themselves around. By doing so they automatically maximize each others' personal space. In Vietnam the exact opposite happens: someone getting onto a bus with only one other passenger will sit close to them, and not doing so arouses suspicion. Such an elementary contrast in habits illustrates profound differences in attitudes and behaviour between peoples. In some cultures women regard it as their duty to provide their men with sex; sometimes marriages are arranged. Concentrating on European behaviour reduces the number of variables.

Two kinds of projection

Finally for this short introduction to the biology underlying Procedural Analysis, a note or two should be added about some of the terms used. Probably the single most important psychological mechanism in humans is *projection*, the assumption we often make that others perceive or act similarly to ourselves. Thus if we see the colour red we expect another person to see red, until we learn that he is colour-blind. By the same process, the easiest

Ignore what people say they do and look at what they actually do.

person to lie to is someone who is always honest. The honest man projects his nature onto others and expects to be told the truth, while the habitual liar is the hardest to convince. Projecting one's undesirable traits onto someone else is just a variation of the same mechanism, and this distinct form of projection is called *Freudian projection*.

A problem with the formal definition of 'strategy'

PA is largely about strategies, and it would be remiss not to mention a difficulty which exists with the formal definition of a strategy. In game theory a *strategy* is 'a complete specification of what an individual will do in any circumstance.' For humans this poses a problem. Only the simplest and most mechanical human strategies can be described for every possible circumstance which might arise, so this strict definition has been abandoned here. Here *policy* and *strategy* are used more or less interchangeably. Major strategies, such as Conspiracy and Disguised Defection, are capitalised.

About Procedural Analysis

The objective is to advance the understanding of human behaviour. The foundations of this approach are sex differences, simple games and the premise that evolution has formed not just our bodies but also our behaviour, which is the cornerstone of evolutionary psychology.

This system is a theoretical framework and as a theory it is consistent – a theory having consistency deserves attention on this basis alone. The reader can decide, according to his own observation and experience, if and by how much the approach applies to everyday life. With a fair wind and a little good fortune the accounts will occasionally be amusing and raise some wry smiles of recognition along the way.

An oil worker for BP was posted to Venezuela and had a flat there. He related how one morning he had been pottering around the flat, showering and telephoning friends to invite them to the party he was having that evening. His cleaner, an attractive Venezuelan woman, overheard. That evening a knock was heard on the door and on opening he saw it was his cleaner and her daughter. 'If we can come to your party you can have both of us' she said. The daughter had no breasts and was probably about 10. The oil worker told them of course they could come to his party and although he declined the offer he was sure that someone else would take advantage of it. In the State of Delaware until the 1920s the age of consent was 8.

2 Signals

Non-verbal communication, especially of a sexual nature

'The female signals, the male responds.' The origin of signals is plain. Signals began with movement. Any animal that moves emits signals, or non-verbal communication, which indicate its intentions. To a prey species the approach of a predator indicates a threat.

Does a dead animal signal?

A first question must be resolved. Does a dead animal signal by its lack of movement? Its inactivity is likely to be interpreted by other animals as death. Is the dead animal signalling? An elementary paradox such as this cannot be tolerated, for it suggests fundamental error. The answer is to accept that the failure to signal can itself be a signal. This is not counter-intuitive, for we know that the absence of a signal can convey a message. Being ignored by someone you know is an example.

Non-human signals are generally unambiguous

Animal signals are generally unambiguous; they are plain and free of artifice. Among animals, feedback operates to maintain the integrity of signals, for example during contests. Bluff is likely to be called. The famous biologist Robert Trivers related an encounter with a monkey which became angry when he gave misleading signals.

Most animals prefer to remain unobserved rather than issue deceptive signals. A predator slinks along low to the ground, approaches downwind or lies in wait for its prey rather than attempting to feign disinterest in its target. Obviously, there is a high cost overhead involved in sending misleading signals. Nevertheless in the animal world some interesting exceptions do occur. Animal signals are overwhelmingly honest, except it seems when a special signal has evolved to counter a specific threat.

Types of human signal

Human signals are here separated into four types: *honest*, *false*, *erroneous* and *dysfunctional*. Further, a signal is called *discriminate* if it is directed to a particular person and *indiscriminate* if it is not. Mode of dress, such as a female dressing provocatively, is indiscriminate signalling. To illustrate the complexity of human signals we need look no further than the smile.

Smiling

A smile might denote not happiness or pleasure but 'I don't want you to know that I'm upset.' It could be intended to obfuscate, that is, as a defence mechanism to prevent one's motives, intentions or strategy from being perceived. A smile can have many meanings, including the following:

Signals List – Mainly Female, Mainly Sexual Signals

ACCIDENT. Things being dropped, bicycle accidents and similar mishaps.
ASSENT. A female subtly conveys her decision to accept a male for sex.
BLANCH. (m/f) A subtle involuntary facial signal indicating attraction.
BODY POUT. A part of the female's body is protruded or displayed.
BODY TREMOR. The body is rocked from side to side to emphasize the breasts.
BRIGHTENING. The female stiffens and smiles as a target male nears.
CHALLENGE. (m/f) A display of defiance; subtle and overt forms exist.
CLICK. Indicates realisation that she is being manoeuvred into sex.
COLLISION. The female attempts to intercept or collide with her target.
DIRECT LOOK. Females tend to reserve direct eye contact for attraction.
DOUBLE BLINK. Both eyes are blinked simultaneously to indicate affection.
DRESS. Indiscriminate signals adopted and imitated as fashion.
DROPPING SOMETHING. A Victorian Lady drops her handkerchief.
EMPTY GLASS. The gentle shake of an empty glass ('Buy me a drink').
EXAGGERATED LAUGHTER. Forced or over-enthusiastic laughter near a target.
EXAGGERATED WALK. Typically, swinging of the hips while walking away.
FERTILE. The female exhibits her fertile state, distinctively by a 'bouncy' walk.
FOOT STAMP. The foot is stamped flat on the ground, audibly or inaudibly.
FREEZING IN PLACE. The head may incline before freezing in position.
GOING QUIET. Falling silent, perhaps in nervousness of signalling overtly.
GRIMACE RESPONSE. A female response to attention, as if in physical pain.
HELPLESS FEMALE. The female directly inspires male caretaking instincts.
HESITATION. Uncertainty is displayed in a course of action or direction.
INCIDENTAL NOISES. Quiet hissing, tsk-tsk or clicking noises for example.
INCIDENTAL TOUCHING. Subtle or overt brushes against a target male.
JOSTLE. A male is aggressively nudged, often after he has failed to approach.
JUVENILE. Characteristic dancing, spinning or twitching by young females.
LEAVING SOMETHING. An item is left behind for the target male to retrieve.
LINGERING. Hovering around or near a target, usually on a pretext.
LOOKING BACK. (m/f) A male or a female looks back over their shoulder.
LOOKING FLUSTERED. While static the female appears agitated or disturbed.
LOOKING SAD. The female appears forlorn as a target male passes.
LOOKING THROUGH. The female is 'caught' with her legs slightly apart.
LOOSE WOMAN. Waving a leg and arm simultaneously while inebriated.
LOUD VERBAL UTTERANCE. A pronounced verbal utterance.
NOT SAYING GOODBYE. Not saying goodbye can be a cue to a male to follow.
OPEN LEGS. Probably the strongest signal a female can issue to a male.

The simple smile: it's multiple interpretations

1. Happiness ('I'm happy');
2. As part of a Brightening signal ('I'm pleased to see you');
3. Gloating ('I let you see my pleasure at your defeat');
4. Obfuscation ('I don't want you to know how I really feel');
5. Confusion ('I don't know what else to do');
6. Nothing (Smiling in automatic response to another or by habit).

Females are a great deal more adept at reading signals than males. When they communicate with each other they can convey more by facial expressions and gestures than by the words used.

Sexual signals

Signals are inherently ambiguous, and with ambiguity comes complexity. This is especially true where sexual behaviour is concerned. Notwithstanding, sexual signals are of singular interest because they have a clear hereditary path.

Hereditary advantage, natural selection

A trait or feature is evolutionarily viable, and capable of taking hold and spreading through a population, if it has heritable advantage. That is, firstly, it must confer advantage of some kind and secondly, it must be capable of being passed to the next generation. If a trait confers advantage then it has a reason

Signals List – Continued

OVERCOME. The female displays loss of control, may be steered into sex.
PERIPHERAL COMMENT. Something is said to which a target male might react.
PLAYFUL ABANDON. Careless and playful attitudes indicating receptivity.
POUT. The lips are protruded, sometimes in false displeasure.
PREENING. The female adjusts herself in the presence of her target.
RAPID LOOK AWAY. This both avoids direct eye contact and attracts attention.
REACHING OVER. Rudely reaching for something to stimulate conversation.
SHORT STEPS. A female trait and display of femininity.
SOFTENING. Similar to Brightening but the facial muscles relax.
SPITTING. Sometimes employed by adolescent girls to attract attention.
TONGUE. The tongue is stuck out as a deliberate sexual signal indicating desire.
WAVE OF HAIR. (common) The Hair Flick. 'I love me, you love me too.'
WAVE OF KEYS. The target male is intended to follow.
WIDE EYE. (common) The pupils dilate (peripheral vision); the eye widens.

to exist; if it is heritable then it has a means to exist. Even if the advantage is slight, individuals possessing the trait will have an edge over individuals that do not, and over generations the trait will proliferate in the population. This is the basis of natural selection, the essential conditions for the viability or persistence of a trait in evolutionary terms.

It is easy to see how a sexual signal is advantageous and heritable; it gives reproductive advantage. This is not true of gestures which display, for example, happiness, embarrassment, discomfort or dissimulation. We can envisage how, say, sticking out our tongue to indicate concentration might give us an advantage in some circumstances, but it is not at all obvious how or whether it helps us bring children into the world, and this is the payoff as far as evolution is concerned. In the game of evolutionary survival the number of progeny we leave behind is the only score that matters.

The obvious hereditary advantage of sexual signals

The normal course of affairs

Normally the female signals, the male responds. The standard signal-response sequence is that the female emits a signal, usually subtly, and the male, unconsciously perceiving it, approaches. He knows to some degree that the approach he is making is not unwelcome, though many males are unaware that the transaction is entirely in the control of the female from the outset. During our evolutionary past, the female needed to secure a protector and supporter, because she was unable to create wealth herself. Her policy is to make the

The female signals, the male responds

> Frequently the nature of a dysfunction provides an understanding of the normal process: when things go wrong it can demonstrate how things go right. Three situations in which the signal-response sequence goes wrong are given in illustration.
>
> A male responds to a deliberate female signal and approaches, and then the female badly feigns surprise that he has done so.
>
> Or the male might approach and then allude to the signal in the approach statement, and the female rather too strenuously denies it ('You looked as if something was troubling you' – 'No I wasn't'), or she similarly denies issuing an obviously deliberate signal.
>
> Thirdly, in subsequent exchanges the female might seek to establish how much of the signal the male consciously perceived, and he recognises the purpose of the interrogation. By such means males can learn of female attraction by signals, although many males are apparently unaware that when they approach a female they almost invariably do so because a signal of some kind has been emitted. At whatever level, the male knows that the approach he is making is not an unwelcome one.

male believe he is making a catch, not the other way around. To this end a subtle signal is more effective than a blatant one.

The conflict between subtle and overt signals

Herein lies a contradiction. Females enjoy signalling, so sometimes their signals are far from delicate. However they will also compete with each other in the subtlety of the signals they emit, for the more comely and desirable the female, the more insinuated is the signal required for her to obtain her desire. It is no coincidence that many words describing female beauty refer to her ability to summon a male: she may be fetching, comely, attractive, alluring, winsome or desirable.

Signals start as involuntary but become less so

Over fifty 'Mainly Female, Mainly Sexual' signals have been identified. The strongest signal a female can issue to a male is the Open Legs signal; combined with a smile, it is stronger still. It is likely that juvenile females initially emit signals instinctively and involuntarily, and she becomes aware of them then. Later, or after repeated instances, she can imitate herself, when the signal may be less involuntary. A repertoire of favoured signals is arrived upon.

Primary and secondary sexual characters. Signals as primary sexual characters of behaviour

Darwin made a distinction between primary sexual characters, those traits or features which are directly connected with reproduction, and secondary sexual characters which are unique to one sex but which are not essential for reproduction. A human male secondary sexual character is the beard: it is unique to one sex but has no direct role in reproduction. It does, however, help to distinguish the male from the female. A woman's breasts are a primary sexual character, being confined to one sex and directly involved with reproduction, while her softened facial features and higher voice are secondary sexual characters. Here an analogous distinction is made between sexual and non-sexual signals. Sexual signals are primary sexual characters in behaviour.

The Accident signal

A woman serves tea to a workman she likes

The following example is a case of a discriminate sexual signal in the form of an Accident signal. A woman serves tea to a group of building workers. She may work inside a mobile trailer which regularly visits the building site, or in a café near the site; she is relatively stationary. Over the previous days or weeks there have been exchanges of looks, pleasantries and so on with a particular building worker. These exchanges have led to a tacit understanding that the two like each other, but there the relationship, such as it is, has stalled. The woman does not want to appear forward and the male does not want to make a proposal in sight of his workmates, fearing embarrassment and ribbing by his colleagues. A public rejection would be even worse.

One day while her target is in the queue being served tea the woman emits the Accident signal. He holds a tea mug before her and she accidentally spills some of the hot tea onto his hand. Her spasm is involuntary and reflexive; it is

> The less likely the male is to respond, the more likely the female is to signal.

perhaps the product of a lapse of attention and a nervous disjunction. The man is scalded and she immediately apologises, but he allays her concerns and tells her not to worry: 'It hardly hurt at all, don't worry about it.'

Some time later the couple meet again, perhaps during a quiet moment while she is clearing tables or outside the café. The incident of the spilled tea is a ready conversation starter. Her apology is repeated and the male again soothes her concerns. The conversation extends beyond this, perhaps talking about other workers they are familiar with or the owner of the café. The relationship is extended. An outing is proposed. Eventually, as a direct consequence of the signal, the couple marry and have children.

He responds to the Accident signal

The female has emitted a particular signal, exhibiting weakness and vulnerability to some extent, probably inspiring *Affection Beneath* in the male; he feels affection for something or someone weaker than him. He has responded to the signal in a particular way: he could have become angry at being scalded, or he might have dismissed her as a potential partner because his target mate was a woman not given to such clumsiness.

The female has inspired his caretaking instincts

Thus from this signal/signal-response couplet progeny has resulted. The female's propensity to signal in a particular way, and the male's form of response to that signal, have been passed to the next generation. An obvious link exists between the signal emitted by the female and the capacity to transmit that feature to offspring. Signalling is a viable strategy – we can clearly see how it is advantageous and heritable. Moreover, not only has she secured a mate, enabling her genes to be transmitted to another generation, she has won a mate of her choosing, a considerable bonus. The signal/signal-response couplet passes on to their progeny. This is why sexual signals are of especial interest.

The signal leads to progeny. The female chooses a mate and retains control

More smiling

When emitting the Brightening signal a female's body posture changes, she becomes more alert and she smiles. The signal may be issued discriminately to a particular male or indiscriminately to a group, say on their entry to a bar.

The Brightening signal

Females smile habitually and this is probably a defence mechanism to compensate for males' greater physical strength. Habitual smiling engenders a cosy, intimate atmosphere. The separation from aggression becomes greater, so anyone disturbing it must traverse a greater distance. The cost of disturbing female comfort is raised. Cosy atmospheres are a typical feature of feminine environments.

Habitual smiling and cosy atmospheres

Disturbing a cosy atmosphere

Imagine a customer had a grievance, and visited the company office to air his complaint. In a masculine environment he would be met with an impartial, business-like manner, and he, equally business-like, would state his complaint and the matter might be resolved. The company's practices might even be improved. If he were to enter a feminine environment however, and find himself faced with a staff of women chatting, drinking coffee and sharing cake on a Friday afternoon, obviously enjoying themselves, he might give up and walk out in exasperation.

Affectionate farewells

The female can become most affectionate on parting

The dynamic is that when the likelihood of a response is low, female signals become more pronounced. In a feminine environment this leads to a preponderance of *affectionate farewells*, sometimes gushing and effusive expressions of affection as people are separating. With the affectionate farewell the female signals most strongly on parting. She signals most strongly at the very moment when a progression to physical sex can no longer take place.

Fear after an affectionate farewell

Immediately after an affectionate farewell she can become fearful of meeting again. Suppose she has kept an admiring male at arm's length, lest he get the wrong idea. She then bids him an affectionate farewell and by doing so elevates the relationship. If she meets him again shortly afterwards she must perform an extrication, a difficult manoeuvre, to restore her former distance and control.

Honest signals

Now the four categories of signals will be discussed. Given the inherent ambiguity of signals, the classification of them into honest, false, erroneous and dysfunctional types is an achievement. Human signals are inherently elusive and making sense of them was a formidable challenge.

Natural systems are usually simple

A basic signal is looking at something for someone to do something with it, for example a visitor looking at a boiling kettle. Honest signals are valid: they accurately reflect an emotional state and the intentions of the signaller. The great majority of animal signals are honest because animals lack the capacity to employ deceitful strategies. Most things in nature are simple because simple systems are robust; they are inherently more reliable because there is less to go wrong. Reliability must be of paramount importance in a system which has survived through thousands of generations to the present day.

Millions of years of unbroken heredity

Any break in the hereditary chain would mean that we simply would not be here. It is no wonder that the human desire for companionship and physical intimacy with the opposite sex is so strong. The intensity of these feelings, i.e. instincts, has ensured the genetic survival of every individual alive today.

Richard Dawkins quotes the cuckoo, or rather, the birds which fall prey to it, as an example of a simple system. Birds have learned to detect strange eggs in their nest by their pattern. In fact as a counter-measure cuckoos have adapted to particular species and changed their eggs to match. However once the chick is born, its gaping beak is fed even when the cuckoo chick is bigger than its 'parent,' never mind any other chicks remaining in the nest. Dawkins argues that the evolutionary advantage of compulsively feeding almost any chick's gaping maw outweighs occasional errors such as feeding the chick of a parasite. Having an overwhelming compulsion to feed young is so beneficial that occasionally feeding the wrong one is insignificant. A simple system may have flaws, but the cost of those flaws is minor compared to the cost of protecting against a few exceptions.

Simple, strong instincts are less liable to dysfunction

The cuckoo provides a useful example of a different kind: since it never has contact with its parents, its parasitic strategy must be entirely hereditary. There is no nature/nurture argument with this bird: its behaviour is entirely innate.

No nature-nurture argument here

An exception to the usual simplicity of natural systems is the immune system: this has evolved to be complex because so many viruses, bacteria and so on are co-evolving with it. However the cost of this sophistication is a catalogue of auto-immune disorders, such as arthritis and eczema, which derive from the immune system not working as it should. The more complex the system, the more there is to go wrong. Excepting a few specific instances such as the immune system, simplicity is by far the best policy in nature.

The complexity of the immune system and its cost

The threat-retreat signals animals emit during contests are honest. The role

The Hawk/Dove game. A basic model is the Hawk/Dove game. Individual Hawks and Doves compete for a resource (food, perhaps) with benefit *b*. If they fight, the cost of the injury is *c*. The strategies are described as follows:

Hawk: Always fight for the resource, whether facing a Dove or another Hawk.
Dove: If facing a Hawk, retreat; if facing another Dove, share the resource.

The two populations reach an equilibrium depending on the values of *b* and *c*. For certain values of *b* and *c* for example, the total population of birds would consist of 50% Hawks and 50% Doves.

This game features just two strategies, but in fact there can be more or less than two. There could be many different strategies in equilibrium, hence a mixture of evolutionarily stable strategies. If there is only one strategy, which cannot be invaded by another, it is called a 'pure strategy.'

the animal adopts depends largely on physical size, and attempts to bluff may result in injury. This can be readily observed when birds feed, say on throwing breadcrumbs onto a flat roof. Innumerable contests take place between the birds. An approach or threatening gesture by a larger bird causes the others to retreat: very few contests lead to actual injury. Only if a resource is considered particularly valuable will a contest be escalated to one which risks real physical harm.

Animal threat/retreat signals and the infrequency of actual injury

Human signals are a great deal more complex and it would be unwise to rely overmuch on them. In some circumstances people signal the opposite of what they mean. Plus, the signals of someone doing something illegal or improper, and the demeanour of someone who merely fears he will be thought by others to be doing something illegal or improper, are difficult if not impossible to distinguish.

Human signals can be misleading. Two signals which are usually honest

The open door is a signal of trust, indicating that the person beyond it is open to visits and conversation, while the playing of loud music is a signal of enjoyment. Both of these signals are ambiguous: the open door may have been left open accidentally, or a thief may have just left. The music could be being played to annoy, or to mask other noises. Nevertheless, the proportion of cases when these signals are invalid is small.

Pleasure encourages females to signal

Pleasure reinforces advantageous behaviour

Females obtain pleasure from emitting signals. She enjoys dressing up and making herself attractive to males. Signals can become more overt if a physical barrier exists, as when females wave to a male from a passing coach or canal boat. If a handsome male strides purposefully past he indicates by his manner that he is unlikely to be diverted. These situations, and many comparable ones, inspire females to signal.

The less likely the male is to respond, the more likely the female is to signal. The pleasure females obtain by signalling explains this apparent paradox. When a female ascertains that a male is unlikely to respond, either because of his manner or surroundings, and indulges herself in emitting a signal, she is playing a game of brinkmanship. Revealingly, a mistake in this game, when she miscalculates, can be beneficial for her. It is possible for progeny to result from it. The tendency to make a mistake is then passed to the next generation.

The female propensity to make mistakes

Similarly with signals like the Accident signal and other instinctive behaviours which advertise her weakness and serve to inspire male caretaking instincts. Mishaps and miscalculations are an inherent female constituent, formed over tens of thousands of generations. For women, mistakes, slip-ups and miscalculations are advantageous. Evolutionarily this is not an insignificant matter.

A party had been held in the Nieuwemeer near Amsterdam, and everyone had got a bit drunk. One very attractive girl who had a boyfriend with her was leading a group of young women about 22-23 and ultimately all of them were dancing around in a circle topless. The man relating this event had gone outside: 'Everyone was doing what they wanted.' However the males were unlikely to have been able to do what they wanted on the sight of a group of young women dancing around with their breasts bared.

Acting

Professional, dramatic and careless signals

Practically any signal can be imitated – we only have to turn on a TV to see professional actors doing so, and some people can even generate tears at will. They can 'turn on the waterworks' when circumstances demand, or to get something they particularly want. Most males have difficulty distinguishing between a female signalling her sincere attraction to a male and signals emitted to invite attention, to tease, or for other reasons.

Blushing as a basic honest signal. The Collision signal

The most basic honest signal is blushing: this is one signal that cannot be imitated. Clearly many human signals are honest: a hand before the mouth can suggest dissimulation or self-effacement, or a posture of exaggerated bravado may demonstrate insecurity. These are honest expressions of what is going on, although we may have difficulty interpreting them or distinguishing them from the gestures of a skilled actor. Perhaps involuntary expressions of nervousness are a better example of indubitably honest signals but, although difficult to imitate, it can be achieved. The nervous tremor involved in the Accident signal may be difficult to feign, but doing so is not impossible. In any case the signal is imitated in the Collision signal, when a female deliberately collides or nearly collides with her target.

The importance of deceit in human relations

Deceit is an important factor in human relations. It has been argued that our success as a species is largely due to our capacity to deceive. Mothers practice deceit while teaching children to read, patiently correcting only the worst and most consistent errors to avoid discouraging the child in its tentative attempts to learn. If every error were corrected the child would become disheartened and give up. We tell 'white lies' ('How are you?' 'I'm fine') all the time to smooth our interactions with each other; they are the oil on the gears of social intercourse.

False signals

False signals in nature

False signals are invalid, and purposely so. They are issued to be misleading. Some animals 'play dead' as a defence mechanism, taking advantage of an adaptation in other species that prevents them eating prey that has become rancid or died of disease. Several birds emit false signals, such as leading a predator away by holding out a wing as if it were broken. Alternatively a bird may give an ostentatious display away from its nest, distracting the predator seeking its eggs. These false signals have evolved to counter specific threats to the bird's eggs or young.

The basic human false signal. Indication of dysfunction

For humans, the proposed basic false signal is leaving a light on when no-one is at home. It is issued deliberately and intentionally. The signal has developed with increasing crime (or fear of crime) to counter the threat of burglary. However issuing the signal indicates a disorder of some kind: either the fear is rational, in which case there is too much burglary, or the fear is irrational, in which case there is too much fear. If the fear is real, a societal problem exists. If the false signal was issued because of irrational fear, for instance if a light was left on at a place with no risk of burglary, that might be classed as dysfunctional.

Pretending to be calm and collected. Formal situations. Overtraining of soldiers

False signalling is the stock-in-trade of actors who mimic authentic gestures. Acting aside, an everyday form of false signalling is to adopt normal gestures of poise and composure to mask internal fear. An individual might be quaking in anxiety at a job interview or momentous social occasion but they suppress their disquiet. The stakes may be high, such as at a public appearance or meeting a much desired prospective partner, and hence there is a high state of emotional arousal. The usual fear is of embarrassment or loss of face which might result if the aroused state were not inhibited, because that arousal might give rise to a clumsy over-reaction. One reason formality exists is to make control of this aroused state easier. In formal situations behaviour is pre-defined and easy to follow even for an individual under stress. This is similar to the soldier who is massively overtrained so that in a time of extreme stress (such as in battle) he resorts to the comforting familiarity of the task he has been trained for.

Emitting false signals during a time of stress

For an ordinary person faced with a sudden onset of danger, becoming the victim of a mugging say, he may suppress his fear and try to negotiate his way out of trouble. At such a time the endocrine system secretes hormones, especially adrenalin, to aid the well-known 'fight or flight' response. But the more common reaction in most crisis situations is to stay put and emit false signals. Then the rush of adrenalin might serve not to motivate action, but to aid inhibition. The requirement in many modern crisis situations is to stay calm, think of suitable verbal responses and keep a tight rein on our bodies to suppress a physical response.

Consider some of the stressful situations commonly faced in modern life: being trapped on a traffic island between fast-moving vehicles; being told off at work; sitting on a stationary train while being late for an appointment; being stopped by police for a traffic violation. In many situations involving nervous arousal, fighting or fleeing will make an already bad situation worse. This is certainly true in a society which punishes almost all expressions of violence. The orthodox psychological belief is that the agitation and shaking which follows an extreme event is the result of adrenalin still circulating in the body, but perhaps this delay suggests that it is a vestige of former times when a purely physical response was required.

Inhibition of a response is often more appropriate

Feigning indifference

Another common false signal is displaying nonchalance. Typical is a shrug of the shoulders but it can also be expressed by a wave of the hand, a tilt of the head or pursing of the lips. Feigning indifference can be beneficial in many situations. When buying or selling, it is used to maximize benefit: deprecate when buying, boost when selling. A trader should never appear too eager (or even eager at all) to part with an item or to buy it.

Falsely signalling indifference. When it is advantageous

Comparably, and more pertinently considering the importance of sexual signals, displaying nonchalance towards a prospective partner can be a way of arousing their interest. The female 'plays hard to get,' suppressing any visible indication of her curiosity about a male to test his commitment to her before she commits her biological resources to him. This is a perfectly standard evolutionarily advantageous game for her. The male may counter with similar insouciance, arousing her interest especially if she is used to being eagerly pursued.

Weakening distress signals

An interesting scenario can be described which combines false signals, criminality and John Maynard Smith's notion of the evolutionarily stable strategy (ESS). It involves a clan of roadside bandits. Their tactic is to signal misfortune at the side of remote roads to waylay passing motorists and rob them. This scenario is probably more common in horror films than in actuality, but it is still a delightful example of majority and minority strategies.

A family of roadside bandits

In the ESS, which is defined mathematically, majority and minority strategies can co-exist, but the population following the minority strategy must remain small. Here the majority population is law-abiding motorists and the roadside bandits are, mercifully, a small minority.

A mixed ESS, MESS

> That season tight, thigh-hugging shorts were in fashion, and a Dutchwoman of about 25 was wearing them accompanied by a female friend of the same age. She was on the terrace of a café on a busy thoroughfare and must have been seen by fifty people at the very least. She was smiling broadly as she sat in a wicker chair, the sort with continuous arm rests and curving back. On the sides of the chair however her legs rested; her knees were spread wide and the curves of her outer labia were easily visible beneath the soft grey woollen fabric of her shorts. The mound was proud and large, the two parallel ridges of flesh separated and clearly discernible. It was still being displayed on cycling past in the opposite direction, my errand having been completed, ten or fifteen minutes later.

The minority strategy is evolutionarily stable, according to Maynard Smith's model of stability: suppose our bandit family were moving around a large, sparsely populated region like rural America repeatedly robbing travellers on remote roads. They could thrive and have progeny following the same strategy, the clan tradition. However their strategy is only an ESS if the population of roadside bandits remains small. If they were to grow too numerous, the majority population would become familiar with the ruse and always drive by, wary of being ambushed.

Falsely signalling an emergency, routinely by British police

More subtle is the false signal of a police vehicle engaging its emergency lights and siren to ease its progress on a personal mission, such as fetching refreshments for an officers' meal break, or for the mundane collection of an arrestee (this latter occurs in Britain). We can imagine the consequences of falsely issuing a distress signal from a vessel at sea, or of setting off a fire alarm in a building. Punishment would likely result, because weakening these signals is discouraged. The masculine strategy is to preserve the integrity of signals, and distress signals especially.

Erroneous signals

The model erroneous signal and its features

Of the four types of signals, erroneous signals are the hardest to rationalise. Erroneous signals are valid but inappropriate. The model erroneous signal is a female signalling to a male when she is unavailable, possibly because she has a boyfriend or is married. Perhaps her partner is jealous, prone to violence, and close by. The male may respond to the signal and approach, then sparks would fly.

The signal is initially valid, because she is genuinely attracted to the male, for that was the origin of the signal. Instinct, desire, whatever has inspired the signal, but the proper course would be to inhibit it. That is, the signal starts with

Summary of signal types and their properties

Honest signals–	Valid;
Erroneous signals–	Valid but inappropriate;
False signals–	Purposefully invalid;
Dysfunctional signals–	Invalid and emitted due to dysfunction.

a valid (honest) origin and becomes erroneous when its progression is disinhibited. Either the signal is consciously suppressed, or the signaller consciously fails to suppress it. These two cases can be distinguished.

An unavailable woman signals, but this time her partner is a safe distance away. In time-honoured fashion, a male responds to her erroneous signal by approaching. Then it is fun to imagine that the male she has signalled is a veritable Lothario, convinced firstly of his irresistibility to women and secondly of his infallible ability to read them. The woman now has to extricate herself from the situation her erroneous signal has created.

A Lothario responds

An erroneous signal is defined as any signal which has a valid origin but by convention or circumstance ought to be suppressed. Making threatening gestures at an adversary at a formal occasion would be an erroneous signal, as would a young surgeon exhibiting nervousness in front of his first patient; nervousness may be felt but it ought not to be displayed.

Some other erroneous signals

Hysterical signalling

A forceful, and quite rare, expression of erroneous signalling is what might be termed 'hysterical signalling.' It has been observed only twice, once by a female and once by a male. By each there was a gradual build-up to an extreme. The first quoted took place during the day and the second in the evening in a small bar.

In the case of a female, the progression seems to follow the following stages. Initially, a female is inspired to signal a male, but either he does not perceive it or he deliberately ignores her. Without a response, she then elevates the level of signalling to elicit one. The amplification may be intended (evolutionarily, not necessarily consciously) to invoke the caretaking instincts of the male, which would be an attempt to inspire Affection Beneath in him. In this case the male response would be to intervene to protect the female from embarrassing herself. In the absence of a response from the male, the signalling can escalate to the point where she is laughing wildly and practically rolling on the floor. That

The escalation of signals that lead to 'hysterical signalling'

is, the girl was laid on the floor, her head resting against a wall, rocking from side to side and laughing hysterically.

More signalling equals more gratification

Females would not engage in overt signalling, or brinkmanship, if the pleasure they experienced by signalling was not in proportion to its degree. The stronger the signal the more pleasure the female experiences on emitting it. The climax of such an intense burst of signalling is euphoric, accounting for the wild laughter.

The laughter is different in character to that in the Exaggerated Laughter signal, which serves to attract attention and invite the target to share in the good humour. That laughter is deliberate and sounds forced.

The 'elephant in the living room' effect

Both instances of hysterical signalling took place in the presence of onlookers, and this first incident occurred in a college computer room. The other students pretended that nothing was happening. The young woman, also a student, eventually collected herself, rose from the floor and sheepishly left the room.

A male engages in hysterical signalling

The event involving a male took place in a student bar of the same college some years previously, and thus alcohol probably contributed to the disinhibition. It involved a male entertaining a female in a kind of unbounded showing off, a display directed at his target. This culminated in him lying on the floor giggling uncontrollably. The nearby onlookers formed an audience with his female target, who seemed the most appreciative. The young man won the girl.

Dysfunctional signals

Effects of childhood sexual abuse

Some dysfunctional signals are the result of childhood trauma, what some would call developmental disturbance. The model dysfunctional signal is the exaggerated sexual signalling displayed by girls or young women who have been sexually exploited in childhood. Attention-seeking is expressed sexually, in signals that the observer interprets as overtly flirtatious. Not uncommonly, a recurrent cycle is established of abuse or promiscuity in later life.

A dark-haired, fairly ordinary-looking Danish girl was in an alternative bar, gyrating around to the music. Sometimes she squatted down on her haunches with her legs apart. She was wearing skin-tight cycling shorts and her movements were quite erotic; some of the time she played with a large shaggy dog and a piece of wood. Once she stood on a ledge on the wall, lowered her hands onto the bar and poked and moved her backside in the air. Later she revealed that she had been raped when she was 7, repeatedly until she was 9, and had been told that this made her more likely to be raped in later life. The signals she had been emitting were testament to that.

Some forms of dysfunctional signalling, such as nail-biting or compulsive picking at the hair or scalp, may be exaggerated expressions of the preening instinct. Many animals spend a large amount of time maintaining their fur or feathers as the animal tends itself against parasites, infection and injury. For example, cats must protect any small injury against invasion by flies, because in the hot climate of their original habitat insect larvae would rapidly occupy any wound. Childhood trauma may trigger a latent compulsion to preen.

A putative link between OCD and preening instincts

Deficient self-image is a feature associated with many obsessive-compulsive disorders. This accords with the idea that some forms of OCD are vestigial preening and grooming instincts from a distant animal past.

Aberrant behaviour can sometimes be seen in zoos, as a consequence of forced captivity, especially among large animals which are normally free to roam. Some of these behaviours, such as rocking the head or body from side to side, can be observed in the mentally ill. An extreme form of dysfunctional signalling is suicide attempts which are intended to fail.

Dysfunctional signals in zoos

Signals summary

Honest signals predominate in nature. Human signals are inherently ambiguous; by their use the female maintains control, for she can always deny her intent. Except for blushing, any signal may be imitated or otherwise false, erroneous or dysfunctional. We follow (i.e. respond to) signals emitted by people we trust.

The signals we respond to. Effect of misleading signals

Confusion and neurosis would increase if a high proportion of the signals in our environment were falsely or erroneously emitted, perhaps for personal gratification, to attract attention, or to confound.

3 Markers

A marker is an unambiguous indication of involvement

The original marker must surely have been scent. Animals mark their territory by leaving scent, and these cues are unambiguous. An animal cannot mask or disguise its smell, which is inherent and often permeates a thick and waxy coat of fur.

Scent as the original marker

A prey species often sniffs the air to check for the presence of predators, and a predator will often converge on its prey from downwind. Animals can distribute their scent over a wide area and many have organs dedicated to this purpose. Animals rely on olfactory cues much more than humans.

The importance of smell to animals

Smell is particulate. That is, it involves particles of the substance. A good tracking dog, such as a bloodhound, can detect scent from a single molecule, an astonishing feat. While the sense organ of humans is the size of a postage stamp, that of the dog is the size of a large handkerchief. Individual animals can be identified, not just species, by the unique aromas of urine or faeces; to the dog such smells are evidently delicious. Although the dog is well-equipped for tracking scent its ability is not particularly exceptional; its value for the task lies more in its domesticated and compliant nature. The common pig has a better sense of smell than the dog, but pigs are harder to control.

Animals likely navigate using an internal 'scent map.' A territorial landscape is stored and updated according to the location of food sources, enemy species and rivals.

The origin of sexual disparity

At the root of the disparity between the sexes is the resource the female provides in the ova she carries and her ability to bear and nurture offspring. At birth girls already carry all the ova they will ever have, about 400 of them. At menarche the eggs start to drop one by one, ready to be fertilised. In contrast to the limited supply of eggs, sperm is continuously produced.

Scarcity of eggs and abundance of sperm

Moreover pregnancy for the female involves high cost. Of greater moment from a male perspective, especially in an age of sexual liberality, is that she provides him with an opportunity for sexual pleasure, also affirming his masculinity and augmenting his sense of self-worth. The pursuit of sexual pleasure is rarely the female standpoint however. Of high value to her is the relationship, which is the female kind of sex. Unsurprisingly therefore, males and females treat markers in different ways.

One girl of Oriental extraction, who had probably been born in Holland, travelled from Eindhoven to Amsterdam for an evening meal, a round trip of about 250km. She refused to drink anything so she wouldn't have to use any other lavatory but her own, back in Eindhoven. Another Dutch girl confessed that when away from home she would desperately want to go but couldn't actually release when the crucial moment came.

Very generally, males tend to mark territory, expressing their territorial instincts, while the female tends to mark people, especially her partner and children.

Human marking

Human marking is sometimes little more complex than smell. People can have a strong preference for using their home lavatory, not wanting to use another. Inner-city graffiti with a distinctive signature, called 'tagging,' can be compared to an animal leaving scent. The graffiti proclaims 'I was here' and the painter's ego is swelled in proportion to its range. The enthusiastic 'graffiti artist' tags every location he can, with hardly a place being passed by without his mark being left. He feels satisfaction on leaving his mark. The wider the extent of his graffiti, the greater the sphere of influence he feels he has.

Unambiguous indications of involvement in humans

Few people will move into a new house and be completely content with its décor. All sorts of changes will be made, some by necessity but many purely as an expression of preference. Moving into a place and filling it with personal possessions, and arranging them in a particular way, marks the territory and makes the empty space a home. That is, it makes it into *your* home, the place one feels 'at home.'

Basic forms of human marking

Leaving a drink at a table in a pub or nightclub, or a jacket over a seat, a pack of cigarettes or even a wallet or purse on show, marks that place as the one to which the owner will return. Such marking might be typical where a group of friends occupy a particular table and members of the group take turns to remain there to mind their base and the markers left behind.

The value of marking property can almost be quantified financially. The sale price of a house which needs, say, £50,000-worth of repairs and renovation will not include the full extent of the reduction. That is, the actual selling price may only be reduced by £30,000 or so, because a buyer will usually be found who is prepared to do a large amount of the work himself. That buyer will not count the cost of his own labour, but is happy to receive as his payoff the feeling of satisfaction which comes on making the house his own. He will have impressed his mark upon it and by doing so he feels proprietorial, the 'lord of the manor,' chief of all he surveys. He has moulded and influenced the restoration of the house and feels a sense of accomplishment for having done so. He has the benefit of having marked the house with his own, personal stamp. In this case it is worth £20,000 to him.

The value we place on marking

A car upon which £2,000 has been spent on after-market accessories never recoups the value of the added items when sold. The modified car expresses the choices and preferences of its owner, and the new owner will invariably wish to impress his own mark upon it. He prefers Brand X bucket seats to Brand Y; Brand B wheels to Brand A. By examining market values of vehicles which have been modified with expensive add-ons, and compensating for their depreciation second-hand, one can almost quantify the value a buyer places on marking to the nearest pound.

Marking by fixing, decorating and gardening

Consider the inept do-it-yourselfer whose confidence exceeds his ability. Or perhaps it is not his confidence which is excessive, but his instinct to mark his territory in a manner which is beyond his abilities. A woman of the Unstable Female type who begins to decorate one room of a house, then another, until every room in the house is being decorated simultaneously, is likely attempting to mark her domain more than actually decorating it.

Gardening or other land management involves marking. In addition to being a hobby or a job, such as managing an estate, an individual is exerting his influence and leaving unambiguous indications of his involvement, such as planting a favoured type of flower, felling a tree or erecting a structure.

Marking boundaries

A farmer may mark the boundaries of his land with fences or boundary posts, and the businessman who operates a chain progressively marks as he opens branches at new locations. The State (a masculine construct) marks its range with road signs and other street furniture.

The marking man. A crazy man was seen walking around Amsterdam carrying a pot of white paint and a paintbrush. (He may have been under the delusion that he was a council worker.) When he saw a piece of street furniture, such as the small grey metal cases containing switchgear jutting out of the ground, he would approach the cabinet, give it two or three wipes of paint, stand back admiring his handiwork and then move off in search of the next. It was pure marking and his handiwork can probably still be seen.

Women can be enthusiastic about erasing former markers. Examples are wanting to obliterate the name of a former girlfriend from their partner's tattoos and unnecessarily removing existing coats of paint while redecorating. There is a female trait, which might be normal, of wanting to have sex in every room in a new house. Some enjoy having sex in unusual places.

Different kinds of markers

Sharing territory

Being in the same place as someone is also a marker: the people are unambiguously involved in some way, perhaps sharing a similar purpose, as are people attending a political meeting or nightclub. More widely, individuals living in the same region are connected by sharing similar fortunes. If food were to become scarce in that area, or extremes of weather were to occur, their basic involvement would increase, whether they were to begin fighting over resources or pooling them.

Inventions as markers. The enormous influence of inventors

Inventions, which are almost always of male origin, are a particularly powerful and sublime form of male marking. For example Bell, the inventor of the telephone, has left his mark in millions of homes around the world. His legacy is huge but by no means unique. Baird, the inventor of television, is in the same category, as are the inventors of thousands of other devices in daily use. These are all male markers. The inventor, be he Tesla, Marconi, Edison or any of thousands of others, has left his mark. Every user of the invention is unambiguously involved with its inventor, each time the device is used.

Marking people

Natural domains, and more types of marking

Here we are not discussing individuals so much as strategies. Procedural Analysis is concerned with male and female strategies, and there will be exceptions to the broad trends. In this antipodal scheme males are territorial, and are interested in things. The natural domain of the male is things, the natural domain of the female is relationships. Thus males tend to mark territory and objects.

Talking to someone is a marker. What is said is immaterial, but addressing someone or exchanging words clearly indicates involvement, whether the words spoken are insults or a trivial conversation about the weather. An employer can mark his subordinates by paying them a wage and obliging them to wear a distinctive uniform.

While the general male tendency is to mark things such as property and places, the sides of vans, shop facias and products with his name or the logo

Male and female marking

of his company or brand, females are inclined to mark people. Incidental touching by a female during the early stages of courtship is marking, and the sex act is certainly an unambiguous indication of involvement, i.e. a marker. A wife marks her husband by buying, selecting and taking care of his clothes. She marks her domestic domain by cleaning and rearranging it, and marks the members of her family by providing their meals.

A mother marks her adolescent son, women avidly pop bubblewrap

Rather intriguing is the strong instinct some women have to squeeze spots appearing on family members. The adolescent son with an acne spot has no hope of repulsing the determined mother, and there is no question but that she acts on her own desire, for herself: 'Oh just let me squeeze that spot' – the youth's discomfiture is ignored. The sight of a ripe spot inspires in her an irresistible urge to squeeze the pus out. If this prevents disease the evolutionary origin of the instinct is clear. It is tempting to compare this behaviour with the common female compulsion to squeeze and pop the pockets of air in plastic bubblewrap.

Altruism

Females often take a distinctive attitude towards altruism – altruism being the rather deep topic in psychology concerned with unselfish deeds. They will often argue that there is no such thing as a truly unselfish act, because an individual performing an act of altruism is rewarded with the sense of satisfaction they experience on performing it. Because females are more sensitive to emotion, and thus instinctive drives, she is aware that by ironing her husband's shirt she is satisfying her desire to mark him, and this is likely her primary motivation for doing so.

The gratification of giving and the Indian attitude toward beggars

From this point of view, the glow of self-righteousness experienced when, say, donating money to charity is directly equivalent to it. The virtuous feeling is the payoff. This was encapsulated in a charity slogan exhorting donations: 'It costs just 60p a day to support a child, but the feeling is priceless.' A similar philosophy exists in India, where a street beggar is regarded as doing his benefactor a favour by enabling him to feel good about himself for what is really a very small amount of money, for the poorer the beggar, the easier he is satisfied. Beggars there are raised for this role, children being deliberately disfigured by amputations and body constraints to increase their income.

Uniforms, badges and ribbons as markers

A uniform worn by a public official is a marker indicating the wearer's specific functions and involvement with the State. Colours worn by the supporters of a football team mark their enthusiastic involvement with their team and their desire to share its fortunes. Similarly a badge bearing a symbol or the name of a band indicates involvement in that cause or cultural style. When Aids became an issue, a charitable organisation distributed bright red ribbons worn to show

Typical appetent marking. A female may ignore a male's greeting or pass him by when she is alone, but when she is with other females she will stop and talk to him. Her desire is to demonstrate the relationship she has with him to the other females.

sympathy with Aids sufferers. The producers of the ribbons were homosexual men and the wearers were predominantly women. Whatever else it was, it was also the mass-marking of women by homosexual men.

Indiscriminate marking

Discriminate, indiscriminate, appetent and inappetent markers

There appears to be a male instinct to distribute markers indiscriminately. Its occurrence may be rare but it is distinct, taking the form of buying drinks for everyone, giving away small gifts, or greeting people at random. Some of these behaviours can find expression during specific public holidays, such as wishing everyone good cheer at Christmas-time. Whether indiscriminate marking is limited to certain dates is not important, the instinct will find its catharsis in some way. That the instinct is acceptably expressed only at designated times of year allows the participants to place markers at random or near-random without those actions being given undue significance. Markers are also *appetent* or *inappetent*: an appetent marker is one for which something is wanted or expected in return.

Weakening and distributing markers

The female instinct to weaken markers

Markers are favoured by males, because they are unambiguous, often material and often involve the wealth that he creates. Conversely, the female instinct is to weaken them, that is, reduce their significance. One way markers are weakened is by distributing them, though in some instances doing so performs a valuable social function.

Widening a conversation

A basic form of distributing a marker is widening a conversation. A man and woman may be sitting at a bar or in a café say, and the man strikes up conversation with the woman. The woman is happy to talk, but doesn't want him to get the wrong idea, so she involves a nearby, second man in the conversation too. If the female is of reproductive age and especially if she is attractive (a 'model' female), then she has accomplished two things: she has set up competition between two males, and she has reduced the significance of her conversation with the first. Or she might have initiated the conversation, and seeks to reduce the significance of that. Opening a conversation is more significant than responding to one, since it constitutes an approach.

Offering sweets around

Perhaps a simpler example is offering sweets around. In an informal setting, say in a waiting room or classroom, a sweet may be offered to a person sitting alongside. The offered sweet is taken, then there may be concern that the offer is attributed with more meaning than intended, so the sweets are offered further afield, to those in the immediate surrounding.

The modern phenomenon of exterior notices advertising a private birthday or anniversary

A behaviour which has become common in recent years is people advertising a birthday or other celebration externally. Decorations are placed not just inside a house or office building but outside, advertising the event within. This involves neighbours and passers-by and is another expression of distributing a marker. There is no suggestion that the passing strangers are invited inside, or perhaps they would not be so keen to advertise what is essentially a private gathering. A notable form of marker distribution practiced by females is *vicarious generosity*, which will be detailed separately.

Another behaviour touching on marker distribution is someone, whom we shall call A, speaking ostensibly to B but knowing that C (and possibly others too) are listening. On the face of it his intended audience is B but he knows that others are within earshot and they are the real intended recipients of his message.

Building on others' markers Distributing inventions

Distributing a marker commonly weakens it, but it may also complete and enhance it, as in the commercialisation and distribution of an invention. Clearly restricting an invention to a single location, or to private use by one individual, would render it of little utility and severely limit its impact. An invention such as a novel device will only become a marker on a meaningful scale once distribution of it has taken place. The men who translate what is probably a bulky prototype, or a device or compound which only works under controlled laboratory conditions, are placing their mark on the inventor's marker; they are expressing their instinct to reinforce, or fortify, or increase the value of markers. The marker has become a collective effort, enabling the inventor to make his mark on wider society.

An academic field as an area to be marked

Novelty can be a marker, almost on its own. Suppose the novelty is the chemical synthesis of a naturally occurring, yet extremely complex, substance. The synthesis has never been accomplished in the laboratory before. The substance is abundant in nature, so the accomplishment is unlikely to have commercial value. Replicating the molecule is a purely academic exercise. If the chemist succeeds he places his mark on his field. Even the terminology of an 'academic field' shows equivalence to geographic territory. The animal ventures forth, leaving markers, and the human does the same.

Females weaken markers

The female instinct is to weaken markers: she seeks to reduce their significance and devalue them. Denial of a marker is the ultimate weakening of it. In the extreme, the female can devalue a marker entirely by denying its existence. One means this can be achieved is by refusing to acknowledge her memory of an earlier event.

The ultimate weakening of a marker. Compound benefit

That event will have involved markers such as sharing time at the same place, talking to each other and so on. A lengthy and memorable meeting has occurred but the female denies memory of it. By doing so she encourages the male to recount his recollection of the event, as he attempts to jog her memory. By this means the female can gather information, enabling her to compare her perceptions and recollections of the meeting with his. This double process – of obtaining benefit on two separate fronts, in this case weakening markers and gathering information at the same time – is an example of *compound benefit*.

Transforming markers

Markers may not only be weakened by females, they may be *transformed*: that is, changed in some way. The term derives from an electrical transformer, made of two coils wrapped around a ferrous core. There is no direct electrical connection between the primary and secondary coils, yet current passes from one coil to the other by electromagnetic induction. Current flowing in one coil induces a current in the other.

Comparison with an electrical transformer

A transformer is capable of various functions: firstly, it isolates the secondary circuit from the primary one, with several advantages; secondly, voltage can be reduced or increased, i.e. conversion takes place; thirdly, phase inversion can be accomplished. They are also reversible: they can be used to either step up or step down a voltage depending on which coil has current applied. A transformer enables alternating current to be isolated, changed and inverted. Thus for a general alteration of a marker, especially one that involves some convoluted process, a marker is said to be transformed.

What is meant by transformation

Females obfuscate – that is, they obscure their strategies by behaving illogically. Often she herself does not understand why she behaves the way she does. But her illogical actions serve an important purpose, and her capricious and sometimes downright perverse behaviour is evolutionarily advantageous for her. Her instincts have stood her in good stead for many hundreds of thousands of years. Making herself confusing to males renders her strategies hard to understand, predict and counter.

Female obfuscation as a defence mechanism

Underneath the layers of obfuscation, females tend to employ the Tit For Tat (TFT) strategy: you do something for me and I'll do something for you. This and

Females tend to employ TFT

Avoiding having to reciprocate

the importance she places on feelings explains her attitude that the sensation of having done good is the payoff for a gift. If TFT applies and there were no transformation mechanism, the female would feel obliged to repay males for the benefit of every male marker. This, for her, is an extremely unsatisfactory situation.

Placing a marker is a basic procedure, but transforming a marker is a more interesting one. A basic form of transforming a marker occurs on buying a female a drink at a bar, when she maintains to herself that she is doing the male a favour by accepting a drink from him. Women admit doing this.

A man buys a woman a drink in a bar

Suppose that a female in a bar is offered a drink, and she thinks that rejecting it would make the male feel bad; that a refusal would make him dejected and diminish his status. Perhaps she feels sorry for him because he is alone in the bar. Projecting feminine values onto the male, she may assume that he is lonely and sad (rather than alone and content), or she may accurately perceive him to be so. In empathy with his desire that his marker be accepted she receives it. She accepts the drink believing she is being kind, because that is what he wants, and also she does not want to issue a rejection, possibly in sight of others.

Certainly at this stage we can appreciate how she can feel that she is doing the male a favour by accepting a marker from him. She values emotion above the monetary or other costs of the marker. By assuming that the male sees it the same way she has projected her attitude onto the male.

A token: When one thing means another

The male in this example however was using the drink also as a *token*, a symbol or representation of something else. In this he is applying largely female-defined norms of social behaviour. Accepting the drink is likely to be symbolic of being prepared to consider further involvement, and this leads to a situation in which the female must issue a firmer rejection later on. The original kindness in not issuing a minor rejection has necessitated a more strident one. The situation has been exacerbated; by trying to be kind, if indeed that was her intention, she has made things worse.

The rationale of transforming markers

In accepting a marker from the male, she has allowed herself to be engaged with him: a relationship of some form has been established and, projecting her own values onto the male, she feels that by that involvement repayment has been made. The cost of the marker to the male (such as a drink or small gift, or the time and effort involved in placing a marker of a different kind) to the female

A Dutchwoman, around 30, reported a daytime outing to a bar with a female friend. She told how for the whole session they had helped themselves to drinks, simply taking them out of men's hands.

The value females place on sensation is evident when they refuse to allow their dog to be stroked. Usually the dog would be happy to be petted, but the female owner is aware that pleasure is obtained by doing so and refuses the amenity. For many, stroking an animal reduces stress. In a feminine environment such refusals become commonplace.

mind is compensated by the sensation he experiences on making it. The female has graciously allowed the male to mark her; he is associated with her. By accepting a marker from him the female is consuming the fruit of his labour and allowed the male to express his instinct to mark. This is the same philosophy as that the giver to charity receives payment in the form of a virtuous feeling – the sensation is regarded as the good purchased. The benefit the charity donation provides to its intended recipients is almost incidental.

Monetary value is dwarfed by sentiment

The essence of this marker transformation is the female projecting her nature onto males. It is a simple extension, in an environment of increased female influence, and in which she has greater confidence in the validity of her emotions, for the female to imagine that the male values the expression of his marking instincts above the physical cost of the marker.

The female projects her attitude onto the male

Taking this a step further, a female who ascribes high status to herself may believe that by accepting a marker from a male she is complimenting him; by receiving a drink from him she enhances his status. In her mind, the value of that enhancement will of course exceed the minor cost of the drink. That is, his gratification in having marked her far outweighs the trivial monetary cost of it. The female thus believes that she does the male a service by accepting the drink from him.

A female with a high opinion of herself

Another circumstance to be considered is when the female indicates to the male, subtly or less subtly, her view that she has done him a favour by accepting a drink from him. During the offer, the female might ask, 'Why should I let you buy me a drink?' After the drink is delivered she might say or imply 'I only allowed you to buy me a drink because you looked sad and lonely and thought that getting me a drink would make you feel better.' Indeed, if a consensus of marker transformation were abroad, the male could hardly fail to be aware of it, even in the absence of explicit statements.

Telling the male that his marker has been transformed

Females mark males

A converse scenario is when the female marks the male: a wife ironing her husband's shirt. The wife expresses her instinct to mark her husband by tending to his needs, and transformation takes place when she maintains (to herself or another) that her activity is solely for his benefit. Undoubtedly, a service is being

The female marks her mate

done for the man who has his shirt washed and ironed, but the trivial effort required when modern devices are employed, when hitherto laundry and mending would have involved several days' work, mean that her instinct to mark her mate is hardly discharged before the task is completed.

This transformation follows a different pattern to that of a male buying a female a drink, otherwise the male would claim that he was doing the female a favour by allowing her to iron his shirt. For both the drink and the ironing, the significance of the marker is modified. The monetary cost of the drink is downplayed. During an argument or divorce proceedings, when it provides advantage to her, we can imagine that the physical cost of the ironing (time and the energy expended) might be emphasised. For the drink, its symbolic component will sometimes be dismissed for general female advantage – females drink for free. The ironing symbolizes the relationship the female has with her partner, but the pleasure she experiences on expressing her instinct is usually unstated. Common to both scenarios is that the significance of markers, and also of the symbolic elements called tokens, are manipulated to the benefit of the female.

Modulating the significance of markers according to particular circumstances

When the female believes she is doing a favour by accepting a drink, or denies that her chief motivation is satisfying her instinct to mark her mate, an inversion of some kind takes place. The transformation mechanism has inversion at its core. When it is amplified by expressing the transformation explicitly to the male then a reflection is applied: the female attempts to impress the inversion she has accomplished onto the male.

The marker as an inversion

The implications of the female ability to transform markers are profound. Buying someone a drink is an act of generosity, regardless of any ulterior motive which may exist. It costs money, reducing the wealth of the provider. The female however, by transforming the marker, is capable of turning this generous act around, to believe that she is being generous by accepting it. Is this mechanism capable of being extended to all markers?

Males have invented almost everything

Males' role in producing practically every modern amenity, such as electrical power, the washing machine, the vacuum cleaner and sanitation, is neglected to the point of dismissal. This is a form of marker-weakening. The female plays down the significance of these male efforts, for before their existence the work

An airplane is about to crash. During its slow but inexorable dive towards the ocean one of the female passengers jumps up and announces, 'If I'm going to die, I want to die feeling like a woman.' She throws off her clothes and asks, 'Is there someone on this plane who is man enough to make me feel like a woman?' A man stands up, removes his shirt and hands it to her. 'Here' he says, 'iron this.'

of cooking and cleaning necessary to maintain a household was a full-time occupation. Is it possible that she not only belittles the contribution male inventions have made to modern life, but that she also transforms them, believing somehow that she is doing mankind a service by using them?

The female capacity to transform markers accounts for the blasé and unthinking manner in which she exploits male-derived amenities such as the motor car and the computer. The purpose and function of the weakening and transformation of markers is their depreciation – to make them seem less important and valuable than they really are. Transforming a marker is by no means the only procedure employed by females involving such convolution.

The purpose of marker transformation

Transforming markers

1. A male marks a female by buying her a drink.

MALE	FEMALE
Pays cost.	Receives drink from male.
The male marks the female as being included in his sphere of influence.	The female weakens the marker by deprecating its monetary cost.
Token: To the male, the acceptance of the drink is a token for being prepared to consider further involvement, or at least to be included in his sphere of influence.	Transformation: The female believes she is doing the male a favour by accepting it.
	The token can be ignored for general female advantage. Then females drink for free.

2. A female marks a male by ironing or mending his clothes.

MALE	FEMALE
Receives service.	Does service for male.
	Marks male.
	Transformation: She claims she is doing him a service rather than satisfying her instinct to mark her mate.
The male can believe it is done for his benefit.	Token: The act of preparing clothes symbolizes her relationship with the male, and her role as help-mate for him. This can be unstated for general female advantage.

4 Tokens

A token is when one thing means another

Tokens are all around us, though we may not always recognise them. A token is a thing which represents or symbolizes something else.

The prototype token was the piece of metal issued by a slot machine in lieu of money. The metal disc may be the same size and weight as a real coin, and be accepted by the machine as if it were a real coin. The token may be redeemable for drinks or goods in the place where the slot machine is located, but it cannot be spent outside.

The prototype token and some of its essential properties

A token becomes meaningless without transactions involving it, but briefly examining its essential properties, divorced from any transaction, will cause much of its mystery to be shed.

The essential features of the token are that firstly, it is defined by the giver and secondly, its value can be different for the giver and the receiver. Being ambiguous and therefore manipulative, tokens are preferred by females, and this accords with the proposed evolutionary origin of the token.

Tokens have an ambiguous component

Even if the token has physical properties it always has some immeasurable, intangible component. When the token is an actual object, and is given to somebody, then it is also a marker, because it unambiguously indicates involvement between the giver and the receiver. However it is the other, intangible part which really makes the token interesting.

The value of a slot-machine token is highly variable

Suppose our slot-machine player has spent a few hours playing and ends up with many tokens, no money, and needing cigarettes. He may exchange his tokens for drinks and snacks but the establishment does not sell tobacco. He must try to sell his tokens and the price he would obtain for them is highly uncertain. It might depend on his appearance, because if he were unkempt a prospective buyer might think they were stolen. Luck would play a part, with the fortuitous presence of another customer who just happens to want his tokens. Another factor is how desperate he is for a cigarette. He could exchange his tokens for money or directly for cigarettes. If his winnings had been in the form of money the situation would be entirely different.

Symbolism

We talk of a 'token of esteem' and a trophy or prize symbolizes a particular achievement or award. The trophy is a physical symbol of success, as in being awarded a medal for winning a race or a cup for winning a game. Likewise with a 'token of affection': the gift is supposed to be appreciated chiefly for its allusive value. It symbolizes the affection one person holds for another.

Some years ago a gang of criminals broke into the offices of the Transport and General Workers' Union near Hull's city centre. Finding the safe, they set about it with an electric drill, attempting to drill out the lock. While this was being done, one of the gang found the key to the safe behind a picture hanging on the opposite wall, but by this time the lock was ruined and could not be opened even with the key. With great ingenuity and resource the old and heavy safe was removed into a vehicle and taken to some waste land, where an expert was brought in to open it with a small amount of explosive. Eventually the safe was opened, and found to contain bags of plastic tokens which had formerly been given to schoolchildren to pay for their bus journeys to school. The scheme had been abandoned a few years before.

Recognised and unrecognised tokens

Everyday tokens – the price of a cup of coffee

The price of a cup of coffee in a café is a token because the cost of the coffee includes many expenses: staff wages, the rent of the premises, the cost of the energy to make the premises comfortable and the amortized cost of the furniture and fittings – the cost of the fittings spread over the entire time of their use. The actual cost of the coffee is probably the lowest of all these. If the price on the menu were not a token, all these separate components might be listed, plus the profit the owner expects to take. Doing this would be patently absurd; the menu would resemble the financial report of a large corporation.

Prices in general

The token nature of the cost of coffee in a café can be extended to any price, though not so obviously because many goods do not involve such high overheads relative to the price of the good. The price of a washing machine in a shop includes many of the overheads of a café, but here the washing machine is a relatively expensive item. For some products, notably cars, beer and jewellery, the sale price is significantly increased by the cost of advertising. The consumer pays the cost of stimulating his desire for it. He may be dimly aware of these components, but to him the price he pays is solely for possession of the good.

Tokens in repair charges

Sometimes repairers will disguise a repair charge in a manner acceptable to the customer. Suppose several hours had been spent locating a troublesome, intermittent fault eventually isolated to a minor component of insignificant cost. It could be a resistor in an electronic circuit (cost: pennies) or a sensor buried deep inside a car engine, requiring almost the entire engine to be dismantled to reach it. The customer would be unhappy paying for many hours of skilled labour with almost no cost of replaced components. Hence the claim is made that a major component has been replaced; the labour cost is reduced and the customer's displeasure is averted. The price of the invented new component is a token for the time the repairman spent finding the fault.

Euphemism

Euphemism and its origin

Tokens are employed in everyday life in another way. Civilised sensibilities lead to the use of euphemism, which are tokens using language. Metaphor is used to avoid directly describing bodily functions and subjects which upset our state of mind. Using tokens, a superficial pretence is maintained that certain things don't happen or are not as bad as they really are. Since female sensibilities are more delicate than males', we can fairly attribute the development of euphemism to females. Euphemisms serve to avoid the discomfort of thoughts being unpleasantly diverted to vivid images of bodily functions, disabilities or similar perturbing topics.

Common euphemisms

Thus we 'spend a penny' instead of announcing that we need to defecate; someone who is mentally deficient is 'not quite all there' and someone with mental illness 'has a screw loose.' A dullard is 'not the sharpest knife in the drawer'; the doctor asks his patient if the 'waterworks are alright' or whether 'everything's alright in the marriage department.' The sex act might be avidly described to a single sex group (probably in greater detail to a female one, and including more personal information), but in polite, mixed society it is 'making love,' a term which within living memory meant professing admiration and devotion. The homosexual who was described as 'not like other men' can now be 'as camp as a row of tents' and is 'gay' regardless of how unhappy he is.

Giving orders politely

Another form of token in language is used between a boss and his subordinates at work, especially in salaried and professional occupations. A boss might tell a subordinate 'I think it would be better this way' rather than issue a direct command. Here euphemism is used to protect the egos of subordinates, to avoid constantly reminding them of their inferior status. The boss who issued curt orders would likely be regarded as arrogant and domineering. A pretence is made that the subordinate has a say in the matter, perhaps even an equal one, and that he has the option of querying the order which has been given in the form of a suggestion.

Hints and white lies

Hints as tokens

Euphemisms are tokens in language made familiar by common usage. Hints, on the other hand, follow no established pattern and convey an implicit message in the guise of, or in addition to, another.

Hints are ambiguous and manipulative. They require a fine ear and that the receiver be 'on the same wavelength' as the giver. That is, a degree of empathy is required for the receiver to correctly interpret the underlying message. Being ambiguous the message is deniable, avoiding commitment and retaining control. As such it is a female policy which has evolved, like a great many female procedures, to compensate for the male's greater physical strength.

Understanding hints and why they exist

Males generally understand the female preference for tokens and allow for it. As an adolescent the male quickly learns that if he asks the female directly for what he wants he is unlikely to get it. In her responses to his proposals, the male appreciates that what is said is often a pretext, that is a token, a symbolic utterance which has the same meaning almost irrespective of the words used. He understands that 'I'm washing my hair tonight' and 'I'm unavailable to you' are synonymous. Sometimes the claim is made that such a pretext is employed for the male's benefit, as a face-saving gesture, but as the excuses increase in whimsy it becomes obvious that they also, perhaps only, serve as an expression of her power. And that power derives entirely from her sexual desirability. The use of a patently false excuse is an expression of her power over males, increasing her confidence in future interactions with them. A teenage girl may claim to be as busy as a high-flying executive, with no gap in her full itinerary. A young Dutchwoman advises another, 'Just tell him anything.'

An early lesson for the male. 'Just tell him anything'

A hint is obviously a token because the person receiving it may not perceive the underlying message. Its implicit meaning is clear to the giver, for the words were crafted to include it, but it is far from certain that the implied component will be understood by the receiver. By the use of hints the female can demand that the male interacts with her on her terms, sensitive to subtle nuances to which a more masculine male would likely be oblivious. By issuing tokens in the form of hints she may preferentially select as mates feminine men over masculine ones, and by this policy she is able to further female influence in the long-term.

The nature of hints and a long-term effect

Origins of the token

Sex is the mechanism with the most direct evolutionary link – it is easy to see how a trait conferring advantage in mating (in other words, sexual selection) can be passed genetically to the offspring which are the product of it. It can then proliferate throughout a population. Therefore it is to mating strategies that we look for origins in general, and of the token in particular.

The importance of sexual selection

A potential origin for tokens exists in the mating gifts found in the animal world. Males of some insect species present the female with a gift of food as a preliminary to mating, or to keep her occupied during copulation. Thus the male scorpionfly gives a 'nuptial gift' to his mate. The bower bird builds a structure filled with bright objects to attract a female. Other male birds of paradise perform complex dances and elaborate displays to attract an audience of

Nuptial gifts as origin of the token

A *hoerenloper* (prostitute-goer) came away from a window without gaining admittance, and I asked him, 'What happened, did she refuse to take you or did you change your mind?' He was a big, strapping man with the flattened nose and puffy face of a boxer, but seemed perfectly amiable. She had told him 'I don't have the time.'

females. As his performance begins the females form a row of spectators, and immediately after his display he selects a female from among them, flies over and mates with her. Among the audience too are young males watching to learn how it's done.

Comparing birds of paradise with a theatre performance

This scenario is just like a showman on a stage, perhaps a celebrated mime artist, giving his artistic display and showing off to the spectators. After the curtain call he may not rush down among the audience and thrust himself upon his favoured female, but there will be plenty of female admirers at the post-performance party. It is there that he can take his pick.

The classic case of the peacock

It is said that bright and exaggerated plumage, most famously of the peacock, is evolutionarily advantageous because it correlates with fitness. Being able to grow and clean such elaborate features indicates robust health, since a weak or diseased animal is unable to maintain such an expensive overhead. This is unlikely to be what the peahen is thinking however. To her, the male's display signifies his desirability as a mate, and she reliably selects the peacock with the longest tail feathers. This has been tested by adding and subtracting a few inches and seeing which bird the peahen prefers.

Elaborately wrapped but empty gifts by insects

Many mating gifts have become vestigial and symbolic. The catastrophic event 65 million years ago extinguished all large animals but insects survived and their long evolutionary history has led to complex behaviours. Some birds also survived which, combined with their rapid reproduction cycle, potentially explains the emergence of mating behaviours involving tokens in birds. In some insects the nuptial gift has become an elaborately wrapped parcel containing nothing at all. The twig a male bird shows to a female represents his willingness to cooperate in building a nest.

When tokens arise

Symbolic rituals seem to evolve when the male seeks to attract multiple females, at which point he can choose between them. Or, more commonly, the female makes a choice from multiple males. Token gifts tend not to evolve when the male surrounds himself with a stable of females whom he dominates. Then the contest is between males, with the victor winning mating rights with the females. In this case exaggerated male secondary sexual characters are not for impressive display but to confer advantage in battles with rival males. Large antlers and massive forequarters are examples.

> Nature has given women so much power that the law has very wisely given them little.
>
> Samuel Johnson (1763)

Here is the essential link: tokens evolve when one sex, usually the female, is afforded a choice of sexual partner. For many species, probably the majority, males fight over territory, and mating privileges with the females it contains come with the territory. Oestrus and the forceful response of the male, coupled with his greater physical strength, mean that the female has little option but to submit.

Males battle for territory, which includes the females within

Pick-up lines as tokens

The analogy is between the token gifts, or mating parcels, used by insects and birds and human 'pick-up lines,' here called *approach statements*. The approach statement is the first words used when a person approaches another. An informal survey of approach statements made by males when approaching females revealed the following categories:

1. The offer of a drink, which is directly equivalent to a parcel of food. The drink is a marker, allowing the male to mark the female, and likely to be a token of his interest. Acceptance of the drink can be a token that the female desires further interaction with him, or is at least prepared to consider it.

Types of approach statement and their general themes

2. A pretext for opening a conversation, such as pretending to mistake the female for another. This enables the male to discover the female's name (a *handle*) and prolong the conversation. The pretext is obviously a token since, initially at least, the male and female interpret it in different ways.

3. A direct enquiry about the target, such as asking her name or how she is. This is a relatively unambiguous approach, but it usually remains implicit that the male is interested in her as a prospective partner.

4. The largest category was of approach statements that involved some mild pleasantry or joke, in one instance referring to an indiscriminate signal the female was emitting. The pleasantry is often combined with flattery. Here the mating parcel has become virtual, and the gift takes the form of amusing the female and making her feel good about herself.

A notable exception to the cases above was the practice of a friend of one of the survey respondents. He would approach a female he was attracted to holding a low-value banknote and ask her if she had dropped it. This was a test to see whether she was honest. If she claimed the money was hers, he would tell her 'No it's not' and abandon. Her truthful denial of ownership of the banknote prompted an explanation of the test and the beginning of a conversation.

An interesting exception – a test of female honesty

Here again a token was employed, but combined a pretext for starting a conversation with a token of his own: that the female who disclaimed the banknote was honest generally, since this was important to him.

In parts of Europe, and in contrast, 'Do you have a light?' seems to be practically the only approach statement a female ever makes to a male. A few European psychology experiments have been done in which a female approached a male, and the males usually reported during the de-briefing afterwards that they thought it was a trick.

Female approaches to males

Successful approaches involve tokens. In an American singles bar the least successful statement tested was 'Let's go back to my apartment and have sex right now.' Such a proposition might be successful, but only if it is delivered as a joke, simultaneously attenuating its bluntness and amusing the female. A clear parallel exists between the elaborately wrapped but empty parcel the male insect supplies and the token involving amusement and flattery the human male gives to his prospective mate.

Results in American singles bars

Along similar lines human, particularly male, endeavour such as music and success in sport can be regarded as sexual display. The originality of the artist, products of the inventor or discoveries of the scientist can all be thought of as sexual displays in more evolved form. These spring originally from the gifts the male provides before the female consents to bear his offspring, or as demonstrations of his fitness as a father of her children. Putatively, tokens derive from this original source.

Male endeavour as sexual display

Tokens for sex

The proposition 'Come back and see my etchings' after a night in a pub or bar is the classic invitation for sex in token form, so hackneyed that it has become a catch-phrase and a feature of jokes. An invitation for coffee is more ambiguous, but whatever allusion is used, by insisting on a token the female avoids any sort of pledge or firm commitment to provide sexual favours. This allows her to retreat if the male fails to fulfil her expectations, becomes demanding, or otherwise alarms her. She retains control by insisting on ambiguity because control of sex is paramount to her.

The female retains control by the use of tokens

In a feminine setting virtually any proposal can be construed as an invitation

An attractive member of the opposite sex approaches you and says, 'Hi, I've been noticing you around town lately, and I find you very attractive. Would you have sex with me?' This was the approach statement tested by Clarke and Hatfield and reported in their paper 'Gender differences in receptivity to sexual offers' (1989). The results were that 100% of the females approached by males refused, while 75% of the males who were approached by a female accepted. Furthermore, many of the 25% of males who declined were apologetic, saying they could not accept the offer because of a previous commitment.

for sex. The more latitude the female is allowed, the more her capricious nature will be expressed, the more she will project that nature onto the male and the more insecure of his intentions she will become. One Dutch girl revealed during an extended conversation that she had been advised not to accept any invitation for coffee lest she be raped. This in broad daylight, actually during a sunny afternoon in a busy city centre.

The more latitude the female is allowed...

The female predilection for speculation, which likely has evolved to allow just this eventuality to be foreseen, enables females to envisage sex occurring in the most unlikely circumstances. For as long as women have had undergarments, men have been trying to get into them. For millennia, resourceful males have sought to steer females into a position where sex could be obtained, and the speculative ability of females has evolved as a defence mechanism to counter this threat. The threat was far from trivial: attempts to induce abortions and childbirth were the major cause of female mortality in prehistoric times. Being manoeuvred into a situation where she is obliged to provide sex can be disastrous for her. In the absence of logic, indeed without logical restraint, unfettered speculation allows multiple outcomes to be foreseen. Her ability to wildly speculate, the female preference for tokens and her desire for novelty (which males seek to satisfy), mean that anything can become a token for sex.

Females love to speculate. Anything can become a token for sex

Tokenism

Tokens exist more generally. Buying a book to show support for its author or subscribing to a newspaper because one endorses its political stance are forms of tokenism, especially if they are unlikely to be read. The money paid is a token of approval rather than a means to obtain the publication. Attendance at a café not because one wants to consume but to show approval of the establishment, perhaps for its ambiance and décor, is a token act. A fan of a musical group

Common forms of tokenism

might attend every performance as a public display of favour, yet another expression of tokenism.

Written and spoken avowals can be rendered insignificant by tokenism. Once the emotion that led to the utterance or writing has dissipated, the actual meaning of the words or promise is considered insignificant. The words have become merely a symbol of the sentiment that was felt at the time.

Effects of tokenism. Reading more into words and actions than exists

Actions can be performed as tokens. It follows that in an environment of great female influence, due to projection, many actions will be interpreted as tokens. Much more will be perceived and implied from ordinary and apparently insignificant acts. A proposal to a female can result in a sense that it has been construed as approval for all the behaviour she has engaged in beforehand, none of which the proposer could possibly be aware of.

Primitive and religious tokens

Superstitious tokenism

Primitive societies imbue physical objects with supernatural properties, often extensively. Trees, mountains, sand and sea contain or embody powerful spirits, disturbance of which can bring forth calamity. Almost every exceptional event is attributed to the spirit of an object or the spell of a witch. Elaborate and lengthy ceremonies are performed to please or placate these spirits and bring good fortune. Objects can become so spiritually significant that their physical existence becomes incidental. The object becomes a token for the abstract and unseen entity which inhabits it.

Tokenism in Africa and London

An African man ill with a fatal disease, beyond the help of the white doctors' medical station, insists on being allowed to lay on the operating table, confident that the act itself will cure him. In contemporary London Negro spiritualism has merged with fundamentalist Christian beliefs and children have been labelled as witches. A number of child murders have resulted.

Asiatics assign great significance to numbers. In China it is common to reject any house or telephone number which includes a four, because that number

Sleeping with the enemy. A fellow Yorkshireman in Amsterdam gave an account of a Dutchwoman who was in the habit of asking a male if she could sleep with him. Then when the time came she would take off all or most of her clothes and climb into bed. When the inevitable advances were made she would 'throw up in horror' (in his words) at the prospect of sex. He knew this to have occurred with six different males. With him it had happened on two or three occasions and each time he had just turned over and gone to sleep. Apparently one Dutchman wrote her a letter afterwards apologizing for his presumption that sex would take place.

During the height of the season in Amsterdam, when the atmosphere seemed veritably thick with sex, a number of young Dutchwomen revealed that they masturbated several times each day. Nevertheless, many Dutchmen reported that they had difficulty meeting their basic needs and a few were personally known to me who had not had sex for years. An Englishman recounted taking a young Dutchwoman out for two nights, paying for all the drinks and a meal, and at the end of the second night she told him she was a lesbian.

signifies death. Eight on the other hand denotes good fortune. In the cabbala, which is Jewish mysticism, every Hebrew letter has a numeric value and thus every word has a mystical, numerological significance.

Numerology as tokenism

The supreme symbol in Christian iconography is the cross and a devout believer in the vicarious death of Christ would not look upon it and see just two pieces of wood. The doctrine of transubstantiation holds that after consecration the communion bread and wine physically becomes the body and blood of Christ. This and much other deep symbolism continues especially in Catholic rituals, in which the remains of saints and other artefacts are treated with reverence and awe. Places, people and objects are credited with supernatural properties, qualifying them as tokens. In Protestant doctrine however transubstantiation has been superseded by consubstantiation, by which it is held that the body and blood of Christ are only contained in the bread and wine, and coexist with it. With this, the level of tokenism has been reduced.

Tokenism in Christianity

Mass tokenism

With established religion in decline we should be wary of unrecognised, *de facto* religions filling the vacuum. A modern, extensive form of tokenism is the reverence paid to actors, singers and celebrities following their appearance in films and on TV. Clearly the actor symbolizes much more than a person performing a role and speaking predefined words from a script. The successful actor is idolized, perhaps because he embodies the aspirations and ideals of his viewers. This is contrived for profit using film and video effects by which the actor often appears to defy reality. He shrugs off bullet wounds, performs implausible feats and is effortlessly charming and witty. At one level this is plainly understood to be an illusion. At another though, a mysterious aura of stardom attaches to the actor who is really little more than a living puppet. This, surely, is an expression of mass tokenism.

The irrational reverence for actors

Soap operas and evidence of delusion

Even the lowliest cast-member of a soap opera is invited to open shops and supermarkets. It seems that for many viewers the fictional world of the soap opera is more vivid and real than their own life. Familiarity and involvement with these dramas far exceeds that with the political personalities and issues of the day. This willing mass delusion has resulted in a number of attacks upon actors. One actor playing a murderer in a soap opera was subjected to shouts of abuse, spat upon and attacked while out shopping by an old woman wielding a handbag. An actor playing a homosexual in another series, out with his girlfriend, was chased and beaten by a group of five drunken young men who believed he was actually homosexual.

Comparing TV tokenism with that in primitive societies

The world of the primitive tribesman is invisible to Westerners, but to him practically every object is alive with spirits and alternate personalities. Another world is soap operas, one with which millions of people, especially women, engage. Can these two be compared? The events portrayed in TV serials, merely figments of a screenwriter's imagination, are discussed as if they are real life, just as the motions of spirits and witches are treated as reality.

No evolutionary precedent for TV

TV has no evolutionary precedent but the roots of viewers' engagement may lie in the tokenism of primitive peoples, or similarly, early man's inclination to impart supernatural properties to people and objects as a means of explaining a universe that was mysterious to him.

Token money

Fiat currencies. The real value of money

Money is a token, symbolizing wealth. It is certainly not a good. Paper money began as receipts for deposits of gold and went on to become exchangeable ('Pay the bearer'). Until the Bank of England abandoned the gold standard in 1931 its 'promissory notes' could be redeemed for gold as of right. From that point on, the actual value of a banknote was zero. Contemporary money systems are fiat currencies, from the Latin *fiat*, an order or decree. The value of the money is decreed and no longer has any link to a precious metal. Governments and central banks now create money virtually at will.

John Law and the ruin of the French economy in 1720

John Law understood that confidence alone was the basis for public credit; that the banknote owes its whole authority to the intangible component of the token. He was surprised by people's willingness to accept pieces of paper solely because the government had defined them as tokens of wealth. Law was an early advocate of fiat currency and he was given royal licence to issue French currency and shares in what later became the American State of Louisiana. His schemes led to the ruin of the French economy in 1720. It is only when confidence in money fails that its token nature becomes evident; when, as in Zimbabwe recently, it became cheaper to use the nation's banknotes as toilet paper than to buy it.

Many more forms of money exist than we think. Pre-payment cards and mobile phone credits are akin to alternative currencies, with numerous impracticalities and inefficiencies. The money represented usually cannot be transferred to anyone else, and it cannot be spent any other way. Some promotions exploit this inefficiency, as when a product carries a '50p off next purchase' voucher. The vendor knows that the promotion will entice many more to purchase the product than will actually redeem the coupon. It may be left behind, lost or accidentally thrown away. Perhaps only ten percent of the coupons are actually redeemed.

Common tokens for money, or tokens of tokens

Mass tokenism with a symbolic common currency clearly confers economic benefit, and examining the balance between money as a token and as a handle is a promising theme for analysis. We can expect that the more notional, that is the more token and feminine, a currency is, the more unstable it will be.

In London in 1993 I met a market researcher who interviewed women between 18 and 25. It was a financial questionnaire (probably a pretext for later selling some financial scheme or other) and he was paid 80p for each completed form. However if any of the essential details were found to be false he was not paid. Initially he had found that a little over 20% had contained incorrect personal details, like the stated occupation or address, or a wrong telephone number, the latter being the first item checked. When interviewing he had noticed dilation of the pupils when the women were being dishonest and also reddening of the lips – both involuntary signals with obvious sexual antecedents. To reduce the number of questionnaires for which he was not paid he now asked for the last digit of the telephone number to be repeated. If the woman could not repeat it he would immediately strike through the form and terminate the interview. Then she would blush with embarrassment.

5 Handles

A handle is a request that generates a fixed and predetermined response

Knowing someone's name is a handle state. The basic handle is calling that name. A handle state must exist, and have been set up somehow, before a valid handle can be issued.

If a name is known, calling the name causes the specified person to give a *handle response* – they will enquire why they have been called or make some other reply. But there are a number of situations when they might not respond.

Possible origins of handles. Animal hierarchies

If calling someone's name is the basic handle, we have difficulty identifying a non-human archetype or original case of the mechanism. While dogs and some other animals can respond to their name being called, there is no indication that pack and other social animals assign names to other individuals in their group. Individual animals are certainly identified, because a large amount of energy is devoted to maintaining or increasing the animal's position in the group hierarchy. Perhaps their 'thought names' take the form of 'Smells like tree bark' or 'He is number three in the hierarchy, I am number four.' In any event, even if animals do assign private names to each other, they lack the ability to call those names out.

Handles involve commitment and obligation, with varying degrees of formality. They concern expected behaviour, applying established norms. In many cases these norms have evolved over centuries, but they are modified as our social environment changes.

Forms of handles and handle responses

Often the response that is made to a handle is less important than that a response of some kind is made. The handle and its response may be in the form of a marker, such as making a verbal request and receiving a spoken reply. Or it could be combined with a token, as when symbolic gifts are given on notable occasions. The handle and its response could be an exchange of signals such as a customary exchange of nods with a neighbour or colleague.

The formal environment of the military

One of the most formal environments is the military and this is a rich source of illustration because expected behaviours are so firmly defined. Orders from a superior officer are issued to a subordinate and must be followed without question. Here the handle state is the disparity in rank, from which comes the authority to issue orders, and the order is the handle. Failure to respond to the handle results in punishment, and the power to punish derives from similar handle states – yet more officers of superior rank. Punishment discourages non-compliance with the handle.

HANDLE STATE	HANDLE	RESPONSE
Know someone's name	Call name	Receive reply
Lend something	Ask for its return	Item returned
In position to make proposal	Proposal	Conclusive reply
Proposal accepted	Later meeting agreed	Turns up
Able to touch or hold	Touch or hold	Not spurned
Marriage	Request for sex	Request granted

Military orders must be followed unfailingly, regardless of how illogical they seem. A less rigid relationship exists between an employer and his employee, but it again is a handle state with numerous presumptions. The employee is expected to attend during certain specified hours, do as he is told by his boss, and work for the benefit of the company.

Working for a boss

Handles are a routine feature of everyday life, though many are implicit. When driving a car in Britain it is assumed that the left side of the road will be taken and this is one example of many handles which are not explicitly stated. Driving on the right would very likely result in serious injuries, if not multiple deaths, and doing so would be an act of such wanton recklessness that criminal prosecution would follow, assuming of course that the driver survived. Even so, it is quite possible that there is no actual law stating that British motorists must drive on the left, and someone breaking this rule would be prosecuted for dangerous driving. Road signs stating the rule are rare, and only seen at ferry terminals and the like where they are provided for arriving foreign motorists. The handle state is the established norm of driving on the left, and the handle is the implicit request to conform to that convention.

Implicit handles, like the expectation to drive on the correct side of the road

Being a boyfriend or girlfriend is another handle state, distinguishing the relationship from a mere casual encounter. A partner in such a relationship can usually assume that meetings will occur regularly; that arranged meetings will be attended; and that some degree of physical freedom with the other's body will be permitted, even if this only extends to intimate gestures. At the least, a partner can expect to be able to hold the other's hand, or put an arm around them, without being rebuffed.

The boyfriend-girlfriend handle state. Expectations of relatives

Being a member of a family is also a handle state which, like the boyfriend-girlfriend handle state, varies widely in the requests each participant makes of another. Nevertheless family members normally expect to meet at important events such as marriages and funerals, and to be able to rely on each other for support in times of crisis. These are all handles deriving from the handle state of relatedness.

Marriage as a handle state

For individuals, possibly the ultimate handle state is being married, a condition in which numerous handles are formalised. Some of the handles which exist in this handle state are that the couple live together, sleep together and share the same fortunes.

Lending

Lending call be all of a handle, signal, marker and token

Offering or requesting a loan of something, and lending it, can incorporate all of a signal, marker, token and handle. For example, holding out a pen with raised eyebrows and a direct look is an offer to lend using signals alone, and there may be a hint of involvement beyond the temporary use of the pen, which is a token. The object or money loaned is a marker, unambiguously indicating their involvement with each other when it changes hands.

Chiefly though, the act of lending establishes a handle state. The handle state is inherent in the definition of lending, because the object or money loaned is expected to be returned. It remains the property of its owner.

Formal handles in finance

When we commit to a financial agreement the terms are often specified in detail. For example a contract may include penalty clauses in the form of overdue charges and elevated interest. A handle state exists between the borrower and his creditor; the expected response to the handle is repayment of the money. In the case of failure to honour the handle, that is repay the loan or failure to keep up the payments, the formality of the arrangement make the consequences obvious.

Informal loans between friends. Implicit handles

More instructive is the informal situation which might take place between two friends. Suppose one has lent some treasured or valuable item, such as a tool or car, to the other. Once the loan has been made, a handle state exists. Normally implicit in an informal loan of this kind are various terms: that the item will be returned when it is finished with, or when the lender asks for it. Then it is expected that a reason or excuse will be given for delay in returning the item.

Also implicit in the transaction is that the lender will not suffer loss by his act of generosity in making the loan. If the borrower crashed the car or lost the tool, the lender would feel entitled to compensation or a replacement. Certainly in the

> A pair of young Dutchwomen were asked for the terms under which our relationship was to continue; their answer was a quintessential expression of the feminine standpoint, 'Our only term is that there are no terms.' There were a great number of implied terms however: they did not expect to be raped or murdered, or other violent or illegal actions embarked upon, and such laws and our civilisation are defined, created and enforced by males.

case of an arrangement between two friends of long-standing, most or all of these terms would remain unspoken. It is another example of implicit handles – expectations which exist but have not been spelled out in fine, precise detail.

Written and unwritten rules

The loan of a key is an especially revealing case. Suppose a houseowner is going away for a few weeks and leaves a key to his house with a friend. He makes a number of assumptions when lending the key: that it will be returned immediately it is asked for; that it will not be copied; that it will not be given to anyone else. These are the unwritten rules associated with the loan of a key: in other words, they are implicit handles. Lending the key is also a token of trust, and of course the key itself is a marker, unambiguously indicating involvement between the owner of the key and the borrower of it.

The special circumstance of the loan of a key

Suppose then that while the houseowner is away sunning himself at some far-away paradise, a mutual friend finds himself without anywhere to stay. The friend has had a blazing row and been shown the door, or simply needs to keep out of someone's way for a while. The temporary keyholder, knowing that the houseowner wouldn't mind, provides the key to the empty house to the friend. He is not left to sleep in an alleyway, or spend money at a sterile hotel, and it is infinitely preferable to be in the bosom of one's friends at such a time. Putting up a mutual friend in these circumstances is all very reasonable, but one of the unwritten rules has been broken.

Unwritten rules are superior because they can be broken in exceptional circumstances

Unwritten rules are superior to written ones because they can be disregarded in exceptional circumstances. What has happened is that the implicit handle of not giving the key to a third party has been superseded by the superior implicit handle of providing shelter to a mutual friend in urgent need. If the handles had been made explicit, by being set down in the form of a written contract, or in law, such flexibility would not have been possible.

Breaking unwritten rules is often manifest in people with mental illness; this is the phenomenon of disinhibition. Hence it is legitimate to quote their actions as examples of basic drives which are normally inhibited by social convention. A mentally unstable person often defies implicit handles such as basic rules of tact or the standard of personal cleanliness expected of him. He may also express emotions, such as jealousy, which according to unspoken rules we normally keep to ourselves.

Disinhibition in mental illness

Weakening of handles

Weakening the marriage handle state

Handles may be lessened in their significance, straightforwardness and unambiguity by being weakened. An obvious example of a handle state being weakened is marriage; the vow of union until death has been weakened by the ready availability of divorce. Marriage is supposed to be a life-long commitment but now is seldom so. It is usually the wife who heads for the lawyer first.

A peculiar form of handle-weakening occurs when a beggar or slight acquaintance asks to borrow something, such as a cigarette or a small amount of money, as in 'Lend's a quid mate.' It is plain that the request is for a gift not a loan; 'lend' has become an informal term for 'give.' Presumably it is thought that the request is more likely to be successful if it is made under the pretext of a loan rather than for an outright donation. In any case the most likely outcome is that the request is denied. As detailed previously, the procedure of lending something is a strong handle, also involving a marker (the thing being lent), and using 'lend' as a synonym for 'give' weakens that handle. In fact since the word 'lend' in this context means something else, it has become a token.

Using 'lend' as a euphemism for 'give'

Suppose someone said 'Lend's a quid' and you gave him one, not expecting it back. If the loan were unexpectedly repaid then the integrity of the 'lend' handle is fortified. Equivalently, the handle is reinforced (in the conventional psychological sense of rewarding a behaviour so that it is more likely to recur).

As a 'joke'

A blatant example of handle-weakening, and one which recalls the basic handle, is repeatedly calling someone's name, hiding after each time to obscure the source of the call. This has been done as a rather poor joke.

Mutating handles

Handles are masculine

Of the four basic components of human interaction, signals, markers, tokens and handles, the most important and masculine component of them all is the handle. The female instinct is to weaken them.

Avoiding commitment by mutating handles

An efficient means of weakening a handle, for the purpose of diminishing it, is to change it into something else. A handle is weakened by treating it as if it were another form of interaction, a less binding element such as a token, marker or signal. The handle is not just weakened but mutated into something different.

> Behaviour progressively becomes abnormal, because normal behaviour involves obligations, which females find advantageous to avoid.

Sometimes a person gives a promise, say to send something on or perform some service, and it does not materialise. This is the mutation of a handle to a token. Then one intangible part of the token is the individual's sincerity at the time he gave the promise. Whatever his intention then or afterwards, the promise has not been honoured: his commitment has become a token.

Broken promises as tokens

The original mutation of a handle to a marker was a female failing to respond to a proposal. This is a continuing theme: as with a female being bought a drink in a bar, we use sexual selection mechanisms, especially those employed by the female, as models for human behaviour patterns generally.

Suppose a proposal is made to a female, for the purpose of illustration, one that is quite vague such as 'May I take you out sometime?' The handle state is the mutual environment of the proposal: possibly the male has engineered a situation, not discouraged by the female, in which a proposal was an expected or not unlikely event. Perhaps they had talked together before, or are engaged in a shared occupation or encounter.

Interpreting a proposal as a statement of interest – mutating a handle to a marker

The handle is the proposal, and requires a conclusive reply. She is not obliged to accept his proposal, but if a handle state exists sufficient for a proposal to be made then she should give a reply. However the female can interpret the proposal merely as a statement of interest: 'He likes me; he wants to be involved with me.' She has interpreted the handle as a marker. Applying her instinct to prevaricate and prolong sexual selection she gives an inconclusive reply, 'I'll think about it' or 'Ask me next week.' With her non-committal response, she either means No (which however is not said) or she expects to be asked again. She may anticipate being asked several times before she assents, for she knows that this has become common practice among her friends and contemporaries.

At the same time, she is likely to tell those same friends that a proposal has been made, and this is *proclamation of enhancement*. This increases her status and has the additional effect of rendering another proposal by the male to another of her female circle counter-productive.

Proclamation of enhancement

Handles in old age

An entirely different handle is the expectation people had of being cared for in their dotage by their children. This handle has been implicit for generations, until in modern Western societies it has been converted to markers. Instead of having the elderly parent live with them, where formerly they were cared for by members of their family, they are installed in nursing homes. The handle has been replaced by markers such as paying the care-home fees or visiting regularly.

Former established handles concerning care of the old

Incidentally, some interesting contrasting practices appear in Darwin's

Descent of Man. In one primitive society the aged, once they had reached a certain degree of infirmity, were buried alive to prevent them becoming a long, lingering burden. In another the aged one would climb a tree and be encouraged to jump by the children of the village.

Crime as the mutation of a handle to a marker

Mutating a handle to a marker is actually as commonplace as everyday theft. Imagine an old-fashioned shop featuring a counter with a shopkeeper behind it. (Originally shops specialised in particular products such as coffees, teas, cutlery or crockery exclusively, but here in mind is a general store.) As soon as the customer enters the shop and approaches the counter a handle state exists. Indeed a visitor enquiring only about a price, or local directions, tends to stay near the door. The customer makes a request – issues a handle – and the storekeeper pulls the item down from a shelf. A pile of goods accumulates on the counter and a further expectation exists that the customer will eventually pay for the goods and take them away.

An old-fashioned shop and the expected roles of the storekeeper and customer

Compare this with a modern supermarket. Being inside the shop is no longer a handle, but a marker. The person is unambiguously involved with the store by being on its property. A person might be there to shelter from the rain, admire the ice creams, or decide on the booze they'll be buying for Christmas. Placing an item into a trolley or basket suggests that the item will be purchased, but there is no obligation to do so. The customer might change his mind and the item returned to the shelf, or the trolley or basket could simply be abandoned. The only handle is that the goods are paid for before leaving the supermarket. Leaving the store with goods that have not been purchased – that is, shoplifting or stealing – is mutating that handle to a marker. The thief is unambiguously involved with the store by stealing from it. Both the act and the goods are markers.

Markers and handles in a modern supermarket

A builder who accepts money in advance for a job is also engaged in a handle. The request is the agreement of terms and handover of money, and the response is the completion of the work. The handle state is the expectation that the builder is honest and competent, and will meet his obligations. Perhaps the housewife who engages him has projected her nature onto him: she would never dream of accepting payment and disappearing without doing the work, so she assumes he would not. However disappear he does, either halfway through the job, or perhaps he never starts it. The marker is the money or work owed.

Unreliable builders

This situation differs from the supermarket example in at least one significant way, the time at which each party to the transaction recognises that the handle has changed to a marker. For the supermarket, the mutation takes place at the instant the goods are carried, unpaid for, over the threshold of the store (and

Are modern women merely Bimbos of the State?

The State-maintained gynaeceum – Unlike normal legal procedures the male is required to prove his innocence if he is accused of domestic abuse or harassment. Advocates for the battered women's shelter, often male-hating militant lesbian types, encourage these domestic abuse complaints. These centres are supported by public money and execute the expulsion of men from their homes, not according to the Christian legal tradition but in a manner which is entirely consistent with the notion of a massive, State-maintained gynaeceum. In effect, females are in the protection of the State, and a male who is obedient to the State might be given licence to one. If he displeases the female however, the State withdraws his licence.

Battered women's shelters and the like take children away from the father and grant custody to the State-approved guardian – the mother. These centres actively prevent reconciliation between husband and wife and promote abortion and divorce. The affidavits offered to women to sign are automated for easy filing and processing. Every technical and legal obstacle which might impede the break-up of a family has been levelled. All a female has to do is claim that she 'fears for her safety' and an *ex parte* order will be signed by a judge or administrative officer to remove the accused from his home. Further contact with his wife and children will be prohibited. A 'fear crime' is ambiguous and extremely difficult to disprove. Evidence of physical abuse is *not* required – all that is necessary is for the female to declare that she is fearful.

Braver, a psychologist at Arizona State University, has documented how allegations of abuse are often invented to gain advantage. Yet incarceration of the male based on accusation alone is common. After the male's release, he is often expelled from his home and ordered not to return. A magistrate will hear the case, but he will not be allowed to return to his house unless she consents. Not since before the Magna Carta in 1215 AD, which guaranteed a citizen's right not to be ordered from his home, have such draconian laws been enforced. Yet in recent years tens of thousands of innocent men have been evicted from their property and onto the street, often on perjured affidavits. Nobody is ever prosecuted for such affidavits, even when evidence of perjury is abundant.

Eduardo on www.heretical.com

The ultimate mutation of a handle to a marker? My 19-year-old Dutch girlfriend of two weeks told me one afternoon, 'I don't want to have sex with you again until I'm not your girlfriend.' Apparently she wished to be released from the boyfriend-girlfriend handle state. Not only would the relationship be modified to one of loose involvement (i.e. sporadic markers) by this conversion, the implied reward for her release from the handle state was sex, itself a marker.

When the change from a handle to a marker takes place

where a store detective may be lurking). For the unreliable builder, he may not acknowledge the handle state at all and only pretend to accept the handle. Or his intention may be to complete the work, but the handle is mutated to a marker five minutes after taking payment. Mutation for the person issuing the handle and the one giving its response can be asynchronous, occurring at different times. The housewife may only realise that the handle has changed to a marker when the builder can no longer be contacted, or after having been fobbed off with so many excuses that she eventually realises that the work will never be completed.

Implicit handles not to steal. Crime as a marker. Primordial spoiling as confirmation

It is difficult to envisage a criminal act which is not a mutation of a handle to a marker. An implicit handle in a well-adjusted Anglo-Saxon society is that personal property is respected. Just as with driving on the left side of the road, the rules are normally implicit – homes do not carry signs saying 'Do not burgle this house.' Burglars who invade a house are marking it: like the daubers of graffiti, they can cruise an area pointing out the places they have made their mark, and take pride in doing so. The territory is marked by their activity and its occupants are marked by their distress at the invasion. The items stolen are markers but in addition, amplified marking sometimes takes place, particularly if the burglars are amateurs. The house is ravaged, with furnishings and other objects scattered about and wantonly destroyed. Sheets and curtains might be ripped up. Sometimes faeces is left behind, which is marking in primeval form. The thieves' influence on the house and its inhabitants, equivalently the thieves' involvement with them, has been increased. That marking is sometimes amplified to this extent affirms that crime is the mutation of a handle to a marker.

Marriage handles and their mutation

The handle of conjugal rights

Marriage may be the ultimate handle state. For centuries this included the handle known as conjugal rights: that a husband had free access to his wife. Abandoning this convention, with husbands now being prosecuted for rape, is

Base and Spoiled Female. Base female is the mould from which all females are cast; she is morally corrupt. Spoiled female is her outward expression after being allowed excessive licence. Some females, such as the DF type, are likely to be slower on the uptake than other females but all will ultimately take advantage of such licence in an environment where it is available.

BSF is unrestrictedly allowed to act upon the dictates of her emotions. It is the ambition of every female to be so spoiled, because such females have the freedom to indulge their impulses. BSF must not only be financially supported but also continuously amused and entertained. She thrives on attention.

Any involvement by a male with BSF will be to his detriment, for it to be otherwise will require inordinate skill and dexterity. Some males are also capable of expressing BSF characteristics.

Single mothers are an example of BSF: they indulge themselves with a baby regardless of the consequences for the child. It is the principal responsibility of the female to control conception and ensure that the male she uses to conceive a child will remain to perform the fatherhood role that is necessary for it.

BSF will go through a male's papers and private belongings to gather information about him if the opportunity presents itself. She will answer the door or telephone only if she feels like it. BSF is quick to complain of boredom or discomfort, and will be the first to point out that one of a group maintains an advantageous position over the others (a trivial example being that one has not bought a round of drinks). She is uncompromisingly selfish and gives the appearance of having no perception of male sensitivities and needs. She wants to be contacted 'on the psychic telephone,' proposes giving the next letter of her name on each chance meeting, or refuses to give her name then flicks her hair in the male's face. BSF is, or seeks to be, totally capricious: 'I don't make appointments, I just go along as I feel' and 'Feelings are never wrong' are typical claims of the genre.

Before I lay me down to sleep,
I pray for a man who's not a creep.
One who's handsome, smart and strong,
One who knows to listen long.
One who thinks before he speaks,
One who'll call, not wait for weeks.
I pray he's rich and self-employed,
And when I spend, won't be annoyed,
Pull out my chair and hold my hand,
Massage my feet and help me stand.
Oh send a king to make me queen,
A man who loves to cook and clean.
I pray this man will love no other
And relish visits with my mother.

another example of the mutation of a handle to a marker. The expectation that the partners could rely on each other for their sexual needs has become degraded merely to their involvement in a shared bed or house. It is also an example of how the weakening of a handle has made life for many married couples worse.

Why many men married

Traditionally, going back to the last few centuries when we have some record, opportunities for sex outside marriage were few. There were grave consequences for the female who fell pregnant: shame, public disgrace or a rushed marriage. Women had to be supported by a man, and often his main motivation for taking on the encumbrance of a wife was that it brought to an end that awful state of sexual frustration that had been his burden since adolescence. If nothing else, at least in marriage he was guaranteed sex.

Marital 'rape' was better than the alternative. Sexless marriages

Consider his situation some time later, after perhaps ten or twenty years of sleeping with the same woman. Now the frustration for the male (and maybe also, without admitting so, for the female) is of a different sort. Sex has lost its novelty; the wife no longer glows with the bloom of youth. Children and other responsibilities weigh upon his shoulders. The obvious target of his frustrations is his wife, but the aggression he might direct towards her is otherwise expressed in violent, forced sex. Inevitably the act leads to further bonding between the two, and the absence of this physical outlet now has resulted in some couples living in marriages in which sex has not taken place for years.

Why women were not supposed to enjoy sex

The old-fashioned ethos was that women were not supposed to enjoy sex, or if they did, they were not to admit it. This was the 'marital advice' given to women as recently as the 1950s. Calling on evolution theory, the reason for this becomes obvious. Female coyness about enjoying sex means that in the long-term, she gets more. Her lack of libido, or reticence admitting it, is evolutionarily advantageous – more sex, and thus more children, result. A husband can use sex as a 'punishment,' replacing other violent actions. In these circumstances if he learns that his wife wants sex, his response is likely to be its withdrawal. The finding that 13% of women fantasize about being raped, and that women can achieve orgasm during forced sex, is evidence in support of this view. As is the modern prevalence of sexless marriages.

Mutating a handle to a signal

Being ignored by a neighbour

A handle can also be mutated to a signal. The following example uses two neighbours, a female and a male whom she wants to avoid. Normally a handle state exists between neighbours such that, when passing each other in a street nearby, or in some other place outside of their immediate neighbourhood, they would acknowledge each other with a nod or a brief greeting. If on seeing the male the female were to quickly scurry away, obviously to avoid him, she would be depriving her neighbour of the ability to issue a handle, and be issuing a signal.

Or, her male neighbour passes by, issues a handle in the form of a greeting, expecting a response, and she completely ignores him. The absence of a response is itself a signal.

Not Saying Goodbye is a signal of great ambiguity. If an extended encounter has taken place, an implicit handle usually exists that the transaction will be terminated with a mutual exchange of farewells. Not Saying Goodbye can be an expression of disdain, exasperation or, in some circumstances, an invitation to follow. This also is the mutation of a handle to a signal. Silence might be the most ambiguous signal of all.

The Not Saying Goodbye signal

The original mutation of a handle was a female receiving a proposal from a male and interpreting the proposal merely as a statement of interest. We imagine the situation of a female made headstrong perhaps by working in a bar or café in which she has regular contact with many unattached males. She receives many proposals. A male makes a proposal and she interprets it as a marker, adding it to her internal tally: 'That's the third tonight.' However she receives the proposal impassively and continues her activity without a pause. She has internally mutated the handle to a marker but her external response is no response at all, a null signal in response to the handle. A shake of the head, the relatively unambiguous signal meaning No, would be adequate satisfaction of the handle, even though the response takes an inferior form.

A bar worker keeping a tally of the proposals she receives

A disobedient child provides a final example of the mutation of a handle to a marker or a signal. It recalls the basic handle of calling someone's name, in this case a parent calling a child into the house. The mother shouts Johnnie to come in, and the proper response is that the child shouts 'I'm coming' and returns to the house. The handle is the command to return inside; the handle state is their relationship and the parent's expectation of being obeyed. Johnnie however

Mutation of handles by a disobedient child

A man in England had been living with his fiancée, he was 24 and she 20. The couple were visited by the police on an unrelated matter, for which no charges were ever brought, but it came out during the interviews that eight months previously the man had come home somewhat drunk and the couple had gone to bed. In the middle of sex the woman had withdrawn consent but he had carried on for a further five minutes. Armed with an admission from the man that this had taken place he was arrested, charged and sentenced to six months' imprisonment for rape. A female professor of law interviewed in the BBC radio report was adamant that the correct course had been followed.

'Body betrayal' is the informal term which has emerged for women experiencing orgasms during forced sex, breast-feeding and childbirth.

mutates the handle to a marker when he shouts that he doesn't want to and runs off to the park. His vocalisation is the marker. If he runs off without saying anything, that is the mutation of a handle to a signal.

Actions and consequences

A feature of a masculine environment

In a masculine environment people have to face the consequences of their actions. Handles are respected and defiance of them is punished or discouraged some other way. Conversely, the female tendency is to weaken handles, because handles involve obligations which females find advantageous to avoid. Normal behaviour involves handles, and if they are routinely weakened then abnormal behaviour ensues.

Females use their natural ability to charm and cajole early in life to win people over and avoid admonishment. Later on, an energetic flurry of excuses, a call to the male's protective instincts, or an explicit or implied recourse to 'I'm just a woman' might be used.

Females largely escape consequences. Female crime is often unrecognised

To a great extent, females inhabit a world devoid of consequences. A woman might initiate or encourage a contest between two men which boils over to serious violence, yet she can simply walk away from the carnage. She can fall pregnant to an unsuitable father, an event which can reverberate its ill-effects for generations, without censure. She can deprive children of the father they need. She can even claim that the killing of her husband was provoked by years of abuse and receive only a nominal sentence. Female imprisonment has risen sharply in recent years but in Britain in 2011 it was still only 6% of the prison population. Males are expected to face the consequences of their actions while females, by and large, escape them. With judicial equality around half of the prison population would be female. It is not enough to say that 'females do not commit crime' because male and female criminality is different.

Females also have a tendency to break unwritten rules, i.e. implicit handles.

Postscript

Primordial and ultimate handles

Possibly the primordial handle is that the female presents to the male. It is debatable whether, at the personal level, the ultimate handle state is marriage or engaging in a suicide pact. Once both were accomplished within the space of a few minutes – Adolf Hitler married Eva Braun then they committed suicide shortly afterwards, rather than fall into the hands of advancing Soviet troops.

Enforcing invalid handles

It is also enlightening to analyse the process of a government exacting unreasonable handles on a population. For example in Scotland it is illegal for a parent to smack a child no matter how naughty the child has been, or needed the smack is. This is a government attempting to prohibit normal human behaviour and impose its political dogma using the force of law. Handles are being issued which are beyond the scope of the handle state.

Summary

This chapter concludes the description of the four essential elements of human interaction. Then we have that males prefer markers and handles, and females prefer signals and tokens. Markers and handles are unambiguous and often involve the wealth that males create, while signals and tokens are ambiguous, manipulative and allow the female to retain control in her transactions with the physically stronger male.

Signals, markers, tokens and handles are basic behavioural elements which can be explored using examples and counter-examples. The components often appear in combination.

An action can be a signal but not a marker (all signals are ambiguous and all markers are not).

An action or object can be a marker but not a handle (e.g. distributing a free gift indiscriminately; making an unreasonable demand).

A handle *usually* involves markers and/or signals forming the handle and its response. (Counter-example: a couple's expectation that they will think of each other while apart, which is a handle without being either a marker or a signal.)

Any marker can have an associated token element, however subtle.

Sitting apart. In a feminine setting the situation will commonly arise when people known to each other will end up sitting at different tables in a bar or similar place, usually within sight of each other. In sitting apart the female is able to spectate with no demands being made upon her. A marker is distributed (being in the same place as not only the person with whom she has some relationship but also the others) and a handle state (the relationship) is weakened.

The bias against male domestic violence victims has been revealed in North American and Australian research, in surveys in this country for the Channel 4 *Dispatches* programme, in a 1999 Home Office Research Study and in a report based on a survey of male domestic violence victims (George & Yarwood, 2004, at www.dewar4research.org/downloads.htm). Considering the seriousness of the abuse compared to the response, the statistics are alarming. Try inverting the sex of the abuser/victim when you consider this: three-quarters were assaulted once a month or more frequently; over two-thirds had been assaulted more than ten times; half were threatened with a weapon, and a similar proportion were severely bruised; a third were kicked in the genitals; one in five were burnt or scalded.

The police response? A quarter of the respondents said that they themselves had been arrested despite being the victim, half were threatened with arrest despite being the victim, and most of the remainder reported that the police had totally ignored what they had to say. In just three percent of the cases was the violent female partner arrested. Most tellingly of all, female assailants called the police nearly as often as did the male victims. Of the few female assailants arrested and subsequently charged – despite the serious injuries some of the male victims had suffered – not one was convicted.

Steve Moxon, *The Woman Racket*

A dysfunctional family. Members of a dysfunctional family have only infrequent contact with each other. An aged family member dies, but no attempt is made to contact one relative, who misses the funeral. The handle state is the expectation of being told, and the handle is the implicit, ongoing request of the relative to be told of such momentous family events.

Violence and threats of violence. In nature, very few contests result in injury. The smaller animal gives way to the larger. All that is required is the larger animal's arrival, or an aggressive gesture, and the smaller animal retreats. Only if a resource confers great benefit will a contest be escalated to a point where actual injury could take place.

The evolutionary imperative of the female is to make the task of the male as hard as she can. By increasing his burden she demands fitness in the male; the fitter the male, the more robust will be the next generation. Both sexes shortly benefit. This is the evolutionary drive which motivates her revolt against the male.

Formerly the female was controlled, just as in nature, by implicit threat. In the vast majority of cases all that was required was threat. The usually rare occasions when physical violence was employed functioned to limit her behaviour and validate the threat.

Following her instinctive imperative the female will challenge any masculine constraint, regardless of its form. Females abhor violence because any conflict involving it they lose. Now, by a sequential but wholly unnatural progression, she will not tolerate even the threat of violence. A man who issues a threat to a woman risks her calling the police, whereupon various State and State-supported agencies will descend in support of the 'vulnerable' female. The male will likely be punished and the family, if there is one, severely upset or even destroyed.

Thus the situation has arisen in which the mechanisms the female has evolved to compensate for males' physical strength can be employed practically without limit, while the male is emasculated by being unable to use, or even threaten to use, his natural power.

Parallels can be drawn with children. Most children probably do not need physical punishment more than a handful of times in their entire childhood. In exceptional cases though, when punishment is called for, failing to give it creates greater problems. A single unruly pupil disrupts and dominates the classroom. Other children, seeing that he escapes punishment, follow his example. Not giving punishment leads to dysfunction, which is where many Western societies are today.

Reasonable physical punishment is also kinder on the child – it is certainly preferable to the alternative. Attempting to reason, adult-like, merely encourages dishonesty and is likely to leave the child with a burden of unresolved guilt. The child longs for security and this entails having the boundaries of behaviour firmly set. The author, who grew up without a father, recalls wanting to be punished as a child, though he would never have admitted it at the time. Similarly woman cannot admit her deep desire to be mastered. However, her unstated desire becomes manifest in the excesses of her behaviour.

6 Neurosis

When one stimulus evokes two or more responses

Females limit physical sex. That much is clear, but what is not obvious are the psychological mechanisms by which this is accomplished for sex, constantly evoked in everyday life, is not enjoyed nearly so often as it is advertised.

Just as signals are primary sexual characters in human behaviour, many procedures – certainly the elementary processes, which are so easy to take for granted – likely have their origin in the reproductive advantage they confer.

Whence Procedural Analysis came

Procedural Analysis details basic, readily observable mechanisms. Many of these procedures were most stark in the sexually-charged environment of Amsterdam where the original investigations took place. Feminism was a potent force, disinhibition was encouraged, and sexual enjoyment was officially acknowledged as healthy and to be pursued. The Dutch encouragement of free expression was in contrast to the traditional British reserve which was the author's heritage.

Trials of various kinds became practically a full-time activity between 1992 and 1994 and the work was often very arduous psychologically. Pavlov did his experiments on dogs, but in these investigations the author was the dog!

Guided by evolution theory

The focus was sexual selection, especially mate-selection by females, and how control is achieved. Constant reference was made to evolutionary principles to maintain consistency and prevent deviation. The challenge now is to generalise the revealed mechanisms, since sexual behaviour must be – evolutionarily – the fount of all behaviour.

Neurosis as internal conflict

This chapter and the next may get somewhat technical, as some psychological fundamentals are defined. The rudiments of internal conflict are established and new concepts are compared with those familiar in orthodox psychology.

Nowadays the term *neurosis* has come mean a generalised state of anxiety, 'a mild mental illness involving symptoms of stress.' The hope is to reclaim the term for a specific psychological reaction.

Skirting the definition

First we shall skirt around the definition of neurosis like a shark circling a wounded seal, before going in with a massive thrust for the killing bite. The wait will be worthwhile, because the reward at the end is the identification of an important new procedure, one with wide application in everyday life.

The following illustration is not of neurosis, but of a comparable process. We imagine an old man becoming bewildered when the telephone rings and someone knocks at the door at the same time. A state of internal conflict is established, because he cannot decide how to prioritize the two demands. Both are urgent: if he answers the phone the visitor may go away, but if he answers the door the person on the other end of the telephone may abandon the call. The psychological conflict established in the mind of the old man can be so paralysing that neither the phone nor the door is answered.

Confusion in the aged

Positive and negative neurosis?

Sometimes an individual exposes himself to two potential responses of his own volition. Risks are deliberately taken and excitement is experienced. The stimulus can be exhilarating, distinguishing it from ordinary neurosis, or perhaps this is a special case of it, because neurosis is generally understood to be depressive. This might be called 'positive neurosis' or 'voluntary neurosis' because the exposure is actively sought after.

Seeking arousal in courting harm or safety, fear or greed, capture or profit

Small monkeys race in front of trucks, competing as to how finely they can time their run under the truck's wheels, and status in the troupe is acquired this way. A punter in a betting shop or casino finds gambling exciting and sometimes ruinously addictive. Conflicting impulses of fear and greed are common to both the financial manipulator and the criminal; the former fears ruin while the latter fears capture, and both activities can be exhilarating and rewarding. There are two outcomes: success or devastating failure, but the danger only adds to the thrill.

Things get even murkier if we consider lap-dancing clubs, which for some men can be stimulating, for others depressing. Indeed a man can be drawn into a form of addiction, compulsively visiting a particular dancer and showering her with money he cannot afford. Sensation-seekers scoring high in extroversion may enjoy being made fearful by a good horror film, though here we touch upon

Lap-dancing clubs and horror films

> It is not Freud but Pavlov who belongs with Copernicus and Darwin as the great dethroner of mankind from its pedestal; it was he who showed that many of our actions are not those of *Homo sapiens*, but are the results of primitive conditioning mediated by the limbic system and other subcortical parts of the brain.
>
> H. J. Eysenck, *Decline and Fall of the Freudian Empire*

Female ambivalence. A half-Negro Jewish prostitute said 'I'm not a racist but I don't take Moroccans or Turks.' She asked me if I had ever been to see a prostitute, I told her I hadn't. 'Don't' she said, 'you're too nice.'

personality types, a separate theme. Nevertheless while men can become devastatingly addicted to gambling and lap-dancers, addiction to horror films is practically unheard of. One can almost imagine a sort of look-up table in the brain determining whether a stimulus produces pleasurable excitement or discomfort. That table could be programmed by life experiences.

A rich mix of emotions on being dumped

A complex mix of emotions would occur on being dumped by a troublesome partner. The relationship has been traumatic, with many upsets and periods of disharmony. Nonetheless a fondness towards the partner exists for the intimacy shared, and this brings a sense of loss. The set of emotions when the relationship ends includes both sadness and relief.

Cognitive dissonance, neurotic stress

Neurosis strictly defined

Here neurosis is defined as the psychological state which arises when one stimulus evokes two (or more) responses. Normally the stimulus is external and beyond the individual's direct control. This is 'negative' neurosis, and it is generally not a pleasant sensation. Pavlov did much of the early work on neurosis.

Definition of cognitive dissonance

Festinger in 1957 defined cognitive dissonance as the psychological discomfort which occurs when an individual has 'any knowledge, opinion or belief' which is inconsistent with another. An implication of this definition is that the cognitions are pre-established. To begin, some elementary principles will be reviewed to examine when an immediate stimulus leads to conflicting responses. That is, how a stimulus can induce a neurotic reaction.

Pavlov and 'war-neuroses'

The dog was the animal of choice for Pavlov because it so readily displays its emotional state. His familiar work concerned classical conditioning but after many experiments subjecting dogs to extreme stress Pavlov shifted his focus to psychiatry. Pavlov's ideas about neurosis found application in understanding the 'war-neuroses' which were commonplace among soldiers during the Second World War.

The stress Pavlov's dogs endured

This example was observed by the author so needs no reference to Pavlov, although it is comparable to one of his experiments. Incidentally, Pavlov remarked that his dogs felt they had been put through a hard situation. Undergoing the stress of conflicting and ambiguous stimuli was evidently an ordeal for the animals.

A split between women's bodies and minds. A meta-study, or review of studies, collated data from 134 separate studies of male and female sexual arousal. The experiments undertaken between 1969 and 2007 involved a total of 2,500 female and 1,900 male participants. The Canadian meta-study concluded that women's minds and genitals typically respond differently to sexual arousal, whereas men gave responses which were much more consistent. Men's reported subjective ratings more closely matched their physiological readings than those of the women, 'suggesting a split between women's bodies and minds.' The review was published in 2010 in the *Archives of Sexual Behavior*.

The tramp who beat his dog

The observation concerned a dog owned by a mentally-ill tramp. He tied his dog to a post when he went on an errand, and beat it on his return. The dog would both cringe in fear and wag its tail in joy at the return of its master. The single stimulus was the return of the tramp, to which the dog responded with both trepidation and elation. After this exchange, which was obviously routine, man and dog were seen happily walking off together.

Internal conflict in the cat

Domestic cats can display a semblance of neurosis and something similar to an erroneous signal has been observed. The cat initially expresses fear, checks itself and then settles back. Exhibiting fear can remind a passer-by of the cat's vulnerability, and his ability to harm the cat. Showing fear of harm may inspire it.

Apparent neurosis in a spider. Cognitive dissonance is too complex a model

Neurotic behaviour has even been observed in a spider. Spiders are binary creatures: a spider's response to a drawing on a piece of card has been shown to depend on its resemblance to another spider. They approach another creature of similar size as either a potential enemy or a mate. A spider was seen repeatedly advancing on and retreating from an object in the grass, apparently torn between its two options and unable to resolve its internal conflict.

That we can quote examples of mental conflict in animals and even the spider suggests that a more basic mechanism than cognitive dissonance exists. We do not normally associate 'knowledge, opinion or belief' with animals, never mind arachnids. The cognitive dissonance model seems appropriate for situations like this actual case of the parsimonious prisoner.

The case of the parsimonious prisoner

A person with a strong aversion to spending money was imprisoned. His incarceration was entirely beyond his control; he had no choice in the matter. His circumstances are unsatisfactory, so he reduced his internal conflict (dissonance) by accentuating the positive aspects of his situation. He said that his imprisonment was a boon because it prevented him from spending money.

The parsimonious prisoner assessed his condition and did not like what he saw. His cognition of his environment created dissonance. Since he cannot change his situation, the only possibility of reducing his dissonance was by altering his cognition. He 'puts a brave face on the situation,' 'puts a gloss on it' finding, dwelling on and exaggerating positive aspects of his circumstances to offset his sense of calamity. This is, of course, a very common process.

Reclaiming the term 'neurosis'

In summary, an attempt is made here to reclaim the term 'neurosis' to describe a process which is primitive in animals and which is an elementary component of human psychology. When a neurosis-evoking stimulus is encountered, neurotic stress ensues. The new (or more accurately, restored) definition is both more fundamental and wide-ranging.

The two fundamental neuroses

Two fundamental neuroses exist, one a consequence of human consciousness and one the product of the essential strategy females employ to guard her limited biological resources against abuse and exploitation by males.

Humans must countenance their own mortality

The *fundamental human neurosis* derives from the consciousness we have of our own mortality. Like any other creature, we have a strong self-preservation instinct. Every creature engages in the 'struggle for life' because the gene-line of the lazy or indifferent one became extinct eons ago. At the same time, as humans we are aware that we are mortal, that our days on earth are numbered. This conflict has been sublimated into religion, for it promises immortality, for instance by ascendance to heaven or reincarnation.

Alternate means of achieving immortality

An alternate means of resolving this existential conflict is to depreciate the self. It may be believed that one's 'soul' or 'essence of self' will be absorbed into some ethereal cosmos, or that ancient, ritualistic traditions will be continued by individuals just like oneself for evermore. These are alternative, non-Western means of achieving a kind of immortality, absent the Occidental emphasis on individuality.

A basic subconscious conflict

This conflict and its resolution will likely be resolved deep in the psyche and mostly subconsciously. In one mentally-ill individual however it was made explicit: he insisted that he was going to live forever. The fundamental human neurosis has been collectively resolved by religious belief, with its promise of eternal life.

The *fundamental female neurosis* derives from the master strategy females employ, the strategy which underlies all others, of increasing the value of sex. The female instinct is to increase the cost of sex, the male instinct is to reduce it. Sex, whether it be in the form of providing intimate and caring relationships, physical sex or progeny, is ultimately the only commodity that females can provide which males cannot. Thus the status of the female ultimately depends on the value of sex.

The second switch. Women are totally sexual creatures who will go to almost any lengths to avoid physical sex. The first switch is physical preparedness: the nipples become erect, the vagina lubricates and dilates. Yet a second switch – conscious acceptance – comes into play whereby a woman can desire, even need, physical sex but her conscious mind will not allow her to give consent to it. Wilson and others have shown that women's level of arousal, measured using vaginal probes, and the level of arousal they report, are different.

The master strategy of females, underlying all others, is to raise the cost of sex. To this end she cannot help but deny her physical desires because this is the strategy which has been so advantageous throughout her forebears' evolutionary history. And this strategy includes being as selective of her companions, especially male companions, as it is within her power to be.

Horses veer from large moving objects such as lorries and double-decker buses because formerly they were the size of dogs. Millions of years ago, huge birds would swoop down on them, catch them in their claws and bash them against rocks before eating them. Similarly battery-reared chickens, which have never seen the sky let alone a predatory bird, are thrown into a paroxysm of terror if something resembling a hawk appears above them. These behaviours were programmed deep in the limbic brain during the course of countless generations engaged in a constant struggle for survival.

An environment where females have complete control of sex is extremely unusual and an aberration in evolutionary terms. She can maintain that control throughout her lifetime, even while being married. Under such conditions women may become even more sexually frustrated than men. This is an alternative explanation for a high level of female signalling. Many adverse social effects follow.

It is possible that contemporary females are applying 'fringe strategies' which formerly were only available to royalty and high noblewomen. More likely however is that they are simply applying normal female strategies to an unprecedented degree.

The importance of sex for the female

Without sex women would have to compete on equal terms with men, which for the vast majority would be impossible. Electrical power, mechanisation and mass production have led to a greatly reduced reliance on physical strength and practical ability, but historically this is a very artificial situation.

The primary sexual activity of the male is physical sex and all is relatively straightforward. He knows what he wants and why. For the female, things are not so simple, for her primary sexual expression is relationships. While relationships are females' chief sexual outlet, at least sometimes she desires physical sex. However, her optimal strategy revolves around increasing its value by withholding it, for scarcity increases the value of anything. Herein lies the conflict: females deny their own desires (indeed, needs) in order to increase the value of sex and enhance their collective status. Thus females as a group advertise sex, and generally condone its constant promotion via the media, which increases its value, while generally withholding it, which does the same thing.

Relationships are females' chief sexual outlet. Withholding the amenity to increase its value

Were relationships and sex readily available at little cost the perceived value of sex would greatly diminish. Hence ordinary women can express antipathy towards prostitutes, for they, by providing the amenity so cheaply, undermine their strategy.

Women psychologists

Another source of female neurosis stems from her failure to understand her own behaviour. This is probably why so many women take up psychology nowadays. The message for them is that women will never understand their instincts except by examining their functions in relation to men.

Female behaviour is purposely irrational

Women engage in actions that are irrational which, though illogical, purposefully obscure their strategy. Females vary less than males and beneath the layers of obfuscation her strategy is essentially simple. If this were perceived by the male, and not obscured by her capricious and illogical behaviour, she would be vulnerable to exploitation by him. Females' irrational behaviour has evolved as a defence mechanism for the purpose of perplexing the male, rendering her actions harder to predict and counter, as well as to test his commitment to her.

> Prostitutes in an area of Amsterdam frequented by locals (not the Red Light District, which was probably busier) reported that they generally took 5 or 10 clients per day, most would take 15 if they could. Just one good client would pay for the hire of the room and window. One half-Scottish, half-Italian woman, dubbed the 'real professional,' could service 25 clients per day, 30 at a push.

Inducing neurosis

Sex is the source of much commonplace neurosis. In light of the male's biological imperative to procreate, he is understandably sensitive to advertisements for it. As previously discussed, sexual signals tend to be more effective when subliminally perceived, yet females often increase the intensity of their signals. We need only look at the way fashions have changed, apparently leaving less and less to the male imagination with each season.

Males' sensitivity to sexual signals

Neurosis is a non-physical means by which sex can be limited and sexual signalling serves to induce neurosis in males. Females abhor violence because their physical handicap means that in any fight they invariably lose. Applying our evolutionary model, even if she were to prevail against an exceptionally weak or retiring male, another stronger one would shortly come along to overpower her. A major cause of male death in prehistory was fights over females. The ambiguity of signals enables the female to retain control and prevail against the physically stronger male.

Using neurosis as a means to limit sex

A signal is always capable of multiple interpretation. It may be emitted as a result of imitation, in jest, due to malfunction of equipment (as in the case of a traffic signal) or otherwise invalid. Inappropriate signals may be emitted as a defence mechanism against the source of the neurosis (as when smiling incongruously). The normal, well-adjusted male instinct is to preserve the integrity of signals, that is, to reduce their ambiguity.

The female transfers her neurotic load onto males. Demanding fitness in males

Signals also serve to distribute neurosis. Especially, females use sexual signalling as a mechanism for shifting their neurotic load onto males. By creating an adverse environment for males generally, females use neurosis as a trial of determination and stamina (i.e. fitness) of the male.

A signal, being ambiguous, induces *neurotic stress* until interpretation of the

> The truth seems to be that *in imagination* the whole female body is a desirable object. In practice this is not so, as anyone can testify who has ever visited a nudist camp. Complete nudity is anti-erotic, as soon as the shock of novelty has worn off; and it does wear off, surprisingly quickly. If complete nudity were common we should probably become seasonal in our impulses, like the animals. Our characteristic *permanent* eroticism is kept alive by clothes.
>
> But clothes can only keep it alive by continually altering the emphasis, drawing attention to all aspects of the female body in turn by exposure, semi-concealment or by other devices well known to every dress designer. This altering of emphasis is the 'Shifting Erogenous Zone' and is the whole basis of Fashion.
>
> James Laver, *Modesty in Dress*, p. 37

How the neurosis induced by a sexual signal can be resolved

signal is established or a decision is made on how to react to it. The ardour of the male and the intense pleasure he receives from physical sex, serving as a reinforcer of that drive, makes him extraordinarily sensitive to sexual signals. This is the model for signalling and neurosis, because it is a primary sexual character of behaviour.

How females discourage approaches. Validity of signals

A male may make an unbidden approach to a female, perhaps mistakenly interpreting her dress, posture or physical features as a signal, only to receive psychological hurt in return. Females employ *transduction* – inducing a false feeling – to discourage unwelcome approaches, and this also discourages unbidden approaches to subsequent females. Nonetheless the signal he has perceived is usually valid in some sense: even large breasts are an indiscriminate signal, because a woman's breasts are considerably larger than is necessary to perform their reproductive function. Their size is an evolutionary adaptation because of their attractiveness to males. Desmond Morris has argued that breasts follow the shape of the buttocks, when copulation took place from the rear, at which time their display to the male was a mating cue.

Perils of approaching

When a female issues a signal to a male, he is faced with two options, to approach or desist. In the absence of other factors, his immediate response would be to approach, in anticipation of sexual pleasure and to add another conquest to his tally. However, previous experience has taught him that things are never that simple: being (as in the usual case) only dimly aware that he has been signalled, he may fear rejection. Or that the female will use him as a trophy, that is to demonstrate her attractive ability to others, to make another jealous, to be flattered and entertained, or with some other motive.

An approaching male must endure an elevation of neurosis

If he approaches he must endure an elevation of neurosis, since a blunt proposition, capable of quickly resolving the matter, is the one class of approach statement which is practically guaranteed to fail ('Come back to my place and have sex right now'). In conversation, his desire is likely to increase by his proximity and association with her, so increasing his neurotic tension. He fears saying something wrong or inappropriate, or evoking some unpleasant feeling in her which destroys his chances. In a trivial but no doubt commonplace scenario, he could invest the entire evening only to be given an invented or illegible telephone number.

A sexual signal induces a particular state in the mind of the receiver

During the time a sexual signal is being emitted, a particular state arises in the mind of the receiver, and it is predicted that a specific area of the brain will be identifiable were his brain activity to be monitored during the reception of a female signal. During the signal the female becomes more attractive (by definition); especially if the signalling is elevated in intensity or duration it becomes impossible for the male to gauge the female's comeliness objectively. Then almost a 'blackout state' can be induced in which perception of the event and its surroundings can be considerably altered.

Neurotic transfer: transferring power to an opponent, motivated by neurosis.

Neurotic transfer

Inadequacy of the cognitive dissonance model

Finally the repast arrives, but the wait has been worthwhile, because this definition of neurosis has taken us to a place we would never have reached with cognitive dissonance. Festinger's model fails to lead to the following elementary, and apparently commonplace, mechanism of human interaction. And whatever else might be said, 'cognitively dissonant transfer' just doesn't have the same ring to it.

The persistent neurotic state, and its effects

If neurosis-inducing stimuli are repeated, or forceful, a persistent neurotic state can be established with long-term, detrimental effects. A neurotic individual might emit spurious signals, unwittingly say the opposite of what he means, or inadvertently express fear. This, as we have seen in the simple example with the cat, leads to a greater likelihood of the thing feared actually taking place. Consider this sequence, a 'boy meets girl in the city' story if you will, which illustrates *neurotic transfer*. Neurotic transfer is transferring power to an opponent, motivated by neurosis. The following is the basic model of the procedure.

A boy meets a girl in the city

A male meets a female, somehow, among the crowds. They share a coffee, or a drink, and get on. He asks her to meet him for an outing in a few days time, and a place and time are agreed. He is greatly attracted to her, in fact he has hidden the extent of it from her (males bond to females much more quickly than vice versa, for obvious evolutionary reasons).

The time of the appointment arrives and with it comes a bombshell, for she does not show up. He has looked forward to their meeting: he has made plans and perhaps even bought tickets. He waited nervously but the climax of the appointed time passes without any sign of her.

The reason for her absence is irrelevant, certainly to the male, for it will probably never be known. She was economical with information so he is unable to contact her. The city includes thousands of people from outlying areas, visitors and tourists and meeting her again by chance, and paying enough attention to recognise her, is quite unlikely. The girl is forever lost.

Time passes. The girl who did not turn up may be a distant memory but the sequence of events is not.

The boy meets another girl

One day he meets another girl. Again the male is attracted to her and again a rendezvous is agreed. By now however, a persistent neurotic state has been established. He fears that, like last time, she will not turn up. His conflict is between his pleasurable anticipation of meeting her again, and fear that he will again be let down. He expresses his fear: 'You will turn up, won't you?' and this is our archetype of neurotic transfer, for in his neurotic state he has made his position worse.

Due to his neurotic state – persistent from the previous occasion when a girl he desired did not show up – he has transferred power to the female. By expressing his fear he has conveyed significant information, and control of information is another important manipulative, non-physical device the female uses to prevail against her more aggressive, physically stronger opponent.

Transferring power to a subsequent or potential neurosis-inducer

His neurotic utterance tells the female at least three things. First, that he has been let down before, maybe several times. Second, the male is evidently anxious that she should turn up, counteracting any pretence of nonchalance he has made; this enhances her and increases her confidence and power. Third, at some point the possibility that she may not turn up to this meeting will occur to her, and she may surmise that it is common practice in this environment for females to not turn up to meetings with males. The probability that she will not turn up is increased.

Males and females are opponents, most of the time

The neurotic male further empowers the female. By the neurotic transfer of power he has strengthened his opponent, and she is his opponent, because although the potential for symbiosis between the players in this game exists, it is still a long way off. Moreover, as is common to many female procedures, action towards a single male is of benefit to females generally. The failure of the first female to turn up has induced a persistent neurotic state, and by neurotically expressing his fear of its repetition he has empowered a subsequent one.

Neurosis as a means of control

Compound benefit. A neurotic environment benefits females

This is another example of compound benefit, where a procedure confers multiple benefits, not necessarily confined to the individual performing the action. Neurosis imposes cost on the male, confuses him and makes him easier to manipulate. In his neurotic state he engages in neurotic transfer, further empowering a subsequent neurosis-inducer. It is of benefit to females generally

> The essential sequence of neurotic transfer is simple. Using the terms of game theory, the Protagonist starts the game by inducing neurosis in the Opponent, and the Opponent responds, not by retaliating, but by transferring power to the Protagonist. That is, the Opponent reacts by strengthening the Protagonist (or a subsequent, similar neurosis-inducer, another member of the Protagonist population). Alternatively the Opponent may disarm himself in some manner. Either way, following a neurosis-inducing event (NIE) created by the Protagonist, the Protagonist is strengthened by the Opponent.

to maintain males in a state of neurosis, all the more so in an environment where females are under pressure to provide sex. A background of spurious signalling would also induce persistent neurosis in males.

Wider examples of neurotic transfer

Now the question arises as to when neurotic transfer is manifest more generally. One potential candidate is the damning confessions suspects sometimes make under police interrogation. That a suspect confesses his crime is not surprising: what is surprising is that, under certain circumstances, the suspect actually exaggerates his crime for the benefit of the police, increasing his own culpability. He may exaggerate his actions or ascribe to himself the blackest motives and intentions. Of course, false confessions can occur after hard interrogation, but most bizarre are the voluntary false confessions which are a feature of highly publicized crimes. People can walk into a police station and confess to a crime they have not committed. After the Lindbergh kidnapping in 1932, 250 people confessed to the crime, but the record is held by the 1947 Black Dahlia murder, for which the police have received more than 500 voluntary false confessions. Neurotic transfer is capable of accounting for these spurious confessions.

A criminal exaggerates his crime, or a person voluntarily confesses to a crime he did not commit

A clearer example of neurotic transfer can occur when a potential partner diminishes herself. On a 'first date' perhaps, the female mentions her unattractive features or habits. The neurosis-inducing event is being examined as a potential partner. By revealing her flaws she is transferring power to the male, making her rejection more likely. In this case demeaning herself serves to test the male, establishing his preparedness to stay with her during the lengthy period of pregnancy and child-rearing which may follow. This is evolutionarily advantageous for the female, and hence this could be the evolutionary origin of neurotic transfer.

Someone being interviewed as a potential partner demeans herself

At a low point in their relationship one of a couple might ask the other 'What don't you like about me?' The answer, if full and honest, is likely to permanently seal the fate of the relationship; it is unlikely ever to recover from a brutally frank reply. This is a specific example of asking a loaded question at precisely the wrong moment. Another situation involving neurotic transfer is when a person lets slip to another the very thing they had intended not to reveal.

Asking the wrong question at exactly the worst moment

A nervous and unimpressive public speaker may lapse to neurotic transfer. Perhaps he has the misfortune to follow a previous speaker who has

The fundamental attribution error – one's own failings are attributed to circumstance while others' failings are attributed to character.

successfully amused and entertained his audience, and he is unable to fill the void. Still, the individuals making up his audience have hardly formed an opinion, especially since he is still in mid-flow. Or, to the degree that a judgement has been made, there may be pluralistic ignorance, in that each audience member believes that their opinion is theirs alone.

A nervous public speaker, hoping to impress, fails, and moreover damns himself

This all changes when the speaker himself comments on the lukewarm reception to his speech. His nervousness has inspired his remark, and that arousal is at least partly the product of internal conflict (he has imagined himself giving a successful performance). His observation makes the audience's inchoate appraisal conscious, solidifying it in their minds. He has empowered them to confidently criticise his performance since what was before a disputable opinion has now been confirmed by the very person delivering the address.

Manufacturing controversy

Other instances are more controversial, inevitably, as defining a subject as controversial is the means by which neurosis is induced. When some subjects are raised, certainly publicly, they are treated as contentious, and a reaction like ink being expelled by an octopus ensues. Transduction (to be discussed) is again employed: outrage is simulated and fuss is made. A taboo is instituted and by this means raising the topic is made costly. Once the taboo is established, perception of the issue can be altered in a tendentious way, and the alteration will always be in a direction favourable to the neurosis-inducer. Rational discourse on the topic then becomes practically impossible, for the traps awaiting a person uttering an unpalatable truth are many.

Raising the cost of discourse by creating a taboo

Role of humour

Exactly the same process operates when a topic is deemed unsuitable for jokes. One of the functions of humour is to alleviate neurosis. The role of humour is to distribute information and release neurotic tension.

Humour counteracts neurosis. Equating speech with action

In the absence of male influence females will fear the worst, and will also equate what is said with what is done. Individuals, usually male, expressing opinions contrary to the female interest will be stigmatised. This holds even if the comments are made in jest, because then they serve to release tension. Humour is practically the antithesis of neurosis and it disrupts the neurotic state, undermining female power. Specifically, once a neurotic state is established it allows perception of the topic to be slanted for the benefit of the female, and enables further benefit when neurotic transfer takes place subsequently.

Learning about incest through humour – How do you know when your sister's having her period? Because your daddy's dick tastes funny.

Public apologies and exploitation

Neurotic transfer also accounts for the peculiar willingness of people falling foul of a taboo to apologize afterwards. Some public figure or person of note (or whom the media considers worthy of note) makes an 'insensitive' comment in front of a microphone. His career is usually finished. The truth of what he has said is irrelevant; even if not strictly true, his utterance was likely an opinion shared by millions of his countrymen. The ensuing furore of media attention and commentary makes him neurotic. In response to the neurosis-inducing shock of media clamour he falls to neurotic transfer in the form of an apology. This reinforces his opponent's stance but as an attempt to recover his former position it is invariably futile. In some cases the apology may be coerced, but the pattern is consistent even so.

Public apologies for stating unpalatable truths

These processes have, for two examples among many, severely constrained honest and objective discussion of racial and sexual differences. The neurotic conflict being established is, on the one hand, a desire to treat these subjects truthfully and objectively, and on the other, fear of accusations of 'racism' or 'sexism.' Pandering to minorities is a form of neurotic transfer, and this is especially likely to take place after dramatic, neurosis-inducing events such as civil riots and suicide bombings. Obsequiousness is evident in the behaviour both of individuals and the Establishment. A further, allied phenomenon is the 'elephant in the living room' effect by which some glaringly obvious factor (such as race) in a political issue or event is studiously ignored.

Limiting free discussion. A common form of neurotic transfer

Neurotic transfer of a physical, rather than a verbal or political, kind may be taking place when Western technology is exported. This enables other nations to grow wealthy selling back to the West the goods and commodities produced using it. An obvious example is oil extraction technology.

Neurotic transfer of a tangible kind

A particular neurotic state, given separate treatment because of the attention orthodox psychology gives to it, will be discussed in the next chapter.

7 Neurotic Suspension

Being frozen in a state of neurosis

Man is first and foremost a social animal. One of the most constant features of life is that in any situation involving several individuals, intercourse between them will take place. The exchanges may reflect fondness, mutual regard or dislike, but that is by-the-by; our social instincts dictate that these interactions will be inevitable.

With a social-psychological slant, this chapter will explore social gaffes, unfunny comedians, altruistic behaviour and some specific ways by which neurosis – and more – is induced.

Human social interaction is inevitable. The granfalloon

Man's social nature is readily demonstrated by the granfalloon effect. A granfalloon is 'a proud and meaningless association of human beings' and such a group is formed with surprising ease. To create granfalloons a pool of people are assigned to groups arbitrarily, such as by the toss of a coin. Despite being assigned to their group using meaningless criteria, members display remarkable loyalty to their granfalloon.

Traits must exist on multiple levels

Human traits are individually and collectively expressed. Crowd behaviour

It is proposed that all human traits must exist on at least two levels: the individual and the collective. If a trait is advantageous and heritable it will spread, and become collectively expressed. Otherwise, not being evolutionarily viable, it extinguishes.

Thus every human trait, be it territoriality, selfishness, parsimony, generosity, aggressiveness, credulity or sensitivity to neurosis, will be both individually and collectively expressed in a population. When traits are collectively expressed they can intensify, as happens with an audience, crowd or rampaging mob. Group behaviour intensifies if restraint is shed or in the absence or suppression of an opposing, limiting influence.

Runaway audiences and gutter humour

Inappropriate responses from an audience

A telling case is that of a theatre audience intent on enjoying itself. Before the play the audience is seated, comfortable, and in pleasurable anticipation of being entertained. The performance begins and early on, an audience member finds some action or gesture on stage amusing and laughs inappropriately. The sentiment spreads with the result that henceforth the audience laughs at almost anything. When this happens a dramatic narrative can be treated by a runaway audience as comedy, while the actors continue in bewilderment at the audience's reactions.

During classical music concerts it can happen that an audience bursts into applause at the wrong moment, sometimes even when they have been specifically instructed not to. The silence during a pause can seem so loaded that resolution in the form of applause becomes irresistible, and one audience member succumbs to set off the others. Sometimes only a small number join the clapping.

Applauding at the wrong time

Then there is the phenomenon of a comedian swearing profusely and his audience bursting into laughter with every expletive. A comedian of this stripe was watched addressing an enormous auditorium and the audience seemed to find every swear-word hilarious. However part of his performance featured a mime routine, which of course denied him the opportunity to swear. In contrast to the reception to his expletive-filled discourse, this was received with almost complete silence, with hardly a titter of laughter being heard.

Comedians whose dialogue consists of expletives and 'toilet humour'

As is routine for TV recording the audience would have been 'warmed up' by a supporting act, but it shows that an audience that is determined to enjoy itself does so, even when the only apparent stimulus for laughter is the liberal use of words, or the broaching of private subjects, not normally expected from a public stage.

The role of humour is to distribute information and relieve tension, particularly neurotic tension. In this case the amusement of the audience was entirely due to the neurotic release on having (now mild) taboos broken: that someone with a microphone on stage is not normally expected to swear or discuss private bodily functions.

Breaking mild taboos

In an audience then, there are several factors operating in conjunction with each other. There are strong social forces with a shared sentiment among a large number of people, and the absence of a contrary influence. The emotion thus becomes intensified; the assembly is carried along, the indifferent being

An actor reported how around 1986 he had seen the comedian Rodney Dangerfield (Jacob Cohen) playing a packed auditorium in New Jersey. A heckler shouted something and Dangerfield replied 'Go fuck yourself.' The audience roared. He took a beat and said 'Blow me.' More roars. Another beat. 'Your mother sucks.' People were now crying with laughter. This went on – no jokes, just dirty words and phrases. Dangerfield then took a brilliantly timed pause and said, 'What the fuck have I been paying writers for all these years?'

Being swept along with an audience or at a religious meeting

swept along in the commonality of sentiment. Similar effects occur during religious meetings particularly, in the West, during Evangelical and Pentecostal services.

This is to approach neurotic suspension by way of its opposite. The response to breaking the taboo against swearing as exploited by mediocre comedians is in contrast to the common response to someone making a gaffe at a formal gathering.

Suspension in neurosis

Ignoring social gaffes

Suppose an embarrassing slip is made by an important dignitary, the guest of honour in fact, accidentally breaking wind at a formal dinner party. Typically a silence would instantly descend, then the incident would be ignored, and a sharp hostess would quickly restore conversation to save the blushes of her guest. If the incident were mentioned again, it would likely be restricted to private conversation between intimates, such as spouses. Or it could be forgotten, blotted from consciousness by some supervening mechanism, by many members of the party.

A cloud descends obscuring the event

This effect is not confined to groups of people, where we can expect it to be intensified, but it may also manifest itself individually. An individual may witness an event which is of severe embarrassment to another – say, observing a male making a clumsy approach to a female and receiving a brusque rejection. Attention to the event is switched away; the incident is ignored and perhaps forgotten entirely. It may be recalled days later or not at all.

Genteel ignorance is maintained in many social situations

Similarly, polite ignorance is maintained about someone's visit to the lavatory. In many cultures attention to a nearby couple engaged in intimate conversation is routinely suppressed. Heed is habitually not paid to another's telephone conversation, for not wishing to eavesdrop. In each of these cases, consciousness is altered, often automatically and without deliberation.

All of these situations involve subtle conflicts. Natural curiosity is opposed by the desire to respect someone's privacy; a desire to maintain social communion is countered by genteel detachment from base bodily functions.

The cocoon effect

The disassociated state of mating animals

Neurotic suspension probably has its origin in the consciousness-altered state which animals enter into during mating. For example a species of American eagle engages in prolonged mating on the ground, during which it is possible for a dog-walker or other rambler to stumble upon the mating birds and approach them. The eagles will only disengage if physically touched. Were it not for their disassociated state, approach so close would be impossible. Many

In 1995 the black TV newsreader Trevor McDonald was reporting the attack on a mother and daughter by a hammer-wielding lunatic. He meant to say it happened in the Kent countryside but instead, before millions of *News at Ten* viewers, he said 'cunt kentryside.' The gaffe was ignored. However when in December 2010 BBC Radio 4's James Naughtie introduced the Culture Secretary James Hunt as 'James Cunt' the slip immediately provoked extensive commentary. The incident was discussed on the radio programme hosted by Andrew Marr an hour later, who made exactly the same mistake. Marr quickly corrected himself and apologised, saying 'It's very hard to talk about it without saying it.'

animals, if disturbed during mating, are difficult to distract or entice to disengage. Their reluctance to do so clearly confers evolutionary advantage for the animals, especially after the investment of a lengthy pre-mating ritual, for if copulation is completed then progeny will result.

Its expression in a human couple

The engagement of mating animals can be compared to the 'cocoon effect' often evident in a pair of lovers in a pub, bar or restaurant. The two are immersed in each other; they are detached from the surrounding hubbub of conversation and the background of routine incidents around them. They are oblivious to anyone who looks their way. The cocoon effect is obviously a precursor to mating, and has direct equivalence to the disassociated state of mating animals. Both involve disassociation from the environment.

The Lingering signal

A primary model for neurotic suspension is a male response to the Lingering signal. A common site for this signal is public libraries which, being fairly sedate and also staffed, are regarded by females as free of risk.

A female signals in a library

A male is sitting at a table studying and a female targets him. She hovers around, feigning interest in the books on nearby shelves and lingering nearby. He however, perhaps due to previous similar occasions, or its routine occurrence, ignores the signal. His susceptibility to neurotic suspension will be increased if he has been exposed to a wide variety of spurious signals, producing in him a generalized neurotic state.

The male ignores the signal

Many conflicting motivations may be present. The library may have become one of the few remaining 'respectable' pick-up places, the others having been exhausted through their use as meeting places for casual encounters, and our male reader disapproves of a place of study and learning being exploited for such purpose. If he were to react to the female lingering nearby his attitude might include an element of annoyance, rather than the gentle and flattering approach she is probably trying to procure. Or, if she is attractive, the male may wish to approach, notwithstanding his reservations, but he is sedentary and perplexed as to how this can be accomplished without disturbing the quietness of the library or being scrutinised by the library staff.

Basis of his conflict

Whatever the precise mixture of conflicting potential responses, it is certainly a neurotic reaction. Like any other signal, the Lingering signal induces neurotic stress. The male continues reading his book, and moreover, his attention to it is intensified, blocking out the presence of the signalling female. Again there is disassociation from the environment. The male has entered into a state of neurotic suspension.

Superjacent attention is given to the book

The effect was observed on a crowded London tube train, where the proximity of an attractive young woman inspired the same effect as the Lingering signal on a man seated opposite her. His scrutiny of the computer magazine he was reading became intense. When she rose to alight, his head swivelled rapidly round to look at her as she retreated through the doors.

On a London tube train

There is undeniably a strong cultural element in these observations, which are based almost entirely on observations in England and Holland. Huge differences exist between, say, Sweden and China; in the latter not only is there a huge surfeit of bachelors but pre-marital sex is traditionally forbidden. Observations of American society will differ again. In any event, extreme manifestations of psychological phenomena are highly useful for identification and analysis.

Cultural variations. The value of extremes

Response displacement

The superjacent attention – the attention above and beyond – the male gives to reading is a specific instance of *response displacement*. The impulse which would be the natural response to the signal is diverted, or displaced, to give intensified attention to the activity in which he is currently engaged. Perhaps it is not a 'displacement activity' by its strict, orthodox definition since the activity is not irrelevant: it is simply a continuation of the former activity but performed to a greater degree.

Continuing the existing activity but with increased intensity

Routine neurotic suspension

Neurotic suspension can take the form of fixedly staring at someone. Typically, a solitary male gazes hard at a female across a room, unable to either arrest his stare or approach. This became so commonplace in some Dutch bars that it became the subject of public, written complaint by females. Their normal reaction to unwanted attention, the Grimace Response, could be effective

A single male in a frozen stare at a female

against a male locked in this suspended state. 'They look at you, they don't do anything, they just look at you' was a more general female complaint, separate from the bars.

Our social capacity can be thought of as 'brain muscles'

Sociability in animals has been found to be related to brain size – social animals have larger brains. It is fair to conclude that a significant portion of our mental capacity is devoted to social interaction. Operation of these 'brain muscles' is normally unconscious but it becomes apparent when a person is sick or when talking to someone who is mentally ill.

In the first case, a patient receiving visitors rapidly becomes tired; the effort of social interaction, usually so insignificant that it is hardly noticeable, exhausts the weakened patient. When dealing with someone who is mentally ill, it is necessary to inhibit the normally automatic process of social communion whereby a commonality of understanding is sought and reached. Achieving this commonality with a mentally-ill person entails sharing their illness. Mental illness can be socially contagious, in the same way as a person can be affected by close proximity to someone who is acutely depressed or anxious.

Being affected by others' state of mind

Because man is a social animal, everyone is engaged to some degree with the people around them, occupied in a sort of diffused social activity. Hence when a crisis occurs a wholly predictable diversion of the impulse to respond is to continue with this diffused social activity but with increased intensity. Similarly it is easy to imagine a passer-by seeing some ambiguous situation (such as a prone body, which could either be a drunk happily sleeping it off or the victim of a heart attack) and the impulse of concern being diverted to renewed focus on their objective, for practically everyone is going somewhere, with some objective in mind. In another scenario, displacement might take the form of continuing an incidental conversation with a stranger with increased intensity.

Diffused sociability can intensify in neurotic suspension

Neurotic suspension takes place when an individual or group is frozen

> *Staring men*. The following note was passed out in December 1992, first in Dutch and then in English, as people entered a large bar in the centre of Amsterdam run by squatters.
>
> 'Don't forget that within these walls we are trying to create other values and norms of behaviour than outside on the street or in other discos. Men who harass women can reckon on being dealt with, and in extreme cases, will be thrown out. Women who don't feel at ease here, because of men amusing themselves with unwelcome advances towards them, whether touching or staring, are encouraged to say something about it to the people on the door. There are always women in the area who will help you.'

between two (or more) possible actions or responses. It has already been noted that during the period a sexual signal is being emitted a peculiar state is induced in the mind of the receiver. Objective appraisal of the female can become extremely difficult and a state of generalised confusion can occur. Perception of the event and its surroundings can be altered: there may be disassociation from the environment or an enhanced perception of it. A possible evolutionary origin for the state of increased awareness is looking out for a predator or aggressive mating rival.

Description of neurotic suspension and its likely origin

Sexual signalling and mating rituals are the likely genesis of the effect. Moreover, neurosis induced by sexual signalling carries over into non-sexual spheres.

Bystander effects

Bystander apathy is the tendency of people witnessing an emergency to ignore the problem. Disassociation from the environment is an obvious potential factor in bystander apathy. Signals of distress are signals just like any other, with inherent ambiguity. They inspire multiple responses, i.e. induce neurosis, in the same way. Screams can be interpreted as playful drunkenness or part of a private dispute. Sufficiently sustained or repeated signals will cause a threshold to be exceeded, at which point the neurotic state is resolved by decision and action.

Distress signals are also ambiguous

With alarm signals we can expect widely varying thresholds, especially with a pre-existing background of similar signals which are not alarms such as, in an urban environment, habituation to drunken revellers' shouts and other noise. The gradual elevation of a signal would lead to difficulty establishing a reliable threshold and hysteresis (delayed) effects would be expected also.

Response thresholds

A female scream or intense commotion is capable of arresting neurotic suspension, spurring hitherto frozen males (especially) into action. However, such extreme female signals tend to be inhibited in an environment in which neurotic suspension is commonplace, a relation which is unlikely to be coincidental.

A female's scream can arrest neurotic suspension

The following incident at a music business party does not involve an alarm signal but nonetheless may be a useful illustration of neurotic suspension. The party was held at the Manor, a residential recording studio in Oxfordshire, though most of the people there seemed to be music business hangers-on. The author worked for Virgin at the time, and was sitting on the floor in one of the large sitting rooms of the country house, when Richard Branson came into the room. He walked in and headed straight for the couch at the room's centre, which had long since been fully occupied, and someone quickly rose to allow him a seat.

Neurotic suspension at a music business party, inspired by the entrance of Richard Branson

After Branson settled himself, over the next few seconds the hubbub of party chatter among the twenty or thirty people scattered around the room ground to a halt. A pregnant silence descended, with doubtless several individuals there being eager to impress the company figurehead with some amusing quip, and easily capable of it, but being totally swallowed up in the reaction of the majority, who fell silent.

Common sociability acts as a damper

It was an example of collective neurotic suspension. The common sociability among the people in the room which had been the underlying theme before the chief's arrival became intensified. Someone making a comment would perforce have felt himself a representative spokesman for the others. After a few minutes Branson left, unwilling to play the role of party-pooper, and conversation resumed.

Diffusion of responsibility experiments

In a series of experiments investigating 'diffusion of responsibility' performed on the New York subway, black and white pretend-victims and responders were employed and race appeared to be insignificant. This will not necessarily be the case in provincial Holland, which was the location of the following incident. As a model of bystander apathy it is far superior to the textbook case of Kitty Genovese, and was more accurately reported.

A Moroccan girl drowns in a Rotterdam boating lake

The incident occurred on a Rotterdam boating lake on 21 August 1993. The man-made lake had a concrete bottom and was not deep. Two Moroccan girls were in a boat in the middle of the lake and one, aged nine, fell into the water. The girl in the boat struggled to keep the drowning girl's head above the water but failed. Meanwhile a crowd of around two hundred spectators at the side of the lake looked on without responding. One recorded the event on a video camera and another, an old fisherman, but who could not swim himself, reportedly tried to get one of the onlookers to go out. Nevertheless except for the old fisherman the crowd remained immobile during the critical period when a rescue could have been accomplished.

Miscegenation induces neurosis

An incident in which race was a central factor occurred in the Hull around 1996. A large crowd gathered at a public space for some kind of sale or fair, and most of the crowd formed a long queue. The crowd entered into a mild form of neurotic suspension on the sight in the queue of a white woman with a Negro partner. The children appeared unaffected however, and in fact exploited the adults' muted behaviour to whoop and gambol close to the source of the neurosis.

Diversion of the response impulse

The default diversion of the response impulse appears to be to continue with the present activity but with greater intensity. This results in enhanced concentration on other people nearby, giving exaggerated attention to their behaviour – or lack of it.

Altruism and Hamilton's rule

The victim was an obvious member of an out-group

Much angst was expressed in the newspapers in the days following the Rotterdam incident, including a proposal that failing to respond in distress situations be made illegal. These recriminations, or certainly the reported sentiments of the participants afterwards, were hysteresis effects. The moral anguish included accusations of 'racism' because the subjects of the emergency were obvious members of an out-group. This brings us to altruism, a subject of such depth that books have been entirely devoted to it. Nevertheless, the following essential element is sometimes omitted.

Hamilton's rule provides an objective test

An objective test by which altruism can be gauged is the following rule, provided by the biologist William. D. Hamilton. Unselfish behaviour occurs when

$$br > c$$

where *b* is benefit, *r* is relatedness and *c* is cost. That is, altruism takes place when benefit times relatedness exceeds cost.

When self-sacrifice is justified

The formula states that risk and self-sacrifice can be justified by its benefit to relatives. This rule accounts for the alarm calls a bird makes when a predator approaches, a problem which occupied Darwin, for it is apparently contrary to 'survival of the fittest.' When a bird sounds an alarm it identifies itself as a target. The predator cares little which of the flock it catches, and the bird which calls draws attention to itself, making itself a likely victim.

However, applying Hamilton's rule, the cost to the alarm-caller is justified by having warned its relatives. Members of the flock carry portions of the caller's genes; if a sufficient number of related individuals survive to continue its genetic line then its sacrifice is worthwhile.

Death can be genetically advantageous

Suppose there are four brothers in a situation where the certain death of one will guarantee the survival of the remaining three. (Most times the cost will be a risk of death, but for simplicity this scenario is contrived to avoid probabilities.) Being siblings, each of the three surviving brothers carry 50% of the sacrificial sibling's genes. One brother's sacrifice – his 100% loss – results in 150% of his genes surviving.

Counting the number of grandchildren

Hamilton's rule can be applied to any resource, but number of offspring is the most definite measure. Reproductive benefit is conventionally measured by the number of grandchildren which result, this being intended to smooth out perturbations during a single generation. If we assume that each brother ends up with four grandchildren we get the same result. The sacrifice of one brother makes evolutionary sense.

We all have Hamilton's rule built into us, deeply embedded, however much influence is brought to bear to encourage us to act contrary to it. For example, it is possible to feel grief on the death of a relative one has never met.

An example of kin-selected altruism codified in religious doctrine appears in an incident recounted by Israel Shahak. Indeed he revealed in the introduction to *Jewish History, Jewish Religion* that it was the inspiration for the book.

Having Hamilton's rule built-in. An example in religious doctrine

An Arab had suffered a heart attack outside the house of an orthodox Jew during the Sabbath and the occupant of the house refused to allow his telephone to be used to call an ambulance. Religious doctrine dictated that this was prohibited during the Sabbath. Only to save the life of a Jew could an exception to the Sabbath rule be made.

On reading of this incident in the press Shahak consulted the highest rabbinical authorities in Israel, who confirmed that the Jew had acted correctly, indeed piously, in accordance with the laws of Judaism.

Loyalty to one's family. 'Civic nationalism'

The everyday expression of Hamilton's rule is loyalty to members of one's family and altruistic behaviour towards them. It would normally also be manifest in national cohesion, but this has been much eroded in recent decades by mass immigration and emphasis by the Establishment on a civic, as opposed to ancestral, concept of national identity. In 'civic nationalism' membership of the nation is solely determined by where one is born, neglecting heredity. This obviously undermines the sense of common kinship. Hamilton's rule can help establish when and if neurotic transfer is taking place.

Potential exceptions

As (perhaps) the final word on altruism, the maxim that 'people will do something for nothing but only under special circumstances and only for a limited time' is offered. It is argued that, save for this exception, Hamilton's rule applies.

Other bystander models

Neurotic suspension is a new term and some mainstream psychological concepts should be mentioned before rounding off this chapter.

Other models involve multiple individuals

'Diffusion of responsibility,' 'pluralistic ignorance' and 'social loafing' have all been suggested as the primary mechanism of bystander apathy. None of these completely account for the bystander effect, because even a single bystander may fail to respond. In 'diffusion of responsibility' trials for example, a linear or near-linear relation has been shown with the number of potential responders.

When asked if he would give his life to save a drowning brother, the biologist J.B.S. Haldane famously quipped: 'No, but I would to save two brothers or eight cousins.'

Fitness. About five different definitions of fitness exist. *Inclusive fitness* is looking from the point of view of the gene, where the gene maximizes its survival through relatives. Thus an individual may behave altruistically to its kin, at cost to itself, as set out in Hamilton's rule. In *reproductive fitness*, an animal's fitness is measured solely by its success in leaving offspring. Thus a sterile worker ant has a reproductive fitness of zero, but a non-zero inclusive fitness because its actions assist the reproductive efforts of the queen, with which it shares genes.

The more bystanders there were, the less likely they were to respond. That is, the more people there were, the more likely they were to be frozen in inaction. However even with a single bystander the response rate was never 100%.

Neurotic suspension in a single individual

We can easily imagine a situation involving a single individual. A solitary worker overseeing a mechanical process sees it going seriously wrong, with disastrous results: a witness, too far away to do anything, might report 'He just stood there looking at it.' The bystander himself may say 'I don't know what I was thinking about' during the inevitable recriminations afterwards. Fixed in neurotic suspension, the worker has been frozen to the spot, suspended in awe at the implications of the malfunction.

Here the primary model involves an individual

'Diffusion of responsibility' and the rest are inadequate for a solitary bystander because when he is alone there is no diffusion and no plurality. However the neurotic suspension model proposed here has an observable precursor in the animal world and a putative evolutionary origin. The basic model concerns a single, neurosis-inducing stimulus and a single responder: the solitary male transfixed by a female in a bar, or the reader in a library exposed to the Lingering signal. The presence of others intensifies the state of neurotic suspension. Neurotic suspension appears to be the basic mechanism, even if other factors contribute.

Inducing psychosis

Inducing not neurosis but psychosis, and for similar reasons

Sometimes not just neurosis is induced but psychosis. Psychosis is departure from reality. Overt Instances in the author's personal experience are few, and consisted of a female using her immediate environment and nearby individuals to invent a situation designed to instill fear in her target. It is an extension of neurosis-induction, for it extends the policy of confusing the male and making him easier to manipulate.

During the Second World War inducing psychosis in the enemy and at home was deliberate policy. Indiscriminately bombing enemy civilians as a means of generating a 'war psychosis' was eventually formalised as the Lindemann Plan. The psychosis at home was to motivate the British to war. This is detailed in F.J.P. Veale's *Advance to Barbarism*.

Probably the most common expression of the induction of psychosis is newspaper 'scare stories.' The oft-quoted example of bystander apathy involving the 1964 murder of Kitty Genovese in New York had many more racial and sexual overtones than the Rotterdam incident quoted here (and is thus again greatly inferior as a model). It is not so much an example of bystander apathy as of inducing irrational fear. The original, lurid newspaper account, which established its subsequent treatment, took the form of a scare story with many inaccuracies and omissions. The implicit message was 'Now you can be murdered outside your door and no-one will come to help.' Such a crime is an extremely rare event, and the sensational media reports generated irrational fear of its repetition. Irrational fear is separation from reality, i.e. psychosis.

Scare stories. Many variables make for a bad example. Inducing irrational fear

An unresolved question is why the public display such appetite for this kind of scare-mongering. It might be compared with the genre of books known as 'misery literature' in which harrowing and usually exaggerated tales of childhood abuse and other tragic events are told, with a predominantly female readership.

Why is 'misery lit' so popular?

Morbid curiosity and soccer prayer

An intriguing and potentially enlightening complement to neurotic suspension is the morbid curiosity of passing motorists when a road accident occurs. The occupants of vehicles driving past are compulsively drawn to view the carnage, with the result that further accidents often occur due to distraction. Possibly the onlookers find relief that they are not the victim, and hence this is tentatively called *neurotic alleviation*.

Morbid curiosity as neurotic alleviation

'Being a New Yorker, I remember the case of Kitty Genovese very well. My understanding is that the courtyard which was the scene of the Genovese murder was arranged in such a way that no one person would have seen or heard more than a part of the attack. Many thought it was a drunken fight. Several people did telephone the police but others didn't because they didn't want to jam the telephone lines.

'By the way, in those days two women living together – unless they were very obvious – would have been considered bachelorettes sharing the rent. It was a common situation. Lesbianism was still very closeted and simply not on people's radar. But the murder was iconic and the phrase "Don't get involved" became shorthand for NYC in decline.'

Yet more mysterious is a phenomenon concerning different kinds of sport. it seems that supporters' fervency is proportional to the uncertainty of a win.

Willing a team to win. Fervency of support. Faith versus fact

In soccer, goals are few and the unpredictability of the ball's movements add a high degree of randomness to the game, regardless of the undoubted skill of its professional players. Winning or losing often rests on a single goal. The support for soccer, in the mass of followers and the huge sums paid for players, far exceeds that for games such as rugby and cricket where success or defeat generally follows large differences in the teams' scores. It is as if the supporters feel they need to will on their team, for the more finely balanced the match, and the more subject to random incidents the game is, the more devoted the supporters become.

Perhaps parallels can be drawn with religious faith, for no evangelist fervently seeks to convert others to the recognition of facts which are plain to all. No-one goes around eagerly seeking to convince others that one plus one equals two.

Common opposites

MALE	FEMALE
Reduce the costs of sex	Increase the costs of sex
Compete	Conspire
Polygamous	Monogamous
Seek rapid resolvement	Prevaricate and prolong
Active	Passive
Conflict	Compromise
Prefer markers and handles	Prefer signals and tokens
Encourage the strong	Nurture the weak
Value old life	Value young life
Primary domain is the thing	Primary domain is relationships
Innovate	Imitate
Hide or inhibit emotions	Display emotions
Endogamous, resist invasion	Exogamous, welcome outsiders
Low population density	High population density
Create wealth	Consume wealth
Desire for privacy	Lack of secrecy
Take risks	Avoid risks
Resolve neurosis	Induce neurosis

8 The Game of Opposites

Male and female influence, the fundamental model and the costs of sex

People's everyday attitudes and actions are much affected by the attitudes and behaviour of the opposite sex. Moreover, the influence each sex exerts on the other takes personal and social forms.

Ways females are influenced by males, and vice versa

A female who is in a personal relationship with a male is said to be *masculinated*. The intimacy of her association with a male affects her, as she becomes empathic to his needs, desires and outlook. A female who is under the societal influence of males, that is males collectively, is said to be *masculinized*. She may live in a strongly masculine society, and be constantly exposed to male perspectives. This type of influence is distinct from the bias affecting her should she be involved in a close relationship with a male.

Similarly for the male: he is *feminated* by an intimate relationship with a female and *feminized* by the collective, societal influence of females. Thus males may be feminated but not feminized, feminized but not feminated, both or neither. An equivalent set of permutations exists for the female.

Fantasies without influence of the other sex

The two following characterizations.illustrate the absence of influence by the opposite sex. A male divorced from female influence can project his drives and aspirations onto females and have wild sexual fantasies in which, in his unfeminated and unfeminized state, he imagines females will partake as eagerly as he. A female who is unmasculinized and unmasculinated might daydream of an idyllic setting while in complete communion with her perfect soul-mate. Physical sex plays little or no part in her romantic fantasy.

The terminology is easily remembered by recalling that the masculinated or feminated individual is sexually sated. However for a male to be truly feminated he must not only be allowed physical sex but also some control of it.

States and speculative extremes for males

Unfeminated and unfeminized – serial killer, *in extremis*
Feminated and unfeminized – macho bully boy
Unfeminated and feminized – spree killer, *in extremis*
Feminated and feminized – loyal and dutiful husband

Women give up physical sex for power, while men give up power for physical sex.

The Prisoner's Dilemma, a symmetric game. Two criminals are captured by the police, who only have enough evidence to convict them on a minor charge but lack sufficient proof of the more serious crime they are suspected of committing. A confession is needed from one of the prisoners, and the one who confesses will receive a bonus for betraying his partner. The payoff array is as follows:

	Prisoner B (Opponent)	
	Does not confess (Cooperates)	Confesses (Defects)
Prisoner A (Protagonist)		
Does not confess (Cooperates)	B gets *R*, 1 year A gets *R*, 1 year	B gets *T*, 0 years A gets *S*, 10 years
Confesses (Defects)	B gets *S*, 10 years A gets *T*, 0 years	B gets *P*, 5 years A gets *P*, 5 years

Games are always framed from the point of view of the Protagonist, who starts the game. The payoffs are called Reward *R*, the Sucker's Payoff *S*, Temptation *T* and Punishment *P*. In fact any symmetric game with the payoff relation $T > R > P > S$ is a 'Prisoner's Dilemma.'

If neither prisoner A nor prisoner B confess, they each serve one year in jail for the minor crime. In this case the criminals have cooperated with each other. The least plausible scenario is that both confess at the same instant, that is, they both defect simultaneously, in which case they each serve five years. Most likely is that one of the pair will defect on his partner, earning a bonus for helping the police solve the major crime and putting his partner away for a decade. The defector's payoff is to escape jail completely.

If the two are 'old hands' who envisage future ventures together then mutual cooperation may take place. Or they may be related, and foresee transactions in the future. Otherwise, defection by one of the two is practically inevitable.

Setting up a game

Modelling behaviour as games

Two players who transact are called the Protagonist and Opponent. The Protagonist is the main player, who starts the game. The transaction may be social, in which case the benefits (payoffs) may be difficult to quantify, or they may be monetary, in which case numbers already exist. The winner is the player with the highest payoff at game-end.

Without conflict of interest there is no game

The terminology does not necessarily imply strife, but a conflict of interest of some kind must underlie the game. Each player can either cooperate or defect, and each choice results in payoffs (benefits or costs) for the players. 'Benefit' and 'cost' are just of opposite polarity: a cost is a negative benefit. In the evolutionary game the crucial payoff is the number of progeny, conventionally measured by the number of grandchildren.

Probably the simplest strategy is TFT

An action is taken, starting a game, and the game proceeds. It could be a wholesaler selling to a retailer: each profits from the transaction, motivating them to continue the game. Probably the simplest strategy of all is Tit For Tat – 'You scratch my back and I'll scratch yours.' If both players cooperate then each gets a Reward payoff.

A wholesaler supplies a retailer

Suppose that one player cheats: he defects. In the case of a wholesaler selling to a retailer, the retailer doesn't pay his monthly invoice. If the other player was attempting to cooperate, the defector gets the highest payoff of all, the Temptation payoff. For the retailer this is being able to sell the goods without having to pay for them. However a defector will normally only collect the Temptation payoff once: only a fool will continue to cooperate when the other side is cheating.

The temptation to defect can be overwhelming

Depending on the value of the payoffs, the temptation to defect can be so overwhelming that one player will always defect. He may fear that the other player will beat him to it. In a single cycle of play, collecting the Temptation payoff is usually irresistible, because there is little to lose by cheating on the deal. In an ongoing or long-term game however the accumulated Reward payoffs can be worth more than a single, large Temptation payoff.

Sticking to two-player games

It is better not to think about games involving more than two players – the model and the mathematics quickly become horrendous. Indeed at any level it is better to reduce the model to just two players. A protagonist can be set against his entire environment.

Only when there is a prospect of future interaction will cooperation occur

The essential point is that cooperative behaviour (reciprocal altruism) only evolves when there are to be repeated transactions. Of course the important game from our standpoint is the male-female game, an asymmetric game – each player has different roles and different payoffs. Like physical sex and a relationship, to the male one is essential and the other incidental, while for the female the emphasis is the reverse.

Females who are in a relationship with a male are much more likely to make direct eye contact with other males; without her partner's influence looking directly tends to be reserved for signalling. Similarly, when a male enters into a relationship with a female he starts to see the world through her eyes, and he can suddenly acquire her acute awareness of single males. Females are well aware of males' physical need, not just desire, for sex. A feminist in North London, the mother of several children, one summer evening said 'They're crying out for it out there' and then later that night had sex with another woman.

Complex behaviour due to long duration

For males and females transactions have been going on for millennia and future interactions are inevitable. Thus we can expect to see a rich variety of game-playing behaviour. In male-female games the female can often be cast as Protagonist because most games are instigated by females, although the male is often unaware of it.

Modern urban life is unnatural, and many instincts which would formerly have been inhibited now find full expression. One instance shall be quoted, which may be telling. During the greater part of our evolutionary past, if a female of reproductive age were to venture out alone, her rape would have been certain. Her solitary presence in a remote place, having placed herself in that vulnerable position, would have been regarded as a valid signal that she desired it.

Female vulnerability to being raped. Casual sex is contrary to the female strategy

One-night stands and copulation purely for pleasure are inconsistent with females' basic strategy. There are exceptions, but such transient relationships typically take place during a period of experimentation, for the purpose of power play, occasional self-indulgence during holidays, or are limited to a few female sub-types (i.e. minority strategists).

Competition between male and female

In a stable relationship which is (or will shortly be) productive of children the male and female are in symbiosis, acting in each others' genetic interests as well as their own. The rest of the time they have conflicting interests. This competitive game could be 'zero-sum' – what the male loses, the female wins and vice versa.

The male strategy is much simpler

Before any further consideration of games though, a foundation must be laid of the basic male and female policies. When modelling behaviour as games, it is female strategies which demand most attention. This is because in pre-history, in fact until quite recently, the male didn't have to adopt subtle strategies, he just used brute force. Thus male behaviour is much simpler.

The Game of Opposites

The sex ratio as an elementary biological game

An elementary game in biology is the sex ratio. In rodents the game includes sex changes taking place *in utero* – a pregnant mouse placed among a group of males produces females, or if placed in a group of females it produces males. Certain reptiles achieve the same end by laying their eggs at different depths, with incubation temperature determining sex. By this means the sex ratio oscillates around its optimum value. The game is cyclic.

Manipulation compensates for physical strength

For men and women, a basic dichotomy is that women are soft and men are hard; softness can be defined as penetrability by something hard. We already have that males prefer unambiguous markers and handles while females prefer ambiguous signals and tokens, because these facilitate strategies which compensate for males' greater physical strength.

Like the sex ratio, the Game of Opposites is a fundamental game. It is simply defined by 'Look at what the other player does and do the opposite.'

Establishing masculinity or femininity

This framework describes overall policies, not the actions of individuals. Whether a strategy is masculine or feminine is established according to whether it is advantageous for the male or the female, evolutionarily and genetically. The crux is that the policies employed by males and females are, excepting certain specific circumstances, utterly the opposite of each other.

Primary domains

Males are interested in things, females in relationships

The primary domain of the male is the thing, the primary domain of the female is relationships. Men can become obsessive about some practical project or objective, while when women become impassioned their focus is usually a single individual. Females' ability to cope with several tasks simultaneously probably derives from her ability to manipulate relationships with several individuals or family members simultaneously.

Modern man's interest in pornography and guns

The male focus on things is expressed in their devotion to repairing cars, building boats, inventing gadgets and scientific endeavour. Probably its progenitors were attention to the male mating object (female genitalia) and weapons used not only for hunting but in contests between males to achieve that goal. This can be seen today in many males' keen interest in pornography and guns. Contrariwise, females' emphasis on relationships explains their appetite for soap operas, portraying dramatic events in the lives of characters they feel they know. These sordid dramas may be directly equivalent to the pornography many males are drawn to.

The costs of sex

According to the model, the male instinct is to reduce the costs of sex, the female instinct is to increase them. Raising the cost of sex is the female strategy underlying all others. Since sex, whether in the form of relationships, physical sex or progeny, is the only amenity the female can provide which males cannot, her status depends ultimately upon it. Sex and sexual attractiveness are promoted by a femicentric media, and considerable sums are spent by women on beauty products, hair care, clothes, plastic surgery and so on. Cost and value are practically synonymous, since the higher the perceived value of sex the greater the cost which can be levied for it. Equally, more regard will be given to a hint or suggestion that sex will be provided in the future.

Sex is the only amenity males cannot provide for themselves

These diametrically opposing strategies – reducing or increasing the cost of sex – derive from the abundance of sperm and limited supply of ova, together with the considerable investment in resources the female makes to bring a fertilised egg to term. Then of course the female invests further resources when she nurtures the child to the stage when it can survive independently of her. The male can indulge in a few minutes of intense pleasure then simply walk away. The female has no such choice, firstly by her pregnancy then by the attachment she acquires to the child she bears.

Males need only make a low investment, female investment is high

Ten costs and benefits of sex have been defined and examples are given of how each cost can be maximized for female advantage. *Control of information* is one means by which the costs of sex can be raised, say by withholding information about an event (especially a sexual event) until that information has the greatest possible impact. Adolescent females tend to divulge information immediately but by maturity females have learned to withhold it to obtain greater advantage and effect. This breakdown into a ten-tuple (ten dimensional vector) is unlikely to be unique, but it appears to be capable of accounting for every possible scenario.

Control of information. Withholding it for maximum impact. Wanting a disease

The concept of a wanted disease may seem perverse, but in love a partner can wish to share everything, including a disease. It may also be a means of securing a lock-in on a partner, the lock-in being a female strategy to secure a male in the role of supporter of the female and her children.

Females cannot give up sex in pursuit of an objective to the extent that males can. A male will forego sex to achieve some goal but a female will never give up relationships, which is her expression of sex, because it is totally essential to her being. The question to a male 'Why is sex so important to you?' is utterly ridiculous, coming from a female.

Competition or Conspiracy

Expressions of the male competitive instinct

Males' aptitude for competition is visible all around – in sporting endeavour, in his pursuit of status, in one-upmanship, in his jostling to become 'top dog.' By the Game of Opposites then, females conspire (literally, 'breathe together'). Competition between males has obvious evolutionary benefit as a means of enhancing fitness, and their instinct to compete is expressed in races, team games and business where prowess is demonstrated and dominance sought. On the other hand females tend to stick together, uniting against their 'common enemy' the male.

Male and female attitudes. The nature of female conspiracy

These opposing stances are encapsulated by the classic male and female attitudes, the competitive and sympathetic responses. Males in a group will seek to outdo each other with stories of exceptional events and tales of derring-do, while a female joining a group of others with a tale of misfortune meets with general sympathy and suggestions how the situation might be alleviated. A conspiracy does not have to be secret, but it tends to be more effective if it is hidden or unacknowledged.

Invoking quasi-religious concepts. Big Sister. The origin of female selfishness

Females conspire when they argue for more power for their kind, often in the form of demands for 'equal rights' or similar quasi-religious concepts. The Establishment is now almost entirely feminine in its policies. By 'the Establishment' is meant the government and media, with the latter probably wielding greater actual power. Big Brother is a myth; the reality is Big Sister. Should this be doubted, in Britain in 2011 there were an estimated 1.85 million CCTV cameras, or about one for every 32 people. The male desire for privacy has been usurped by the female longing for safety, and this despite official admissions of the ineffectiveness of CCTV in solving crime. The female desire for safety, and her selfishness, originate from her role as bearer of a limited resource: her ova. While males produce sperm continually, females are born with a limited supply of eggs. Biologically speaking, she tends not just herself but for many, as yet unborn, children.

Just as important as acting together is failing to limit each others' behaviour, which is another expression of the Conspiracy strategy. The criminal activity of the early suffragettes is rarely mentioned: hundreds of arson attacks, including against churches and ancient buildings; vandalising a priceless work of art, the

> A tipsy employee flirts with his boss's wife at the office Christmas party, which she construes then or later as a pass. Rather than divulge the incident immediately to her husband, when it might have been laughed off, she waits until the employee is being considered for promotion, at which point instead of being promoted he is dismissed.

The ten costs and benefits of sex, with examples

COST	EXAMPLE COST WITH PHYSICAL SEX	COST WITHOUT PHYSICAL SEX	BENEFIT WITH AND/OR WITHOUT
1. *Unwanted child*	Unwanted pregnancy after intercourse.	Artificial insemination, resulting in an undesirable increase in population.	Procreation, to further the species.
2. *Unwanted disease or other physical disorder*	Contraction of a sexually transmitted disease.	Catching pneumonia during a trek to find a female.	Securing a lock-in or satisfying a desire to share everything.
3. *Unwanted relationship*	Continuing a relationship out of habit or politeness after passion has expired.	Continuing a relationship with a desired female which is unconsummated.	(Relationships without procreation are null in evolutionary terms.)
4. *Disturbance of an existing emotional relationship or activity*	Sleeping with a friend's girlfriend who then discloses the encounter.	Making a pass at a friend's girlfriend and the information being strategically divulged.	Friendships can be enhanced by becoming more sociable as a result of having sex.
5. *Disturbance of an existing business relationship or activity*	Missing a business appointment because of having sex.	Making a pass at the boss's wife at an office party in jest and being passed over for promotion because of it.	Large companies prefer their male employees to be married because they are more stable and thus more productive.
6. *Money*	Maintaining a woman.	Entrance charges to a discotheque, drinks and other incidental costs incurred while trying to win one.	Professional sex confers the benefit of money, or a person might marry into money.
7. *Information*	The 'Honey Trap' in which a female spy seduces a target to obtain information.	Giving excessive information in attempts to impress a target female.	Information about females and particularly how they feel to the touch.

COST	EXAMPLE COST WITH PHYSICAL SEX	COST WITHOUT PHYSICAL SEX	BENEFIT WITH AND/OR WITHOUT
8. *Diminishment of Self*	Having sex with an older or unattractive female and the event being cast abroad.	Being used as a trophy before being ditched. Psychological stress endured while trying to obtain a partner.	Feeling good about oneself.
9. *Energy*	Energy expended in the act.	Travelling a long distance to see a girl unproductively and back again.	Children working for a parent.
10. *Time*	Duration of the act and in recovery.	Waiting or being at a place hoping that a girl will appear.	Learning of a time-saving device while meeting someone socially. Children working for a parent.

'Suicide bumming' (as one guy I spoke to put it) refers to the practice by which healthy individuals deliberately have sex to contract HIV. They achieve this by engaging in prearranged, systematic penetration with a succession of HIV-positive partners. One after the other. And then plug up the rectum to prevent the semen escaping. It's called, on the scene, 'the gift.'

In a bar in San Fransisco, I ask one guy why he did it.

He has no hesitation in telling me.

'You feel, I don't know, more part of things,' he says. 'Like you belong more.'

A friend – young, beautiful and also HIV-positive – comes over to join us. I ask him the same question. He smiles.

'It's a sign of commitment,' he says. 'Of solidarity. It's turning a negative into a positive. It's like getting a tattoo, only on the inside. It's like an immunological tattoo.'

Kevin Dutton, *Flipnosis*

Rokeby Venus; breaking hundreds of shop windows, and planting bombs. That very small but extremely vociferous minority met no serous opposition from other women. In the same manner, and by a similar progression, a woman with perfectly moderate views today, who would never claim to be a feminist or identify herself with radical opinions, in fact performs actions and holds views identical to those proposed by militant feminists a decade or two ago.

Modern women hold views identical to earlier extreme feminists

A married woman with a family has no shortage of relationships and, having achieved this goal, she often uses her influence to increase the costs of sex for other females. Female conspiracy may be as surreptitious as meaningful looks undermining males, and many subtle messages are conveyed via the media intended for females and which pass entirely over the heads of males. The women of some American Indian tribes had a special language which could not be understood by their menfolk. This exists for us in milder form as 'women's talk' which many males find practically unintelligible. Themes of babies, children, emotions and the reactions of individuals to minor events are almost a foreign language to many men.

Females increase the cost of sex for each other. 'Women's talk'

If the female were to possess an innate sense of grievance, this would cement the policy of female conspiracy. The conviction may have grounds or it may not; it could exist regardless of circumstances because its origin would be the advantage it confers not its validity. Just as a rabbit finds it simpler, easier, more conducive to a long life and the transmission of its genes to assume that every rustle in the grass is a predator, a female predisposition may be to believe that her discontent is due to males, or perhaps one male in particular. An inbuilt conviction that she is hard done by could make her regard every weapon available to her as legitimate for use.

An innate sense of grievance

Biased perception is by no means rare: national lotteries are popular because of our tendency to believe that we are lucky, rather than a rational appraisal of the odds. It is advantageous to believe that good things will happen to us while the bad will befall someone else. All sorts of predispositions exist because they confer general advantage, independently of their validity or invalidity in a particular circumstance. Plus of course, many of the situations in which we now find ourselves have no evolutionary precedent – travelling faster than a galloping horse and watching TV, to name but two. They have never occurred before in the history of man; we have hardly begun to develop a suitable response to them.

Instincts can be irrational, often existing solely because they are advantageous

Polygamy and monogamy

While the primary sexual expression of the female is relationships, the primary sexual activity of the male is physical sex. Both are sex, or equivalent gender expressions of sex. Maintaining relationships with a husband and children,

Gender expressions of sex

Raising the cost of sex is the paramount female policy. Moreover, all of the costs of sex can be incurred, in full, without physical sex taking place.

relatives and others is, to the female, sexual activity. As essential as her biological functions are, most of her time is spent maintaining relationships in either a virtual family circle or an actual one.

The female tests the male

Achieving a family of her own follows the process of sexual selection, which for the female is a critical process. She needs support during gestation and child-rearing. Her optimal strategy is to secure the best possible mate for long-term procreation, obtaining for herself a single monogamous partner and a stable and comfortable environment for raising progeny. To this end her policy is to test the male, obliging him to prove his loyalty and commitment to her. That, at least, is the evolutionary and traditional scenario.

If she can secure an alpha-male, that is a male of exceptional ability or power, this gives even greater facility for the proliferation of her genes. In the evolutionary game, gene-proliferation is the only payoff that matters.

The male proceeds by resolving and progressing

Males are polygamous and females are monogamous. Allied to his polygamous instincts, the male seeks rapid resolution while the female instinct is to defer it. The optimal strategy for the dispersion of a male's genes is to impregnate as many reproductive females as possible, while females tend to a singular emotional focus. This is demonstrated with the birth of a child, at which time the husband often finds himself ignored.

In furtherance of his polygamous drive, males seek resolvement, and this is demonstrated in their approach to business. The male polygamous drive is expressed by concluding one deal as quickly as he can and progressing to the next. By this means he aims to proceed (acquire property, or wealth in another form) as efficiently as possible.

The male seeks to bring things to a head, the female instinct is to prevaricate

By *resolvement* is meant the impulse to force a decision or cut to the chase in a complex situation and demand a decision resolving it. An agreement is finally settled in forceful negotiation and a contract signed. A failing company is shut down and its assets auctioned, so that the businessman can cut his losses and move on to his next venture. Opposing this male drive for resolution is vacillation and prevarication, in which caprice plays an important part.

In dealing with a female, the male seeks to optimize his resources by bringing things to a head; either the female will submit to him or she will not. If he allows himself to be played along he could expend a great deal of time and effort on her for nothing, so he seeks to resolve the matter as soon as he can. The quicker he resolves, the sooner he can move on to the next. The female, pursuing her opposing policy, seeks to test the male's suitability as a long-term

The Perfect Day for Him

6:00	Alarm.
6:15	Blow job.
6:30	Massive, satisfying shit while reading the sports section.
7:00	Breakfast: steak and eggs, coffee and toast – all cooked by naked, buxom wench who bends over a lot showing her growler.
7:30	Limo arrives.
7:45	Several beers en route to the airport.
9:15	Flight in personal Lear jet.
9:30	Limo to Mirage Resort Golf Club (blow job en-route).
9:45	Play front nine (2 under par).
11:45	Lunch: steak and lobster, three beers and bottle of Dom Perignon.
12:15	Blow job.
12:30	Play back nine (4 under).
2:15	Limo back to airport (several bourbons).
2:30	Fly to Bahamas.
3:30	Late afternoon fishing expedition with all-female crew, all nude who also bend over a lot showing their growlers.
4:30	Land world record Marlin (1234lbs), on light tackle.
5:00	Fly home, massage and hand job by naked supermodel (bending over showing her growler, naturally).
6:45	Shit, shower and shave.
7:00	Dinner: lobster appetisers, Dom Perignon (1953), big juicy fillet steak followed by ice cream served on a lovely big pair of tits.
9:00	Napoleon brandy and Habanos cigars in front of wall-sized TV as you watch football game.
9:30	Sex with three women with lesbian tendencies.
11:00	Massage and jacuzzi with tasty pizza snacks and a cleansing beer.
11:30	Night-cap blow job.
11:45	In bed, alone.
11:50	A 22-second fart which changes note four times and forces the dog to leave the room.
11:51	Laugh yourself to sleep.

She tests the male and keeps her options open in case a superior male comes along

supporter of her and their potential offspring, prevaricating before she commits to bearing his children. She will also often attempt to keep her options open should a superior (fitter) male come along, at which point, having avoided committing herself, she can rapidly change her allegiance to the superior male. A now seldom-used word describing this behaviour is *tergiversation* – combined prevarication and disloyalty. The female can rapidly change allegiance to whoever is willing to devote the most attention to her.

Serial monogamy

Serial monogamy. Wrongful paternity

The modern female strategy is serial monogamy, where the female maintains a monogamous relationship with a male, insisting that he remain faithful to her. Evolutionarily of course, female loyalty was far more important. The male could be working to raise the offspring of another, and then practically his entire motivation for supporting his wife is nullified. This would certainly be the case if only a single child had been produced which was not his.

Advantage of serial monogamy. 'Trading up'

In serial monogamy the female becomes more adept at manipulating the male with each successive partner. She will sometimes engage in 'trading up,' securing a male who she sees as a better partner for herself and finalizing the transition even before she has dumped the old. By this means she can ensure she is never without a partner and supporter, even if that support, due to modern welfare systems, is only emotional.

Activity and passivity

Physical sex reaffirms masculinity and femininity

Males are essentially active while females are essentially passive. In the feminine way of things she waits for males to present themselves to her, from whom she selects her favourite. These active-passive roles have an obvious origin in the sex act, where usually the female takes a passive and receptive role and the male is active, intrusive and overbearing. It was ever thus.

How males and females acquire status

Another, more subtle dichotomy concerns the status of males and females, or rather how it is acquired. The male acquires status from his abilities or success in various endeavours, such as business or sport, the latter deriving largely from collective male activities such as hunting. Many sports still retain the essential elements of running and aiming, and status within the tribe was dependent on these skills. In contrast, the dominant female in any female group is almost invariably the one that is most attractive, and this measure directly follows from male perception. The status of the female is proportional to the status of the male she can attract.

Often the female is not so much interested in the male's action, she only wishes to be reassured of his willingness and preparedness to act.

The Perfect Day for Her

8:15	Wake up to hugs and kisses.
8:30	Weigh-in 2kgs lighter than yesterday.
8:45	Breakfast in bed: freshly squeezed orange juice and croissants; open presents – expensive jewellery chosen by thoughtful partner.
9:15	Soothing hot bath with frangipani bath oil.
10:00	Light work-out at club with sexy, amusing personal trainer.
10:30	Facial, manicure, make-up application, shampoo, condition, blow-wave.
12:00	Lunch with best friend at fashionable outdoor café.
12:45	Catch sight of partner's ex and notice that she has gained 17kgs.
1:00	Shopping with friends – unlimited credit.
3:00	Nap.
4:15	Massage from strong but gentle hunk – says he rarely gets to work on such a perfect body.
5:30	Choose outfit from expensive designer wardrobe.
7:30	Candlelit dinner for two followed by dancing, with compliments received from other diners and dancers.
10:00	Hot shower, alone.
10:50	Carried to bed. Freshly ironed, crisp white linen.
11:00	Pillow talk, light touching and cuddling.
11:15	Fall asleep in his big, strong arms.

Old life and young life

The male inclination is to encourage the strong, while the female tendency is to nurture the weak. Males value the old, for their wisdom and experience, while females value the young, for their appeal and future promise. Some historical examples can be given.

Nazi and Dutch euthanasia

The Nazi euthanasia programme, whereby mental defectives and the severely handicapped were killed, was a masculine expression. Nonetheless that programme was rapidly aborted due to public disquiet. A feminine counterpart can be seen in the modern Dutch practice of killing aged and dying patients, occasionally simply to free up a hospital bed. This is accepted in Holland and apparently continues to this day.

Foundling hospitals

By around 1880 foundling hospitals had been firmly established mainly in France but also in Britain, where tens of thousands of unwanted babies were

The practice of 'overlaying' in earlier, more masculine times

consigned by their mothers to death. This continued a long-established practice of 'overlaying.' Whole families slept in one bed, and 'accidentally on purpose' asphixiating a child the family could not afford to support was commonplace. At the time it was a hard-living, masculine society: females were masculinized and masculinated.

Only the State may kill

Marvin Harris pointed out in *Cannibals and Kings* that by establishing foundling hospitals the State was claiming a monopoly on the right to kill. Now the State is all but claiming a monopoly on the right to punish, and killing a child seems to be regarded as more heinous than the murder of an adult.

Innovation and imitation

Origin of male innovation

The male policy is to innovate, the female's is to imitate. The origin of male innovation is obvious: contests for mating privileges with females. This is evident in troupes of gorillas, where an aging male trying to retain his position as patriarch of a harem of females must use cunning and intellect to prevail against the young male seeking to replace him. The challenger is physically stronger, but the older animal relies on his experience of previous contests and must employ innovative tactics to compensate for his failing strength.

The male imitates the female regarding relationships

This dichotomy should be elaborated. Because the primary domain of the female is relationships, an area in which she manifestly excels, the male tends to imitate her, in the same way that she imitates him in his activity and treatment of physical things. Females influence and define personal transactions, even remotely. A procedure a female has used against a male is likely to be later employed by him against a subsequent female or even another male.

The female policy of imitation also has relevance to the Tit For Tat and Disguised Defection strategies, to be discussed shortly.

Emotional intelligence

Displaying and inhibiting emotion. Males prefer precision

Another opposite, of known physical origin, is the male tendency to hide and inhibit emotion. Just as the female policy is to signal and the male's is to respond, the female policy is to display emotion and his is to inhibit it. Its physical basis is the wider corpus collosum in females. This connection between different parts of the brain explains why females are adept at vocalizing and expressing emotions. Females' 'emotional intelligence,' that is, the efficacy of their instincts as a driver of behaviour, separate from logic, has served to protect her from violence and abuse for millennia. Now feminine caprice meets with little restraint, and her claims are given a great deal more credence than hitherto. While females prefer feelings, intuition and ambiguity, males prefer logic, rationality and precision.

Inbreeding and outbreeding

With perhaps just as solid an origin is the male policy of endogamy, that is inbreeding, set against the female policy of exogamy, outbreeding. Because of the physical strength and greater aggressiveness of the male it was incumbent on him to defend the tribe against invasion and conquest. Males fought to preserve the integrity of their tribe. Historically the female was regarded merely as a spoil of war.

Males' role as defenders of the tribe. Naked mole rats

The naked mole rat is a good example of exogamy in the natural world: it was found that, of a sample of 1,000 animals, 1.9% were strongly predisposed to outbreeding with neighbouring, normally isolated colonies. All were female.

Our model is a tribe or village of a few score or a hundred people. There, a small degree of exogamy was necessary to prevent excessive inbreeding. Females then would be under great constraint in their choice of partner, their husband maybe having been selected for them years before. Long-standing assumptions between families would have existed: it was understood that the blacksmith's son would marry the farmer's daughter.

Enter a visitor, perhaps on horseback who, having travelled a great distance by the standards of the time, would likely be an alpha-male. The local maidens are greatly attracted to him, for he seems strange and exotic to them. Their eagerness for such a mate reflects the difficulty they would have extricating themselves from their existing binds and obligations. If the exotic stranger were secured despite these, throwing in her genetic lot with an alpha-male would be highly advantageous for her. Now, in an age of mass mobility, people travel not scores of miles but thousands. Females' enthusiasm for immigration and miscegenation is an anachronism.

An alpha-male rides in on horseback from a faraway town. Anachronistic female impulses

Big dick for sale. On the Leidseplein in Amsterdam for several days was a man, short and stocky and probably of South American origin, pressing a notice into women's hands. I asked to see and a little reluctantly he showed it. It was a piece of cardboard on which was written, 'Big dick for sale, *f* 5,–.' I smiled and corrected the 'for sale' to 'for hire' for him. He assured me that the dick really was big. Some time later I saw him again, sitting on the Leidseplein but by this time without the notice, and I asked him the outcome. He told me that eventually a German girl had assented; they had gone to the nearby Vondelpark and done it behind some bushes. 'Did you use a condom?' I asked but the question was redundant because I already knew the answer. I wanted to know whether he had received the five guilders and, laughing, he said 'No.'

Population density

Male territorial instincts are frustrated by high population density

Males are territorial, and a low population density gives the male the ability to express his territorial instincts. Freedom to express instincts confers a sense of power and control, which the male desires. On the other hand, a large population provides 'safety in numbers' for the physically weaker sex, quelling many of her irrational (and often anachronistic) fears. She is unlikely to be overpowered and raped while in a crowd. Great numbers of people also disrupt male targeting strategies, specifically, making his target harder to isolate or identify. This may seem trivial, except that females devote great attention and expenditure on clothes and cosmetics changing their appearance to achieve a similar end. With the aid of such accessories the female can change herself almost beyond recognition.

There is clearly a limit to the female preference for high population density since the white birthrate is currently falling. Possibly the limiting factor is our innate need for space.

Born to shop

Females' role as leaders of consumerism

Finally, the male policy is to create wealth, the female policy is to consume it. In Holland it was found that females accounted for 70% of the welfare budget. It is rare for a female to start work at sixteen and continue an unbroken work record until retirement, whereas millions of males do. Females tend to prefer part-time work and are more often sick, pregnant or otherwise absent from the workplace than males. Females' role as leaders of consumerism is well-known to advertising agencies and should be obvious.

Females generally imitate

Lest it needs repeating, here we deal with overall male and female policies, not individual behaviour. While the Game of Opposites describes male and female policies in the main, there are undoubtedly many exceptions. Nevertheless, when females perform male roles they are generally imitating.

Male deference exploited in Marginal Defection. Man's attitude to woman, broadly speaking, involves two major factors: Affection Beneath and deference. Regarding deference, Steve Moxon quoted a study in *The Woman Racket* of the behaviour of female lemurs. The females were observed taking food out of males' hands and, very unusually for wild animals, there was no aggressive response: the males just carried on as if nothing had happened. The paper's authors interpreted this as female dominance, but Moxon pointed out that it was actually deference. This is based on the female's role as carrier of eggs and nurturer of young, and is instinctive in these lemurs just as it is in us. Hence gentlemen hold doors open for women, traditionally tip their hats to them and, in extremis, give them priority in the rush for the lifeboats.

An example of Disguised Defection. The following purports to have taken place in rural Ireland many years ago. A labourer was hired to work on a remote farm for £10 per week, with meals and lodging included. The farmer was a wily soul while the labourer was a little slow. After a time the farmer noticed that when his worker had been given his weekly wage he disappeared, so one week he followed him. He saw that his worker was using a hiding place in a stone wall to save his wages, removing a stone and placing his £10 note on top of a pile of banknotes within. Thereafter every week, once the labourer had deposited his wage in his primitive wall safe, the farmer would secretly follow and remove a £10 note from the bottom of the pile. This was used to pay the labourer the following week. The notes were being recycled.

This continued for a couple of years, until the labourer sensed that something was amiss and left to find work elsewhere. The farmer had been playing Disguised Defection but had been unable to resist the temptation, perhaps unwittingly, to drop a hint, inwardly gloating that the labourer was working for him for nothing, maybe showing a mischievous gleam in his eye. Or perhaps he had played some sub-game of making one of the notes distinctive and watching it come round again, and this had aroused his worker's suspicion. By whatever means, perhaps only by subliminal perception, the labourer became aware that something was wrong, though he never appreciated the manner and extent of the swindle that had been perpetrated against him.

9 Basic Strategies

Cyclic games, alien roles and forms of defection

In nature, cyclic games are common. Nature requires push and pull, a conflicting dynamic of to and fro, to adapt to surpluses and deficiencies. This implies oscillation, a cycle. A dynamic system is the means by which a balance is reached and then maintained, because nothing exists in perfect equilibrium for very long, if indeed it ever does.

The 'Battle of the Sexes'

One of the most important cyclic games for our purposes is Dawkins' 'Battle of the Sexes.' John Maynard Smith suggested that this is a long-term game, but perhaps it is not so long as all that.

If females are fast, it pays males to philander. Females are 'easy,' they pair with males and submit to sex without delay. In this case the male makes only a small investment in the female. 'Easy come, easy go' applies and males will follow their polygamous instincts and sample many females.

If males philander, it pays females to be coy. When the male attempts to sample many females, they will demand increased investment by the male to discourage abandonment by him. Abandoning the female would require him to make a costly investment in a female all over again.

If females are coy, it pays males to be loyal. Having made a costly investment in a particular female, such as a long period of courtship before procreation occurs, it benefits the male to continue his relationship with her so that multiple progeny can be produced.

If males are loyal, it pays females to be fast. If males are loyal, that is monogamous, it benefits the female to secure a partner quickly to begin procreation as early as possible and maximize the number of progeny. She also seeks to secure a loyal partner before she is beaten to him by another female.

Cyclic games are probably common

Thus male and female populations react to each other and a cyclic game is established. At the end of this sequence the players are back where they started, and the cycle repeats. The likelihood is very high that cyclic games proliferate in the natural world and between human populations.

Tit For Tat

One of the simplest games is Tit For Tat, a game that is ubiquitous in nature and has been shown to be extremely reliable. Probably the best known example of TFT is the symbiosis which exists between groupers and cleaner fish. Cleaner fish are parasite-eaters, grooming the body and even inside the mouths of the much larger fish. Each provides a service for the other, and groupers regularly stop at particular coral reefs where cleaner fish congregate. This illustrates the cooperation which evolves when future interaction is likely.

Symbiosis between groupers and cleaner fish

The TFT strategy is completely described by 'Cooperate on the first move, then do as the other player last did.' Thus the Protagonist initially cooperates, the Opponent reciprocates, and an unbroken sequence of cooperation ensues. In the case of groupers and cleaner fish, this means that the grouper continues to be cleaned and the cleaner fish do not end up in the stomach of the grouper.

Definition of TFT

Problems can arise with the TFT strategy however. An inadvertent defection may be made, or a perceptual error may occur which leads the other player to interpret a cooperative play as defection. According to the definition, any defection, or perceived defection, leads to an unbroken chain of defections thereafter ('Do as the other player last did').

Suppose Paul is paid on Wednesday, Oliver on Friday, and Paul regularly lends Oliver £20 to tide him over the extra couple of days. One week Oliver cannot repay the money as usual because of another commitment, so he gives the £20 to a friend to give to Paul. The friend forgets, or squanders the money, with the result that Paul believes that Oliver has defected. According to the rules of TFT, that is the end of the game. No further cooperation takes place.

When TFT fails

Generous Tit For Tat

This dead-end can be resolved with Generous Tit For Tat strategies, which are capable of resuming cooperation after defection, or mistakes in perception or execution. Simple GTFT strategies include overlooking an occasional defection and forgiving an old defection to resume the game anew.

Advantage of GTFT over TFT

Religion can be viewed as the formalisation of the characteristics of a people, a sort of 'cultural carrier bag' of racial traits. The policy of forgiveness which is a cornerstone of Christianity avoids the practice, in many cultures, of family or tribal feuds continuing for generations. Codification of the forgiveness policy in the form of religious doctrine makes it more likely to occur, conferring advantage to a population.

Religion can encourage advantageous behaviour

GTFT is not, and cannot be, precisely defined because doing so renders it susceptible to exploitation. Suppose our GTFT strategy was specified as 'Overlook defection so long as it does not occur more frequently than every fifth

Why GTFT cannot be formalised

play.' Once this was ascertained an opponent would be able to safely exploit the other player and maximize their payoff by defecting every fifth round, but never more frequently.

Males tend to play GTFT

Females play TFT while males play GTFT. Typical examples are a male buying females drinks in a bar; he discounts the drinks for which he receives no return (that is, little further involvement with the female), providing he succeeds occasionally. Or in business, an entrepreneur invests capital in perhaps half a dozen businesses which, once established, results in one profitable one and maybe one which is borderline. The successful business justifies his investment in all of them, because it will provide an income for many years to come. The failures, involving losses, are rationalised away with the dictum that 'Nothing ventured is nothing gained.' The same strategy is employed by companies when they continuously introduce new products. If they did not, the company would stagnate as its products became outmoded or otherwise fail to satisfy changing public tastes. Problems only begin when all the new ventures or products fail since not only is this very unprofitable, it is intensely disheartening.

Females obtain compound benefit and usually initiate games

Females rarely transact with a male for no reason, even if she is only gathering information or satisfying her instinct to perform some procedure conferring advantage to females generally. Executing procedures individually which benefit females generally is not only compound benefit but an expression of the Conspiracy strategy.

Most games are initiated by females, often by signalling, whether the male is aware of it or not. Hence the female is usually cast as Protagonist.

Marginal Defection

Males give females the benefit of the doubt. The 'ratchet effect'

A powerful strategy, *Marginal Defection*, exploits males' natural tendency to give females the benefit of doubt and overlook minor infractions. The female executes a measured, minor defection which the male ignores or dismisses as inconsequential. Time passes, sufficient to establish a new threshold dividing cooperation from defection. Once that new level is consolidated, further Marginal Defection takes place, and the process is repeated. This is the so-called ratchet effect whereby change is subtly executed by small, almost imperceptible steps.

When the female miscalculates things can go seriously awry

In this game, the female optimally proceeds at just below the level at which the male is provoked. She advances in her power play with finely calculated gambits which she thinks, weighing her opponent, will not trigger a response. If she miscalculates during one of these iterations the game is disrupted and the consequences may be severe. They may include violence, family break-up, court appearances and imprisonment for one of the players, usually the male.

In Disguised Defection the female imitates the male, adopting roles and exploiting technologies which males have defined and developed once they become sufficiently facile, in order to disguise her defection from her natural functions.

Disguised Defection

Normally, in a TFT game, the payoff for defection (the Temptation payoff) can be collected only once. By far the most profitable policy for a player, if it can be achieved, would be to collect the Temptation payoff repeatedly. This can be accomplished by convincing the other player that their defection is in fact cooperation. This is the strategy of *Disguised Defection*.

Collecting the best possible payoff

Suppose a con man is in a bar, out for a little sport with the objective of drinking that night without spending any money. He could execute a short-term con on the barman, using a familiar manner and manipulation to induce him to offer a free drink, and go from bar to bar. Or he could use a longer-term con and claim to be the silent partner of the owner, in which case he might drink all night for free without having to change opponent.

A con man out for a bit of fun

In their dealings with things, females imitate males. The female is only interested in things to the extent that they are of utility to her, while for many males, say designing, building or repairing a device such as a car or computer, its essential interest is exhausted once it becomes a mere commodity. An analogy can be drawn with a duck floating down a canal on a large piece of polystyrene: the duck has no awareness of oil extraction technology, of the derivation of that polystyrene from oil, or of the chemical processes involved in its creation. To the duck it is merely a floating platform, with no appreciation of the science of its production.

Things as objects of interest or utility

In Disguised Defection the female imitates the male to disguise her defection from her natural functions. She exploits male technology and systems, and imitates artificial media role models (AMRM's) to assume roles hitherto occupied by males. This can only take place once those roles are sufficiently safe and physically undemanding, but male inventions such as power tools, power steering and hydraulics have greatly reduced demands on physical strength. Even so, her performance will rarely be exceptional and often, as masculine influence diminishes, less than competent. The strictures of equality dogma dictate that the working environment must change rather than any innate properties or shortcomings of the female be admitted to.

Artificial media role models. Political correctness

In the early months of a female adopting a male role she is likely to express EBIAR, *exaggerated behaviour in alien role*. After that period, if there is sufficient masculine influence, she will settle into a more normal pattern. The

When females first take up male roles. Later they occupy bureaucratic positions

ticket collector will be assiduous, the policewoman will frog-march petty criminals to the station, the female security guard will strut and swagger, the new female driving examiner will be inordinately strict.

Due to residual physical demands in many jobs, such as occasional heavy lifting, and her innate passivity, females will tend to gravitate to sedentary administrative roles. Excessive female influence results in institutional incompetence, and a female-dominated bureaucracy leads to a mediocracy – rule by the mediocre.

Wrongful paternity

Another common form of Disguised Defection is allowing a husband to support and otherwise adopt the role of father for a child which is not his. A large body of evidence has accumulated showing that women tend to schedule their adulterous liaisons for the time when they are most likely to conceive. Data provided by the Child Maintenance and Enforcement Commission (formerly CSA) revealed that between 1998 and 2011 an average of 17%, or one in six, DNA tests showed wrongful paternity. There was surprisingly little variation in the yearly figures (min. 14.2%, max. 20.9%).

Women are constantly reminded of their reproductive role

Women of child-bearing age are reminded of their essential reproductive role every 28-day menstrual cycle. Explicitly, her natural functions, for which she is biologically and psychologically adapted, is as a manager of relationships, supporter of her partner, bearer and nurturer of children and maintainer of a family home. The vast majority of women would be happiest in such a role. Feminism, particularly the second wave which started in the 1960s, by its source and media promotion, was an example of the strategy called Malign Encouragement.

Recall that Kinsey found that women were almost twice as likely to achieve more orgasms with their affair partners as with their husbands. A recent British study (Baker and Bellis, 1995) found that women have more frequent high-sperm-retention orgasms (those that occur within two minutes after the male orgasm) with their affair partners than with their husbands. The clincher, however, may be the *timing* of lunchtime romance at the No-Tell Motel: Women who have affairs appear to time their sexual liaisons to coincide with the most fertile phase of their cycle – prior to or at ovulation. Indeed, rate of sexual intercourse with an affair partner during peak fertility is three times as high as the rate that occurs during the low-fertile post-ovulatory phase.

David Buss, *The Evolution of Desire*

A 2002 paper by Gangestad et al. of the University of New Mexico is one of several studies showing a tendency to female infidelity during ovulation. Women reported a big increase in attraction to, and fantasies about, men other than their regular partner when they were fertile. The study also appeared to show increased guarding of females by their partners during their fertile period. More recently Gangestad and Thornhill (2008) and many others have found evidence of facial preferences and behaviour suggesting that women select staid, caring males as husbands and more masculine men for affairs.

Malign Encouragement

Malign Encouragement is encouraging an opponent to pursue an adverse policy. For the ME player, 'What's bad for you is good for me.' ME is one of four policies in a two-by-two array describing the overall strategies, or meta-strategies, in which two players can engage. The policy names describe the behaviour of the Protagonist, who starts the game and hence defines it.

Encouraging an opponent to pursue an adverse policy

In the policy array below, the Protagonist's policy is fixed and the variable element is in italics. As generally, intent is irrelevant; only the outcome matters. What is surprising, indeed shocking, is that the Malign Encouragement strategy appears never to have been formally defined.

In Loser, payoffs are minimized. The Protagonist in a Loser game maximizes the costs of the Opponent, either deliberately or incidentally. War is an example of a deliberate Loser game, with the winner being the player with the least losses. The game is invariably at cost to both, even if the only cost to the Protagonist is the cost of the bombs he drops on a primitive village, which cannot retaliate.

War is a game of Loser

More subtle is a game of Loser in which the Protagonist is what is commonly known as a 'loser' or 'shit magnet.' The Perfect Loser takes the worst possible choice at each turn, thwarting every attempt the Opponent makes at cooperation, and dragging the Opponent down with him. The Opponent may be kind-hearted and well-meaning, but be a poor judge of character, so that even a well-intentioned Opponent also becomes a loser. One or both players may have unconscious destructive drives.

Losers are people to avoid

In Perfect Charity, the Protagonist maximizes his Opponent's payoff. The perfectly charitable Protagonist gives an anonymous donation to some worthy (he believes) cause. He may deliberately minimize his benefit by foregoing public recognition or other benefits of having his generosity

Giving without anything in return

acknowledged. He may be unable to avoid the sense of self-satisfaction and gratification he feels, i.e. enhancement of self, but his overall policy and intention is to maximize his Opponent's benefit by giving as much as he can afford.

The Protagonist's and Opponent's interests coincide

In Symbiosis, the Protagonist maximizes his Opponent's payoff and thereby his own. The Protagonist effectively maximizes benefit for both players. The cleaner fish maximizes its benefit by efficiently cleaning the grouper, since it feeds by doing so. The grouper maximizes its benefit by visiting the cleaning site, remaining stationary and not eating the cleaner fish. Then there is the symbiosis of a man and woman in a stable relationship rearing children. Their cooperation assures well-adjusted progeny which themselves will be able to form stable relationships and produce offspring of their own. This augurs well for the genetic success of both parents.

Encouraging detrimental actions

In Malign Encouragement, the Protagonist minimizes his Opponent's payoff. A Protagonist playing ME maximizes the cost to his Opponent. Obvious examples are encouraging an overweight person to eat, or recommending an illegal act, perhaps under the pretext of friendly advice. A nation could aid the pacifist movement of a country with which it is at war. An insular and intensely self-aware nation promoting mass immigration to other nations also qualifies as ME.

Array of policies

Fixed, *Variable*

Loser	**Malign Encouragement**
P minimizes O's payoff	P minimizes O's payoff
O or P minimizes P's payoff	*O or P maximizes P's payoff (CB)*
Perfect Charity	**Symbiosis**
P maximizes O's payoff	P maximizes O's payoff
O or P minimizes P's payoff	O maximizes P's payoff

CB = compound benefit

Malign Encouragement might be involved in any promotion of adverse or injurious behaviour. An obvious adjunct policy for a Protagonist playing ME is to argue that the behaviour he promotes is not injurious so that his strategy is unrecognised and his game can proceed without restriction.

Are orthodox psychologists naïve?

One must wonder why Malign Encouragement has not been defined hitherto. It certainly does not feature as a mainstay of elementary behaviour analysis where it belongs.

Kamikaze pilots and suicide bombers

A revealing situation is the kamikaze pilot or suicide bomber, who seeks to inflict maximum damage on his opponent by his self-sacrifice. As an individual in his game with his compatriots he is playing Perfect Charity (neglecting any acclaim he receives or belief he has in an eternal reward); in his compatriots' collective game against their adversary he is playing Loser. In this second, longer game, where the players are two warring populations, the policy may be successful.

The set of pure combinations in a game are detailed. The Protagonist can either minimize or maximize the Opponent's payoff, and the Opponent can either minimize or maximize the Protagonist's payoff, so we have four permutations. Extreme examples are given in each case.

Protagonist	**Opponent's Response** *Min P's payoff*	*Max P's payoff*
Min O's payoff	Total War	Malign Encouragement
Max O's payoff	Greedy Charity	Symbiosis

The first entry is the game of unrestrained war, i.e. Loser. Both sides try to inflict maximum damage on each other.

In Greedy Charity, the Opponent (the charitable organisation) is insatiable, constantly seeking more donations and neglecting any recognition of the Protagonist's generosity.

Malign Encouragement appears again, except that here the Opponent is a perfect dupe, conferring benefit on the Protagonist for his malevolent actions. Religion might inspire such irrational, self-destructive behaviour – the Protagonist could be the leader of a suicide cult who convinces his followers to bequeath all their money to his church. He, of course, avoids the suicide ritual.

When both players are in the happy situation where their actions are to mutual benefit we have Symbiosis.

Choosing your opponent, and your allies

Of paramount concern, especially in an adversarial game, is the selection of opponent. During the Second World War ostensibly Churchill, Roosevelt and Stalin all had Hitler as their opponent. As revealed in Paul Johnson's *A History of the Modern World* however, Stalin privately added Axis and Allied losses in the same column. Stalin's game was in terms of Communist versus non-Communist, and he apparently played Malign Encouragement to maximize non-Communist losses.

The sexual archetype of Malign Encouragement

If Procedural Analysis is consistent, forming a coherent system of interlinking parts, then Malign Encouragement must have an archetype, that is an origin, in sexual behaviour. Its putative precursor is a player encouraging their opponent to follow not an adverse strategy, simply the opposite strategy to theirs. (We could call this *Opposite Encouragement.*) Females, who conspire, encourage males to compete. This has obvious evolutionary advantage for the female since it increases the fitness of her progeny, from which both sexes benefit. The procedure can sometimes be harmful however. The female can find it thrilling to have two males fighting over her, a situation she can manipulate for her own gratification.

Conspiracy amongst males

A conspiracy can exist among males not to encroach on another's partner. By this a male is discouraged from, or naturally averse to, stealing someone's girlfriend or making a cuckold of a husband. The conspiracy is strictly enforced in some cultures. If we regard this policy as beneficial (which it is to males, since it fortifies a handle state), then undermining it, which females sometimes do, is Malign Encouragement.

Conspiracy amongst females

There may be a more robust consensus among females not to steal another's partner and this would conform to the general female strategy of protecting each others' interests, i.e. conspiring. Failing to limit each others' behaviour by criticism or censure, acting in each others' interest, or lending credence to absurd proposals which confer benefit to females generally are all expressions of the Conspiracy strategy.

Compound benefit

We can expect to encounter compound benefit often

Compound benefit occurs when benefit accrues in multiple ways. The Protagonist may impose cost on the Opponent and simultaneously obtain benefit by doing so. Or a procedure may be beneficial to an individual and for other members of a population at the same time. This latter class includes many female procedures which confer advantage not just individually but to females generally. Because of its efficacy, providing double benefit, we can expect procedures involving compound benefit to be commonplace.

Simple parasitism is primitive ME and CB; it imposes cost on the host to the benefit of the parasite. A tapeworm occupying the gut of its host reduces the payoff of its host, taking benefit to itself. However the tapeworm does not seek to minimize its opponent's payoff since to do so would jeopardize its comfortable position; it is not in the parasite's interest to kill its host.

Animal parasites as precursors of Malign Encouragement and compound benefit

Some parasites have evolved complex behaviours akin to ME: a parasite of the ant hijacks its brain to make it climb to the top of a blade of grass, where it is eaten by a sheep, completing the parasite's life-cycle. This of course results in the death of the ant. Many examples of parasitic manipulation of a host could be quoted. However here we are really only interested in the animal world as a source of precursors, and ME is a human policy. Only humans are capable of verbally encouraging an opponent to pursue an adverse policy, which he then adopts of his own volition.

Malign Encouragement combined with compound benefit

A country encouraging the pacifist movement in a nation with which it is at war is ME but not CB, since that encouragement costs money, when it secretly finances the pacifist organisation. The best that can be hoped for is a reduction or cessation of hostilities. However a Protagonist producing heroin to be exported and sold to its Opponent is both ME and CB since it is both harmful to the Opponent and a profitable endeavour.

Similarly with the dealer of an addictive drug: giving it away to get someone addicted is ME, later selling him the drug is ME and CB.

Supra-maximization of advantage

Obtaining maximum benefit

The game of Disguised Defection is potentially cyclic. The Disguised Defection player, due to insecurity or other motivations, tries to monopolize all advantage and this exposes her strategy. *Supra-maximization of advantage* is the policy of extracting the last possible morsel of benefit from a situation: to collect the absolute maximum payoff which can be achieved.

We all maximize advantage, either by maximizing benefit or minimizing cost. Supra-maximization is the process whereby maximization is taken to an elevated and inordinate level.

Examples of supra-maximization

Being unable to throw anything away and obsessively recycling everything are common expressions of supra-maximization. A government or management might impose repeated efficiency drives and be unable to tolerate incidental expenditure (such as the cost of workers' refreshments). Supra-maximization is a feminine policy – the normal male attitude is to dismiss relatively inconsequential costs provided a healthy profit is being made.

Female as Protagonist

Deceiving the Opponent

A player employing Disguised Defection still does not collect the maximum possible payoff. The accumulation of Temptation payoffs is very high, but for the strategy to succeed during multiple iterations, that is, for any length of time, the Opponent must remain unaware that defection is taking place. The male Opponent must be kept in a state of illusion that the Protagonist is cooperating while in reality she is defecting.

Religion as 'true myth.' Revelling in exploitation

Here an interesting Biblical analogy exists with Eve's inability to resist temptation. Religious writings can be thought of as 'true myths' because they contain truths in the form of allegory, encouraging beneficial policies such as forgiveness. The Disguised Defection player achieves perhaps 99% of the maximum possible payoff, but she cannot resist the temptation to collect the last 1%. That remaining part is enhancement: the sense of superiority, the pleasure of gloating, the gratification of seeing that the Opponent is not only being cheated but that he knows he is being cheated.

Supra-maximization is applied in both Marginal and Disguised Defection

Supra-maximization is also applied in Marginal Defection – supra-maximization is applied in Marginal Defection and Disguised Defection in a similar way. In either game, if the bounding value is exceeded then the Opponent is provoked and the game is disrupted. Both games involve approaching, but not usually reaching, a limit or threshold. In Disguised Defection the limit is 100% of the Temptation payoff, which is approached but rarely deliberately reached; in Marginal Defection the threshold dividing cooperation from defection is approached nearer and nearer so as to proceed more quickly. An attempt might be made to take greater steps with each successive iteration until one day the threshold is inadvertently crossed and the male is provoked.

A supremely powerful, long-term female policy

Effects of female mate-selection in the long-term

One of the most potent forms of female influence, effective in the long-term, is the female policy of selecting males with female characteristics as mates. The most obvious example is the female preference for monogamous males, with the result that many males now admit to monogamous preferences. However this is only one of various modifications females have made to the male character by cumulative mate-selection over millennia.

Mate-selection is normally the prerogative of the female

The opposite case, long-term modification of the female character through historical selection by males, is probably less, for two reasons. Firstly, mate-selection is usually the prerogative of the female; as Darwin said, 'It is the female who normally exerts a choice.' This is true even within the constraints which would traditionally have been placed upon her, such as requiring paternal

The lonely man advert. The TV advertising campaign for Strand cigarettes which ran between 1959 and 1960 is regarded as one of the most disastrous tobacco promotions of all time, even though the ads were liked by the public. The theme tune was so popular that it was hurriedly re-recorded and reached number 39 in the British singles chart. The ad featured a man walking alone on a dark, wet, deserted London street with the slogan 'You're never alone with a Strand. The cigarette of the moment.' Consumers associated Strand cigarettes with being lonely and no-one bought them.

consent for marriage. Darwin quoted cases of native societies in which women were ostensibly traded like cattle but on closer examination were found to exercise complete or near-complete control over their choice of husband.

The second reason is that less feminine females tend to be less fecund. Masculine females have fewer children, which is obviously evolutionarily disadvantageous. Females who did not want children, or were otherwise deficient in maternal instincts, disappeared from the population.

Masculine women will have less children

North American women may be exceptional, seeming to exhibit many masculine traits. When North America was colonised women were a rarity, with perhaps several dozen male emigrants for every female. The women who ventured into what was then dangerous and unknown territory were atypical, countenancing danger and hardship. The more feminine, stay-at-home women did just that – stayed at home. It is from this subset of adventurous women that today's American women largely descend.

American women may be exceptional

Physical beauty

Interestingly, physical attractiveness seems to be a function of a feminine society. Females place great emphasis on physical appearance while the classic male grouping is the gang, to which members are admitted solely because they are useful. Glenn Wilson wryly observed that even the most unattractive woman in a village manages to get pregnant from time to time. It seems that the more feminine the society, the more beautiful its people, although this is by no means the only manner by which this can be achieved. A more direct, and thus masculine, means of achieving physical beauty was the practice of the Jollof negroes. Darwin noted that this tribe was exceptionally handsome from their tradition of selling their unattractive women to other tribes.

A feminine society seems to lead to greater selection for physical attractiveness

Traits undesirable to females

Traits females are likely to select against. Females demand dishonesty

Male traits which females find intolerable and which we can expect to have been diminished by progressive female mate-selection include boasting, aggression, polygamy and honesty. Boasting is hated because it evokes feelings of female inadequacy. Females abhor aggression because in any conflict involving physical force and violence she loses, and polygamy is rejected for reasons already discussed. Honesty diminishes because females oblige males to be dishonest in order to obtain sex – the male who approaches a female with a direct request for what he wants, or fails to hide his enthusiasm, or emits any number of other honest expressions, fails.

Females' support for male homosexuals

Incidentally, this preference for males with female traits explains females' support of male homosexuals. A barber, who had previously worked as a hairdresser, related that if a woman customer thought he was homosexual he would receive bigger tips! Many males disdain homosexuality not because of 'homophobia' (a taint-word implying fear) but because males transact with each other in a non-sexual way, and doing otherwise is unnatural to him.

What goes around comes around

Our present extreme position

A cyclic game similar to the 'Battle of the Sexes' almost certainly exists in sexual influence, with alternation taking place between male and female dominance. The pendulum at present is at an unprecedented extreme due to the influence of the mass media, particularly television.

Impact of television. Likelihood of reversal

TV has no evolutionary precedent and hence mankind has had no opportunity to become inured to it. The hitherto unimaginable power of film and television to change attitudes has created opportunities for employing Malign Encouragement on a huge scale. One of the most powerful policies is to create a false normality, portraying aberrant attitudes and behaviour as normal. Man's inherent tendency to conform, especially to power and authority, results in these perceptions being adopted by the admass, that proportion of the population which is susceptible to media manipulation. However the dynamics of the male-female game suggest that even under these powerful influences a return to masculine mores is inevitable.

The proof of the Dynamical Laws is the inability to find a counter-example. The closest there has been to a successful counter-example so far, of a woman committing suicide, will illustrate.

How is her power to kill herself obtained from males? A person's ability to use will to over-ride their naturally strong self-preservation instinct involves logic and reason, which are male traits. According to Darwin, what capacity females possess to defy their natural instincts is derived from males.

If she jumps off a cliff, all that is involved is will; there is nothing more to add. If she uses a tool, e.g. a gun, this is a thing, which belongs in the male domain. The natural domain of the female is relationships, the natural domain of the male is the thing. Every thing, almost without exception, has been discovered, invented or developed by males.

Suppose a) The female is young, reproductive and attractive; then her power is derived from males; she is perceived by them as desirable: male desire establishes her status; or b) She is old and ugly; then her status is low; in evolutionary terms, she is practically worthless (some primitive tribes ate their old women during times of hardship before they ate their dogs).

In case a), by killing herself she is depriving males of her function. In case b) she has little or no utility to males in any case. If the female who is killing herself is pregnant, this also has been facilitated by a male, by sex. Then she further deprives the male of his progeny.

From *All About Women*

A woman badly treated by her husband has been known to hang or drown herself in revenge, thereby not only putting the man in jeopardy of evil spirits, but also requiring him to pay her family a substantial compensation.

Jens Bjerre describing a custom of the Kuman tribe of New Guinea in *The Last Cannibals* (1956)

10 General Mechanisms

Perceptions of cost, perceptions of difference and the dynamics of power

Apologies in advance if this chapter gets somewhat technical. Whoever said that human behaviour was simple? This is an attempt to cut to the chase, and some aspects of perception, and human behaviour in general, are explored.

Definition of a procedure

A *procedure* is a sequence of human actions, which should be capable of being modelled as a game, and which is executed to advance in that game. Ultimately every human action and response should be able to be broken down into simple steps and analysed in this way, as a game. Women will revolt at this philosophy but people are generally a lot more predictable than they like to suppose.

Equivalently, a procedure is employed by a protagonist to proceed in their competition with the opponent. The notion of the procedure sprang from manipulations of markers and handles, such as the transformation of a marker and the mutation of a handle to a marker.

Whether acts are conscious or unconscious is immaterial

Whether procedures are consciously executed or not is a fine distinction. People seek to satisfy their instincts, and a behavioural sequence which originates instinctively will inevitably rise to consciousness when repeatedly performed. In a simple example, a female may emit a signal impulsively but then, especially with her greater sensitivity, she will become conscious of it, and perhaps later do so intentionally.

The difficulty is setting up the models

Here the mathematics of the games people play are hardly touched upon but in the future, I hope, the mathematics of human behaviour will be a recognised field. First though, the hardest part is to set up the models. From them the mathematics readily follow. Establishing some basic models of human behaviour is the goal which Procedural Analysis seeks to achieve.

Perceptions of cost and benefit

Difficulties in enumerating costs

Ten costs and benefits of sex have been defined and the scheme appears applicable to all human activity. One difficulty is in assigning numeric values to the payoffs. Giving a numeric value to something as subjective as enhancement (diminishment in the negative) is especially problematic, but this could be tackled by assigning a value ranging from –5 to +5. We might assign

> The cost of a human action can be expressed as a ten-dimensional vector, where each component can be either positive or negative, according to whether the component is wanted or unwanted, beneficial or costly.
>
> Cost = child + disease + relationship + emotional disturbance + business disturbance + money + information + diminishment + energy + time

a value of –1 for a minor snub and –5 for wishing the ground would open up beneath us. In a long-term game involving progeny of course, the payoff is well-established in the number of grandchildren which result.

In enumerating the various costs as a ten-dimensional vector, a ten-tuple, a further difficulty arises in the perception of these costs: the two players may view their respective costs differently. We already have numeric values for time and money, but their impact on the players might be unequal. A prison sentence of three months handed down by a judge may be meant to be severe, but to the seasoned criminal regarded merely as a respite for rest and recuperation. A repair bill of £500 to a man of modest means can be devastating but to a millionaire it is just small change. One potential solution to this problem, if the game called for such a scheme, would be to cast the money element of the ten-tuple cost vector as a percentage of the players' wealth.

Differing perceptions of cost

Expected payoffs

Another game where costs are perceived differently by each player is when a false expectation of a payoff in the future is promoted. The archetype of this procedure is a maiden maintaining a circle of hopeful suitors, entertaining each in a Victorian drawing room. Each suitor nurtures hopes of winning the comely maiden, and she maintains each in expectation with subtle cues. Each is lulled into a belief that he is the favoured one, or at least that he stands a chance. However despite all their hopes only one of the circle of suitors can be successful, and perhaps none will if a tall, handsome alpha-male were to appear before she has settled on her choice. Maintaining a false expectation of a payoff in the future is a procedure routinely employed by politicians at election-time. It is also (arguably) a feature of religion and certainly of political ideologies.

Promoting a false expectation of a payoff in the future. Politicians at election-time

Time is an element which is sometimes neglected in orthodox game theory. Any game will involve a progression of different states through time. Payoffs or expected payoffs can vary with each passing second or day, say in a fast-moving game or contemplating whether a loan will be repaid. The proverbial

The importance of time

glass can change from being half-full to half-empty within a few moments, and that perception can alter according to completely unrelated events.

Although time immutably progresses, the perception of time can be altered. A clock might be changed. Or another example of this policy is the exhortation 'You only live once, get your kicks while you can' which encourages an opponent to dismiss the long-term, adverse effects his actions are likely to have on himself, his progeny or his society.

Altering the perception of time

Displacement of cost

It is proposed that costs are never annulled, they are only displaced. Numerous examples of *displacement of cost* could be quoted deriving chiefly from feminine environments in which costs are more finely measured (cf. supra-maximization). A volunteer working in a community centre or behind a bar can offset the fact that they are not paid with attempts to control their workplace or otherwise stamp their influence upon it. Voluntary workers in charity shops often compensate for their lack of pay by taking first pick of the donated items. In a place where prostitution is common females, aware that they are providing an amenity that males often pay for, will insist on total control before and during sex.

When there is no monetary payment, the costs can be very high

The cost the unpaid worker levies is often unpredictable, and may greatly exceed the value of the work he undertakes. For instance, a volunteer for a political organisation may feel justified in helping himself to a copy of a confidential database, especially if he feels that his work has been unappreciated or he has been offended, with disastrous results.

The modern practice of saving old newspapers, glass bottles and so forth for taking to a recycling station has an unforeseen consequence in the displacement of the *clearance instinct*. By this instinct we are motivated to purge old projects and materials every so often to make way for new activities. When material is taken away for recycling however, this is cathartic of the clearance instinct, depleting and displacing it.

Displacing the clearance instinct

Tit For Tat/Take Back

A procedure which is particularly difficult to model in conventional terms is Tit For Tat/Take Back in which a female, expressing her tendency to employ TFT strictly, retracts a gift or even attempts to retract a meal. Retracting a gift, or seeking retrospective benefit for it, is popularly known as 'Indian giving.'

Retracting a gift

Distribution of guilt

In a similar frame to displacement of cost is *distribution of guilt*. This is a process by which an individual assuages the guilt they feel by distributing it. A telling incident was the behaviour of a slightly unstable Dutchwoman who lived on a boat. Her dog had produced a litter of puppies which she could not keep. She went to a nearby alternative bar, which on Saturdays served as a vegetarian restaurant, and went from table to table asking each of the clientele if they would take a puppy. If no-one assented the puppy was put into a weighted sack and cast into the river. This was repeated for three consecutive Saturdays until all the puppies were gone. The woman felt guilty about having to destroy the puppies so she distributed her guilt around the people in the bar.

Reducing guilt by sharing it around

Also in Holland, a practising psychologist observed that women would express remorse for their behaviour towards animals, children and other women but never about their treatment of men. Perhaps when females apologize to males they are only admitting to the forces of circumstance.

Expressions of guilt. Saying 'Sorry' all the time

In contrast to this reticence concerning apologies for behaviour towards males, there is an obvious female propensity to say 'Sorry' during minor encounters, even when an apology is unnecessary. This would be deemed trivial except that the practice is so widespread that an underlying mechanism is indicated.

Another potential expression of distribution of guilt is attempts in the courts to legitimise euthanasia; these legal challenges may be attempts to secure State complicity. In a masculine society, with a less intrusive government, authority would be allowed to devolve to the individual or individual's family. A family doctor could weigh the unique personal circumstances of the situation and act according to his conscience without fear of a charge of murder. This was in fact the position until a few decades ago.

Attempts to legitimize euthanasia

A phenomenon apparent in feminine environments is *compulsive confessions*, where individuals find irresistible the urge to reveal to others some former incident or private condition. These are matters which from a masculine background would remain private. Lack of secrecy and disinhibition are general features of a feminine society, the former due to female insecurity and the latter because historically it was always males who limited female behaviour, not females themselves. Female insecurity and irrational fear may in part derive from wanting a male to quell her concerns and reassure her, evoking his caretaking instincts and increasing the bond between them. Certainly a male who failed to comfort a distressed female would be unlikely to be selected as a mating partner.

Urges to confess. Evoking male caretaking instincts

Affection Beneath

The mechanism underlying the caretaking and protective instincts

One of the most consistent and powerful human mechanisms is *Affection Beneath*, the mechanism which underlies the caretaking and protective instincts. Children, especially females, become inordinately attached to their teddy bear (some report that the attachment extends well beyond childhood) and all children express their caretaking and protective instincts towards domestic pets. Affection Beneath is expressed by mothers towards their children and men towards their wives. On the assumption that God is our notional creation, deriving from the fundamental neurosis, Western man projects his caretaking and protective instincts upwards with the concept of a heedful and merciful Supreme Deity.

The Helpless Female signal

Given its strength and ubiquity it is inevitable that Affection Beneath will be exploited. Females fall back on evoking male AB when displaying incompetence or inability, with characteristic signals, although nowadays, when the idealized female role is of her as a competent equal of the male, doing so is unfashionable, and hence these signals have become less evident recently.

For AB to be properly invoked the object of affection must be weaker, but the natural order can be subverted, as when a female is in a position of authority over males. Still the males are likely to harbour caretaking and protective instincts towards her, especially if she is attractive and likeable. If a female officer commanding a squad of soldiers is injured in battle, extraordinary risks will be taken to recover her, potentially jeopardising the lives of the soldiers and the mission, simply because she is female.

Affection Beneath

(God)					
	man				
		woman			
		(child)			
		thing			
			child		
			animal		
			thing		
				animal	
					thing

If females become inordinately elevated, and so privileged that expressing AB towards them becomes absurd, these instincts will be displaced and directed towards alternative recipients, such as immigrants. Affection Beneath is so strong and innate that it must be expressed some way, even if towards a grotesquely unappealing pet dog.

Affection Beneath can become absurd

EBIAC and EBIAR

Allied with EBIAR is EBIAC, *exaggerated behaviour in alien culture*. This is commonly evident in the behaviour of tourists abroad, for example Western tourists dressing provocatively in Muslim countries. One of the most telling demonstrations however occurred in London some years ago, when the wives and daughters of Arab diplomats took up shoplifting. This of course is highly discouraged in their culture but the women had learned of it in Britain, and went at it with great gusto. Its official discovery was highly embarrassing to the Arab dignitaries. More subtle expressions of the mechanism will not be so easy to identify.

Examples of exaggerated behaviour

EBIAR, exaggerated behaviour in alien role, has already been mentioned but its scope is greater than may have been suggested. Perhaps because of disinhibition and females' recent adoption of many male roles it is more apparent in them, but the effect can also be apparent in males. The possibility remains however that males exhibiting EBIAR are merely a sub-population of males expressing female characteristics.

The question of who expresses EBIAR

Men have been observed pushing prams with exaggerated jauntiness, or earnestly kissing the baby in their charge. A more general example is people who have recently stopped smoking becoming dogmatically anti-smoking. Those who have never smoked, or stopped many years ago, are usually indifferent, but a recently stopped smoker can become an eager supporter of smoking bans and other restrictions.

Males pushing prams. Recently stopped smokers

In the infamous Zimbardo mock prison experiment male students were randomly assigned as either prison guards or prisoners. It was intended to investigate obedience to authority but it most tellingly demonstrated the enthusiasm for wielding authority people can exhibit when it is new in their hands. The experiment had to be prematurely terminated. Re-interpreted in this light, it suggests that EBIAR is a general phenomenon, not just a female one. Recent converts of both sexes to a political ideology or religious belief are also likely to display exaggerated behaviour in the form of exceptional fervour.

The Zimbardo prison experiment. Exceptional fervour

Also a potential expression of EBIAR is when a person insists 'I'm telling the truth, honestly, really I am, I'm not lying.' The listener can justifiably suspect that if the person is not lying right then, then he has certainly made a habit of it in the past. This bears comparison with contemporary advertisements for

Declaring something too emphatically

cosmetics telling women 'You're worth it.' Here, as Shakespeare put it, 'the lady doth protest too much.' In his day the meaning of *protest* was to 'vow' or 'declare solemnly.' With truly psychological insight Shakespeare observed that a claim which is made too emphatically is not credible.

Women expressing EBIAR

Recently appointed, swaggering female security guards were a common manifestation of EBIAR but there was also the female airline pilot who harangued her passengers from the cockpit 'as if they were recent arrivals at a reform school.' This astonishing incident was recounted by the internet columnist Fred Reed in May 2007. Reed added, 'Men of course do not behave that way, the cost of dental restoration having become prohibitive.'

Expressions of female power

EBIAR exists because females are unused to wielding power; her only power historically was her authority over children. When she has power, and she is in a feminine environment, her inherent insecurity ensures that any power available to her will be used, if only to confirm to herself that she still has it. Power will be exercised simply because it can be. Plus in the feminine way of things, power tends to be used to stop something from happening rather than make something happen.

The Dynamical Laws

Male and female measures of success

How male perceptions govern the status of females has already been discussed, especially since sexual attractiveness is the major measure. It was proposed that the status of the female is proportional to the status of the male she can attract. Even if a female is able and successful (e.g. in business) she has adopted masculine values; expected feminine measures of success are that she be beautiful, have many admirers, a wide circle of friends, a comfortable life-style and perhaps a successful, loving partner. All authority and power derives from the male: the very notions of hierarchy and status are masculine. The masculine structure of the military with its strict hierarchy can be invoked, and status is something males compete for. The Dynamical Laws are stated as follows:

1. The only power which females have is given to them by males;
2. The only thing females do with that power is use it against males.

Proving the Dynamical Laws

The proof of the Dynamical Laws is in the inability to find a counter-example. No case of female power which does not derive from a male source, or rely on male enforcement, has been found.

All things (tools, devices, inventions) are of male origin and we have Darwin:

'With many closely-allied species, following nearly the same habits of life, the males have come to differ chiefly through the action of sexual selection, whilst the females have come to differ chiefly from partaking more or less of the characters thus acquired by the males.'

Even her ability to propagate (which relies on male input) is used against males in the form of over-population, which diminishes male freedom and power. The origin of the laws could be that they increase fitness in the male by forcing him to compete with the female.

Origin of the Dynamical Laws

Marvin Harris concluded that until 10,000BC human population numbers were limited by female infanticide. When this practice stopped, likely due to female pressure, the rise in population led to an immediate decrease in health, measured by the height and teeth of skeletal remains, food no longer being abundant. It could be argued that this denoted the end of patriarchy.

When patriarchy ended?

The laws are manifest even in the terms female workers adopt. Female titles seek to draw authority from the male: the manicurist is a 'nail technician' (technician being traditionally a male role), the hairdresser is a 'hair designer' (ditto), the salesgirl becomes a 'sales consultant' and so on. Then we have *product*, formerly a manufactured, tangible thing, used to describe financial schemes; *research* instead of study, reading, or investigating, which invokes masculine, original science; and *tools*, again lending on masculine practicality to describe information, training or 'counselling skills.'

Masculine authority is invoked for feminine roles

Females acquire power only to acquire more power. The essentials of this power game are described by the Dynamical Laws in general and neurotic transfer in particular. The advantage of such a strategy is obvious: the benefits, akin to those gained in compound benefit, are potentially exponential. Suppose we had a psychopathic politician (this of course is an entirely theoretical conjecture) who will say absolutely anything to achieve the power he craves or, once his position is secured, keep it. How could a normal, reasonable and honest person compete with him?

Obtaining power only to acquire more power. Psychopathic politicians

Concepts of truth

A mainstay of Western civilisation is the notion of objective truth, and this firmly underpins our scientific and technological achievements. Acknowledgement of the primacy of objective truth is often assumed and projected onto others; it is 'taken as a given.' However, it is not a feature of Western civilisation so much as a product of Occidental male influence. Females and other cultures maintain different concepts of what constitutes truth. The following is an excerpt from *The Great Sex Divide* where Wilson quotes a number of prominent feminists as they assault male notions of truth:

Scientific, provable truth, a product of male influence

'Truth, reality and objectivity are all in trouble from our point of view; we see a male-created truth, a male point of view, a male-defined objectivity.' (Ruth Bleier in *Science and Gender*)

'The postulate of value-free research, of neutrality and indifference towards the research objects, has to be replaced by conscious partiality.' (Renate Klein)

'Feminism withdraws from the patriarchal construction of reality.' (Blanche Dubois)

The scientific rabbit gets eaten

An obvious alternative to objective truth is believing that whatever is to one's immediate benefit, or evolutionary benefit, is true. The timid rabbit quoted earlier always assumes the presence of a fox. Suppose there were to arise, by random mutation, a rabbit with a scientific bent. It decides to count how many rustles in the grass are actually foxes – now our mutant rabbit has a clipboard between its paws. Squatting on a hillside observing, it would likely become a fox's dinner before it completed its survey. For the rabbit the rustle in the grass is truly a fox, and no survival or evolutionary advantage exists for it to believe or discover otherwise.

The female brain intermingles logic and emotion, and this has likely contributed to the unabashed assertions of the feminists above. Females tend to believe what they want to believe, because doing so avoids uncomfortable truths which she finds painful to countenance. This trait alone is grounds for questioning the orthodox dogma of sexual egalitarianism.

Notions of truth in different cultures

It is perfectly feasible that other populations follow this feminine pattern, that what is advantageous is true, what is disadvantageous is not. A fixed conviction of being unfairly persecuted, or an innate sense of grievance, would also be beneficial, at least in the short-term. This might be used to justify stealing from someone, or exploiting another population in redress for an imaginary or grossly exaggerated injustice.

In some cultures something is true if people believe it, and a large number of prisoners in Central Africa are incarcerated for witchcraft. The prisoners themselves are firm believers in the existence of witchcraft, even if denying their own role as a witch. Men in West Africa regularly report having their penises stolen due to witchcraft.

Manipulation of public policy with emotional appeals

The ascendancy of objective truth as a mainstay of our civilisation is a precious jewel, often taken for granted, but which is under challenge. One form of threat is *emotional appeals* publicising individual tragedies, particularly involving a missing child or murdered young woman, which whatever their supposed newsworthiness are inconsequential in the context of a population numbering many millions. Nonetheless the clamour roused by such media attention often threatens to influence public policy, which should properly be science-based.

The DSoD theory

The DSoD theory is hypothetical, and it is said that 'Every man has a scheme which will not work.' However the theory does have the advantage of calling on evolutionary precedents, if not direct observation.

The DSoD theory (pronounced dee-sod) attempts to describe distortions in perception specific to males and females. That perceptual distortion takes place should not be surprising, since practically everything we see is distorted in some way, the most common alteration being size. Objects we see are subject to *size constancy* (also called *constancy scaling*). An item's apparent size is maintained even though the size of the image formed on the retina varies greatly according to whether the item is nearby or far away. Hence the same item can appear smaller or larger according to its position relative to other objects. Human perception is notoriously easy to trick using false size and depth cues, and this accounts for many visual illusions. The Ames room, a room constructed of wood and which is far from square, is one of the most dramatic.

The likelihood of such perceptual distortion. Size constancy

Mechanisms giving rise to perceptual distortion can only have evolved because they confer advantage. Evolution often takes 'short cuts' which achieve an advantageous function by cheating, when the process works 99% of the time. For example if our eyes were to work like a television, reproducing every pixel in the field of vision, more than our entire brain would be required to process the data. Instead we see shapes and textures which we have learned to recognise, making many assumptions about our surroundings. Close attention is only devoted to a small area.

How we see

> *The education of women* – The whole education of women ought to be relative to men. To please them, to be useful to them, to make themselves loved and honoured by them, to educate them when young, to care for them when grown, to counsel them, to console them, and to make life sweet and agreeable to them – these are the duties of women at all times and what should be taught them from their infancy. Unless we are guided by this principle we shall miss our aim, and all the precepts we give them will accomplish nothing either for their happiness or for our own.
>
> Rousseau, *Emile* (1762)

The Ames room: all three men are the same height. The room is constructed to appear square, but in fact the 'smaller' man is further away

How others saw

Clearly our perception of difference can be fluid: the famous philosopher Rousseau, whose ideas were incorporated into the French Constitution, was one of a group of people who believed that apes were man. The fact that they had no language was regarded as unimportant. Darwin routinely referred to Negroes as 'savages.'

The most significant distortion is in female perception

DSoD is shorthand for *the dishonest submergence of difference*, this summarising what is probably the most significant of four distinct effects. Particularly, this effect describes errors in female perception. All the mechanisms have a putative evolutionary origin, according to the different male and female roles. Hopefully these effects will be confirmed empirically, although a difficulty is that experimental confirmation will necessarily involve comparing disparate objects. For the present the theory relies on historicism and observation which, of course, is subject to the very phenomena we seek to confirm.

1. Males make large differences larger and small differences smaller;
2. Females make large differences smaller and small differences larger.

A prostitute in Amsterdam would bring her little dog to work and use its reactions to determine whether to admit a client or not.

The enhanced female perception of small differences is most evident in her meticulous selection while shopping, perhaps especially when choosing clothes. Small differences are amplified. The female is sensitive to subtle nuances of taste and smell and she has a greater sensitivity to these stimuli. With a likely origin in mate-selection, and of utility in managing relationships, she perceives subtle differences in character and temperament. Her acute perception of small differences aids her reading of body language, at which she is adept, her ability to see dust and grime and her superior ability when performing fine and detailed work.

Females see fine detail

The female seeks to select a father for children and needs to know whether her prospective mate is suitable as soon as possible. Since she is physically weaker than the male, and vulnerable, her instincts warn of losing control at any moment and finding herself pregnant by a male who thereafter will leave her to fend for herself. Any small deviation she perceives in the male will be regarded as an omen of this eventuality.

Role of perception in mate-selection

The dishonest female submersion of large differences involves large differences being minimized. A likely origin is avoiding conflict, promoting a stable and stress-free environment for having a baby, and it also facilitates the Disguised Defection strategy.

Females wish to avoid conflict

Once a male perceives a difference as large enough to warrant aggression the female loses her ability to manipulate, because such subtle skills pale to ineffective insignificance when set against brute force. It is in the general female interest to disclaim differences in age and attractiveness, as well as the wide disparity in practical ability between males and females. Thus females minimize and deny large differences between males and females, children and adults, different races and between humans and animals.

Disclaiming large differences

The claim that humans are all of a kind is absurd: it is estimated that around 12,000 species of ant exist, some so subtly different that DNA testing is required to distinguish them. This can be contrasted with the feminine denial of glaring disparities, both visible and behavioural, in human types.

Claims that humans are all the same

The practical male submersion of small differences largely accounts for males' ability to work together. The classic male grouping is the gang, and relatively

Males work together. Justifying male sacrifice

small differences in personality are ignored to admit a member who is useful to it. Females socialize with individuals they like, while males work together with people who are skilled or of practical benefit. Males will fight to preserve difference but will not risk injury and death over issues they perceive as trivial.

Males compete

The inordinate male amplification of large differences probably originates from the male role as fighter and warrior for his tribe. Waging war involves risk of death, and to justify that risk a difference must be perceived as large enough to be worth fighting and possibly dying for. Thus males are exhorted to war 'to defend freedom of speech' or 'to make the world safe for democracy' – high ideals which he can believe makes his sacrifice worthwhile.

If one man makes a ship, another man makes a bigger one. Males always try to make things bigger, faster, grander or more compact because they compete and are interested in size (or even the lack of it).

An analogy with compression and expansion as used for audio signals

These mechanisms can be compared to an expander or compressor as used to process audio signals. These devices alter the dynamic range, the difference between the quietest and loudest sounds. An expander makes the dynamic range of music wider, increasing loud sounds and decreasing quiet ones. A compressor, always used for radio broadcasts, reduces the dynamic range by making loud sounds quieter and quiet sounds louder. The perceptual effects proposed for the female are analogous to a compressor, for the male they are analogous to an expander. These mechanisms could be established in the same way the width of the corpus callosum and the functions of the hypothalamus are fixed during sex formation of the brain.

Defective Female is the female type most likely attributable to some kind of hormonal imbalance – she is defective only in the sense that she is not quite wholly female. DF appears to have three essential characteristics: she is only as capable as males at manipulating relationships; unlike normal females, she is interested in things; attempts by her to lie go wrong.

DF's are able to maintain successful non-sexual relationships with males, which can result in jealous animosity being expressed towards her by other females: to males she is 'one of the lads.' Extreme DF's cannot even lie on the telephone while moderate DF's can. DF's may also have a higher sex drive than normal.

A young woman squatter in North London said, 'I'd rather a squaddie died than a dog.' The reasoning was that a dog would not harm anyone but a soldier was a willing instrument of war.

General strategies

A few words may be added about some very general strategies humans adopt. Many people's life-course is thoroughly described by the policy of 'following the path of least resistance.' Then our behaviour is governed by creating paths of high resistance by imposing legal or social costs. Fines and imprisonment discourage illegal acts and social ostracism operates to promote conformity. One of the most powerful weapons the media employs is the creation of a false consensus, defining particular views as unfashionable or 'unacceptable to all right-thinking people.'

Imposing cost to discourage undesirable acts. Creating a false consensus

Behavioural establishment is the process by which the essential dynamic of a relationship becomes established. Whether a person is dominant, another submissive, or whether one is attracted to the other and not vice versa is often established within a few seconds, sometimes even less. Behavioural establishment can be evident when reuniting with an old friend, when modes of address or other behaviour which has long since fallen away suddenly reappears.

The early formation of behaviour patterns in relationships

A game which models a significant element of human behaviour is the Dollar Auction (from William Poundstone's book *Prisoner's Dilemma*). Under the right conditions a dollar bill can be sold for more than double its value with this game.

A crowd, preferably having imbibed a little alcohol, is invited to bid on a dollar bill. The only special condition is that the under-bidder – the person who has just been out-bid – must still pay the amount he bid. The bidding goes swimmingly at 5 cents, 10 cents, 20 cents... then as the bidding reaches $1 a pause occurs as the terms of the game sink in. At this point the under-bidder bids again to try and minimize his loss.

Getting almost $5 for a dollar bill in a Dollar Auction

Bidding tends to stall between two and three dollars. The cost to the auctioneer is $1, but his take, assuming the bidding reaches $2.50, is $2.50 (the winning bid) plus $2.40 (the under-bid), almost $5!

The Dollar Auction demonstrates our reluctance to abandon once an investment has been made. It models and illustrates our propensity to 'chase losses.' Persevering in a telephone queue having waited 20 minutes to speak to someone, being unwilling to hang up having invested so much, is an example of a Dollar Auction. So is continuing with a costly and unwinnable war. Many thousands of men have been lost but there is no realistic chance of victory; the

Our reluctance to abandon once significant investment has been made

prospect of abandoning after paying such a heavy cost, with nothing to show for it, is abhorrent. The Vietnam War is often cited as an example of a Dollar Auction.

Creating, moving and solving problems

We constantly struggle against problems of various kinds and it seems that there are three approaches to them. Or perhaps, three kinds of people. People can create problems, move them around or solve them. In a simple example, someone in a house does something foolish and blows the fuse on the electric iron. There are no spare fuses. The next person who comes along, a problem-mover, needs the iron, so he removes the fuse from the toaster and fits it to the iron. The fuse is swapped around from appliance to appliance until a problem-solver arrives with some fuses.

Often people just move problems around

Few problems are so simple and the ability to solve problems is a rare talent, requiring perspicacity, resources and will. Most people, lacking that talent, move problems around, because by doing so they gather information which in the long run enables a solution to be found. The complications and costs of unsuccessful remedies impels the search for the source of the problem and eventually a solution is arrived upon.

The importance of habit

Finally we should not neglect the importance of habit in influencing human behaviour. Habit is closely allied with DWWLT: Doing What Worked Last Time. The owner of a broken-down car often flattens the battery in his futile attempts to start it; he presses the accelerator hoping to be propelled forward as he was before.

> Since women have no respect for exact scientific data and are interested only in what is of immediate benefit to them, they will say what seems to be convenient or opportune at the time. Consequently, any facts acquired on the subject of a woman's reactions – whether, for instance, she is frigid, to what degree she can enjoy sexual intercourse, or whether her own orgasm can be compared to that of a man – tend to be extremely contradictory.
>
> Esther Vilar, *The Manipulated Man*

Anonymously reported sexual fantasies (in percentages)

FANTASIES	MEN (*N*=291)	WOMEN (*N*=409)
Group sex	31	15
Voyeuristic/fetishistic	18	7
Steady partner incorporated	14	21
Identified people (other than partner)	8	8
Setting romantic/exotic	4	15
Rape/force	4	13
Sado-masochism	7	7
None	5	12
Everything	3	0
No answer	21	19

Glenn Wilson, *The Great Sex Divide*

Elevated to the status of paragon by the tribe – It is around 1961 and the Beatles are playing a venue in the north of England. The hall is filled with girls and the point arrives when they start screaming and rush the stage, with only the janitor of the building present to stem the tide. He, feeling overwhelmed, threatens to tell their mothers if they don't retreat. This is practically common lore except that the mayhem has been triggered by Gerry Marsden of Gerry and the Pacemakers, the headline act, removing his tie and unbuttoning his shirt, while the Beatles, third on the bill, have already performed their set to a phlegmatic audience.

Interview with one of the audience, *Feedback*, BBC Radio 4, 27 January 2012

11 Mate-Selection Strategies

Sexual fantasies, paragonism and the mechanics of mate-selection

The ideal sexual object, particularly for the male, need not be a single individual. Having multiple partners is a common male fantasy while female fantasies usually feature romantic settings or a specific, long-term partner. Some women quote being raped as a fantasy.

Shown are the results of a survey undertaken by Glenn Wilson of male and female sexual fantasies. The respondents were anonymous and the figures shown are percentages of the sample of *N* individuals. The total is not 100% because some categories overlapped.

Male sex targeting is learned

Much of male sexual targeting is learned, Wilson says, suggesting that learning accounts for the wide variety of objects and materials males can associate with sex. Males can be excited by footwear, uniforms, rubber and any number of odd triggers of arousal.

Some paraphilias derive from males expressing female traits

Notwithstanding, some paraphilias – which is what such fetishes are – have an obvious biological or evolutionary origin. Physical intimacy with children is perfectly normal and natural for the female, but when a male exhibits the trait he wants to express it with sex, making it paedophilia. Coprophilia probably derives from the old practice, evident in a photograph of isolated natives, of a mother cleaning the rear-end of her baby with her mouth. This used to be normal for a mother, and when the trait reappears in a male it becomes coprophilia. Thus the same mechanism, of a female trait appearing in male form, potentially accounts for both coprophilia and paedophilia.

Paedophiles and the 'sexually indiscriminate personality'

Paedophiles are notoriously difficult to type; the only apparent commonality among them is that they are sexually attracted to children. However one recognised category of sex offender is the 'sexually indiscriminate personality' – a person, probably a male, who regards practically everyone they encounter as a potential sexual partner. This syndrome may be due to dysfunction of the sexual targeting system, much as dyslexia likely results from lack of development of the language centres of the brain.

Attraction to youth

Males are naturally sexually attracted to youth for obvious evolutionary reasons. Pairing with a forty-year-old female might result in one or two children at best, but a teenager could easily produce a dozen. This accounts for the perennial theme of busty girls in school uniform. Attraction to youthful targets is also common among male homosexuals.

Wilson also points out that if women were so minded, an impersonal fantasy could be realised almost the instant it was conceived, because women face little difficulty finding willing partners. This attests to the view that women get most of the sex they desire in the form of relationships. Intriguingly, sado-masochism is one of the few entries in Wilson's survey which was equally rated by both sexes. Human sexuality is enormously varied and much more could be said on this theme, especially on female fantasies of being forcibly taken, but that would be to stray from the objective of describing behavioural strategies.

Females' non-romantic fantasies can be quickly realised. Sexuality is extremely variable

For the male, being sexually frustrated is almost his natural state: few males are able to satisfy all or even most of their sexual desires. An obvious first category includes film stars, powerful politicians and celebrated sportsmen who are given prominence in the mass media.

Few males get all the sex they want

A second category enjoying great sexual success is the gangland figure, often operating on the criminal fringes of society. His illicit activities may enable him to run a nightclub or lead a gang. With a physique formed with the aid of steroids females flock to him, attracted perhaps by his masculinity, confidence and domination of other males. For him and members of the first category little or no effort is required – females pursue him.

Gangland figures and the like, whom females pursue

Rape. Perhaps rape is analogous to being locked in a room being forced to listen to a recording of children in agony. There would be no physical damage, only psychological stress. Whether she consents or not the female invariably lubricates so unless there is violence employed (not just the threat of it), or an ensuing pregnancy, or a disease transmitted, there is rarely any physical effects. The reason females abhor rape so much is that she is, above all, selective and rape sets the cost of sex at nought; it is the complete antithesis of the female strategy.

A comparison may be made between rape and childbirth; in childbearing there is months of physical deformity, and often her figure is never fully restored. There is a painful labour and still more painful parturition. Further, some women report achieving orgasm during forced sex. It may further be that by the sensations she experiences, such as bonding and other instincts such as disclosure, the female is forced to confront the invalidity of her emotions and this she cannot countenance. Sex is a natural function: it may be not so different to being forced to eat a banana, except that 13% do not have fantasies about being force-fed a banana.

If rape is the main way that men supposedly oppress women, then the impact of rape must be serious, but research shows that generally it's not. Typically there may be some mild depression, but not usually lasting beyond four months. The most recent overview of studies was over twenty years ago, and it showed a range of effects so wide and bound up with pre-existing conditions, that the research was worthless.

The idea that rape is the quintessential form of 'oppression' of women is denied by the fact that men rape men. This is on such a scale in US prisons that there is much more male rape in the USA than rape of women. What's more it's for sex, not to express 'power.'

Steve Moxon, *The Woman Racket*

The third, probably the largest, subset of sexually successful men are those who are adept at emotionally manipulating women. Like talented chefs and exceptionally loquacious males, these males express female characteristics more strongly than do females themselves. The trait is obviously advantageous for gene proliferation but, much like politicians who pursue power for its own end, the strategy confers no social benefit. One man in Leeds had as his only goal getting a woman pregnant, and once this was achieved he moved on to the next. An informal and certainly incomplete count of children he was known to have fathered reached 17, it being reported that he even managed to knock up the social worker of one of his former conquests. He was also a conscienceless thief, a trait which was observed in one of his sons.

Men adept at manipulating women

These three groups combined still comprise only a tiny fraction of the male population. One category of male practically certain to be unsuccessful is the desperate, completely unfeminated male who surely (and obviously) needs feminine intimacy the most. The situation is exacerbated if he is geeky, smelly or unkempt; he fails to display the feminine markers of cleanliness and detail. Given a choice between him and another, the female will always prefer the male who is feminated already. Possibly the feminated male is regarded as safely manipulable and unthreatening. Plus he has demonstrated fitness and success by already having been selected by another female.

Females always prefer the male who needs sex the least

The unfeminated male fails to conform to, or is unaware of, the rules of *television vision*, TVV. In television, the camera almost always avoids the breasts or groin in close-ups or an actor's bottom when they retreat. If the male does not adopt TVV, and dwells on the female's body, he will immediately be regarded as lustfully ogling her. 'Creepyness' is a difficult to define trait which females also find intolerable.

Television vision and creepyness

Traditional marriage had the advantage at least of sharing out males and females one-for-one. Attempts have been made to redress the situation for males with on-line discussions of 'game,' where bachelors share ploys intended to further their sexual success. Perhaps the most concrete suggestion was that when contemplating marriage, a man should insist that the woman ask him, rather than vice versa, as a defence against future recriminations and female discontent. It is, after all, invariably the female who has selected him.

An advantage of marriage. Bachelor forums

Plays and subterfuges employed by the male in attempts to reap a sexual harvest will inevitably rebound, if not on the male himself then on subsequent ones. Relationships and sex are females' natural domain, for which she is vastly better equipped. Relationships are at the centre of her being and the ruthlessness she can apply in their manipulation follows from having no thing else. Notwithstanding the categories of exceptional males above, attempts to compete with the female on equal terms will fail. The costs, especially psychological, of pursuing a large number of females are considerable and, unless he is a complete brute, will leave the male noticeably damaged. It will certainly be discernable by females in subsequent encounters.

Trying to prevail against the female in her natural domain is hopeless

Paragonism

The *paragon* is the ideal sexual partner or ideal state. Love is paragonism, particularly that kind which sees the love object as ideal, perfect and flawless. Adolescents can direct their paragonic instincts at a picture of a beautiful model or famous pop idol, with only superficial, if any, consideration of character. Perhaps maturity brings only minor changes, since a well-known finding was that couples meeting for the first time establish their mutual attraction within the first few seconds. Everything occurring after that is mere play. The female wishes to discover the temperament of her prospective mate, establish control and prolong sexual selection (*protraction and postponement*, P&P). On the other hand the male typically only needs to be shown a panel of photographs to select his favourite.

The ideal mate. Superficial attraction. Game-playing

> If young girls might always choose their own husbands, we should have the best families intermarry with coachmen and grooms; and young heiresses would throw themselves away upon the first wild young fellows, whose promising outsides and assurance make them set up for fortunes, though all their stock consists in impudence.
>
> Cervantes, *Don Quixote* (1605)

The paragon effect

Many males cannot help but be drawn to the fairest female in any group. This might be called the *paragon effect*, because although she may not be a paragon, she is the closest thing to it at the time. Possibly an element of this is that winning her would confirm, although it is certainly not guaranteed to elevate, his status among other males. However, it is the male who appears nonchalant that is likely to excite her interest.

Doing Whatever It Takes to win a paragon

If a male perceives a female as a paragon, and believes or convinces himself that she is attainable, then this is the quintessential situation when the Doing Whatever It Takes strategy is likely to be employed. Many operations in DWIT are obvious, such as refusing to take No for an answer, showering her with flowers and gifts, and devoting every attention to her. If a long-term, likely procreative, relationship is envisaged by the male then significant investment by him is justified.

Waiting in line for a female

When a highly desired female is already involved in a relationship, the male may find or place himself on a 'celestial waiting list.' He waits for her to end her current involvement and hopes that he will be next in line. This is comparable to the circle of hopeful suitors discussed previously, in which the female maintains males with false expectations of a payoff in the future.

Following a female around

A notable, but not at all masculine, version of DWIT is 'Klingon' where the male simply follows his target around, sometimes watching her engagements with other males, and acting as her friend and confidante. He must be close enough to his target to be able to provide her with a sympathetic shoulder to cry on when his rivals fail to live up to her expectations. Eventually the shoulder is literally provided and the Klingon can then look forward to a long-term career as a house-husband.

Giving all control to the female

Similarly ceding all control to the female is the Male Extremely Honest Strategy, MEHS. Here the male abandons any pretence he has maintained previously, confesses that he has not had sex or a relationship for some specified duration, is desperately attracted to her, and so on. He is not in one of the categories of male with whom the female would never countenance a relationship, otherwise he would not be in a position to deliver such a personal outburst. This being so, the female is offered an affair on such favourable terms that she is unlikely to refuse. The male's extreme honesty leaves him defenceless and the female is able to dominate the relationship.

A female last resort strategy

A female equivalent is the Female Last Ditch Strategy, FLDS. She stands apart from the group, sits on or near a boundary, or retreats to an unoccupied room hoping that her target (who may have hitherto failed to approach) will follow. In this situation an opportunistic or rival male may perceive the move and approach instead.

Being 'in love' and being 'in a loving relationship' are clearly distinct. A couple 'in love' see each other as paragons; hormones are flowing like beer

Pet healthcare. In 2011 Americans will spend $50billion on their pets. The largest growth is in veterinary care, up from $13b actual spending in 2010 to reach an estimated $14.1b in 2011. Bob Vetere, President of the American Pet Products Association, said: 'Veterinary and health related services are growing at a fast rate because pet owners are treating their pets as they would their children.'

from a tap and, for the male, semen production is dramatically increased. This state can involve such a distorted perception of reality that it has been described as a state of madness and derives, of course, from the evolutionary advantage it confers.

Hormones rage when in love

In this scheme the *alter ego* is the paragon's paragon, a version of the self deemed to be a suitable mate for the paragon. An individual may adopt manners, appearance or the career he believes will make him a suitable target for his future paragon.

The alter ego

Paragonamy (or perhaps *paragony*) is the state, possibly a disorder in some cases, in which an individual is incapable of attraction to, or bonding with, anyone but a paragon. During examination of a potential target some flaw is found and the target dismissed as a prospective partner. Anything less than a paragon is insufficient. It is easy to envisage an environment in which males are seeking casual sex for pleasure and females are adhering to paragonamy. 'I only have sex when I'm in love' is an actual female expression of paragonamy, an attitude encountered more than once. Sexual indiscriminacy is the antithesis of paragonamy.

Paragonamy, or extreme discriminacy

Another entity is the *remote paragon*, where a relationship with an idealised love object is maintained at a distance with correspondence taking place by letter or telephone. Such an arrangement may be exploited by the female to avoid physical sex and use the remote paragon as her rationale for rejecting proposals from males closer to hand. This is especially likely if she is in a male-dominated environment in which proposals are frequent.

Using a remote paragon to avoid sex closer to home

Substitution and sublimation

By far the most profound expressions of paragonism however are manifest in its substitution and sublimation to practical objectives. Sport and other physical activities involving strength, skill and competition are a major form of substitution of male sexual drives. Winning the race is the paragonic goal of the athlete, winning the cup is the collective paragonic goal of the team. All will be well when the goal is reached; everything else is subservient to it. Males also use risk-taking as a sex substitute and to gain status.

Male sex substitutes

At a higher level, when substitution is raised to sublimation, concepts such as a perfect god, high art or the quest for a scientific breakthrough have developed as expressions of paragonism. Perfectionism is obviously allied to paragonism. Shortcuts to the blissful sensations of having reached a paragonic peak, however fleetingly, can also be obtained through music or drugs. Using drugs is indeed the easiest means of achieving this state and their role as male substitutes for sex seems obvious.

Sublimation of sexual drives by males

Paragonism is a powerful motivating drive which fuels male resourcefulness and inventiveness. The same ingenuity is applied to the scaling of a mountain, the solution of a challenging technical problem, or the creation of an ultimate work of beauty and expression. DWIT is likely to be applied in each case. The importance of the paragon to the human, especially male, psyche cannot be overestimated.

Female sex substitutes. Adopting others' appraisal. Female plasticity

In contrast, the major female sex substitutes are food, substituting for sexual pleasure, and domestic pets, substituting for relationships with children. The first category of sexually successful male, those who appear on TV and in films, have effectively been defined as a paragon by the tribe. Females are plastic and often use others' reactions to an individual to appraise them. They are strongly influenced by power and authority, and can adopt their partner's views uncritically. The attitudes and roles females adopt are very much defined by authority and the media, especially the latter. During the Victorian era middle and upper-class women were idealized and revered, and usually conformed to the role which had been defined for them. Of course not all women are so impressionable, but it cannot be denied that the tendency exists.

> The degree of self-confidence a man displays, however, is responsive to feedback. In singles bars, men rebuffed by women in their first few attempts produce successively less confident approaches. Rejection produces a downward cycle of resentment, hostility, and sometimes a cessation of all tactics. One man in a singles bar commented after a third woman had rebuffed him, 'You need steel balls to make it in this place.' Apparently the psychological pain and lowered confidence experienced by rejected men trigger psychological mechanisms that cause them to reevaluate their sexual techniques, lower their sights to women who have lower appeal, and wait until circumstances are more propitious for further attempts.
>
> David Buss, *The Evolution of Desire*

'Like Jill' is the male's target specification at $t = 1$.

At $t = 2$, Kate comes along, making a strong impression.

Finally the template has adapted at $t = 3$.

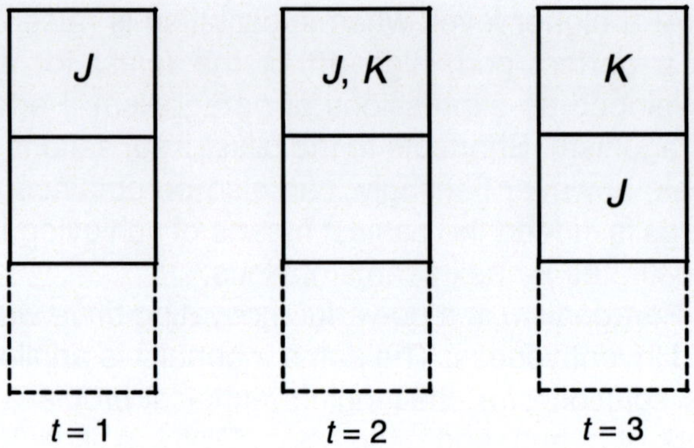

Proposed operation of an adaptive template. It may operate as a 'stack' containing images of mating partners in order of priority

Mate templates

It shall be restated, because it is so important: paramount to any consideration of procedures, policies or strategies in a game is the choice of opponent.

Choosing the opponent. Specifying a mate

The *template* is the mental image or specification of a mate. Relationships often arise because of a resemblance to a former partner, and this has inspired the initial attraction. It is proposed that various templates exist, with varying degrees of permanence.

Dream partners

The *primary template* may be biologically predetermined. Males have a demonstrated and apparently inherent preference for a specific female body shape.

Partners one can fall in love with

The *secondary template* contains the image of a member of the opposite sex who has made a strong impression in the past. The person may become a paragon by the process of adaptation. *Copulation bonding* may also contribute, where repeated intercourse elevates the attachment. Examples of adaptive paragonism in action are thoughts such as:

Thoughts while falling in love

'She's just right for me because...'
'I didn't know she felt so delicious.'
'We understand each other.'
'I love her because she takes my sperm' (copulation bonding).
'I love him because he makes me whole' (copulation bonding).
'He needs me.'
'I love her because she accepted me.'

Sex pals. Changes in template contents

The *tertiary template* contains an actual or prospective sexual partner for whom there may be attachment but who can never become a paragon.

The contents of all the templates, except perhaps the primary one, may be replaced (displaced) by subsequent impressions.

Approaches and approach effects

By an *approach* is meant going up to someone, especially a target, and making an approach statement. Several phenomena associated with approaches, indeed a complete set of them, have been observed. They are noteworthy on their consistency alone, even neglecting their influence on subsequent behaviour. The foursome follows a pattern comparable to the four DSoD components, and conceivably has a similar origin in the early sexual definition of the brain.

Four distinct approach effects

Transmission of diminishment, ToD, is trivial and consists of displaying sadness or disappointment on receiving a rejection. Expressing disappointment to any event which is adverse to the individual is transmission of diminishment. The individual conveys his diminishment by displaying it.

Looking sad or disappointed

Inverted transmission of diminishment, IToD, is often expressed by a male smiling on receipt of a rejection, even though no happiness is felt. If a prolonged sequence of approaches are made, each being rejected, the instinct to express IToD can accumulate to inspire a verbal outburst. The exclamation has no deliberate audience but may be heard by people in the vicinity. Such a sequence is also likely to give rise to a sense of detachment or disassociation.

An effect of repeated rejections

When a person smiles or laughs on receiving a rebuff or insult (unless the insult is truly amusing, or the ego genuinely dismisses it) this is IToD; the slur or disappointment is felt but its outward expression is inverted. Spectators may find the inversion inexplicable. IToD may be employed as a defence mechanism, to confound the opponent.

Smiling inappropriately

Proclamation of enhancement, PoE, occurs when a female advertises that an approach has been made. This may be to a confidante, most likely another female, or publicly ('I have a boyfriend!'). She is enhanced by being desired and wishes to raise her status in the eyes of her contemporaries by making that enhancement known. PoE also ensures (compound benefit) that the male is unable to make further approaches to other females in her circle: if he did he would be exposed as approaching several females in turn hoping that one will take him. This will reduce his status in the eyes of his targets considerably so PoE makes this 'Round Robin' strategy impractical.

The female proclaims that she is desired

PoE, an element of 'Kiss and Tell,' is one of many means by which the costs of sex are raised. Adolescent females use 'I think I might be pregnant' to boast to her contemporaries that she is both desired and sexually active. An individual announcing their promotion at work is an elementary expression of PoE.

An adolescent expression. The general case

Shop dives. If girls believe, rightly or wrongly, that they have been targeted, they will dive into a shop, which is a retreat into safe female territory. Shops with multiple exits are favoured. If there is only one exit, they may attempt to skulk away unseen, and often succeed, even if the likelihood of an approach is zero or almost zero. This is especially characteristic of girls in pairs, but single women may deliberately signal and then hurry into a shop. Shop dives are part of the game which females love to play.

Inverted proclamation of enhancement, IPoE, comparable to IToD, is when the proclamation is inverted. Typically the female will advertise that an approach has been made by complaining of the male's attentions to a third party. In other words, she proclaims her enhancement using the pretext of a grievance. By so doing she simultaneously advertises her enhancement and makes approaches more costly for the male, raising the cost of sex. This, then, is another procedure with compound benefit.

The female proclaims her desirability while simultaneously increasing the cost of sex

After the male has made a successful approach, saying anything the female does not like, and which induces any unpleasant feeling, irrespective of how truthful the statement is, immediately sours the male's chances. His error is often irrevocable. This is a likely source of male dishonesty, and indeed the male may, from adolescence onwards, adopt female perspectives in order to improve his success. The most convincing liar is one who has deceived himself.

Females oblige males to be dishonest

Ambiguity of intention

Ambiguity of intention, AoI, is the ambiguity individuals possess when they transact with others, especially on approach. Ambiguity directly relates to control. In a very neurotic, feminine environment, disquiet will be evident on approaching any individual when the approacher's motive for starting the conversation is not immediately obvious.

Ambiguity in transactions

Suppose a male makes a jocular comment to a female. He may be placing an indiscriminate and/or inappetent marker, merely being friendly, but the remark is interpreted as a sexual approach. The female derives benefit from this interpretation – she feels desired. In the language of Procedural Analysis she is enhanced, and her confidence is raised. If her interpretation is perceivable, which it usually is, the male is likely thenceforth to restrict his friendly comments to females he actually desires.

Why females interpret friendly comments as approaches

By this means she also acts for females collectively by removing ambiguity of intention from males; she seeks to conserve all AoI for females exclusively.

Repeated over time, the outcome is that females can be confident that every incidental comment is a sexual approach, and testament to her attractiveness.

The male receives a double blow

The situation is compounded if the male makes a purely friendly comment, it is interpreted as a sexual approach, and she uses the opportunity to deliver a rejection. In this case he suffers the diminishment of a rejection when he was not even trying to win her, a double blow.

Monopoly as female strategy

Females attempt to impose monopolies

Females seek to remove ambiguity of intention from males and monopolize it for themselves. Instituting a monopoly is a natural extension of the Conspiracy strategy, where procedures executed by individual females benefit females collectively. Her desire to establish monopolies derives from insecurity and her heightened perception of potential threats. Females will also attempt to monopolize Affection Beneath.

Divorce from reality

In a highly feminine environment females can fall into a belief, then an insistence, that their feelings are precious, invariably valid and paramount, while male sensibilities are dismissed as inconsequential. This has been dubbed *emotional fascism*. 'My emotions are always correct and are sacrosanct. Your feelings don't matter. You're only a man.'

Diversionary purpose

Unstated intentions

A wider form of ambiguity of intention is *diversionary purpose* whereby females go to work or college with the primary but unstated intention of securing a partner, especially a paragon. One report was of young women recently arrived at a prestigious American college using a copy of *Who's Who* to discover which of their male counterparts came from wealthy families.

Males use diversionary purpose in crime

Females use diversionary purpose to secure advantageous relationships and control by keeping the motivation for their presence ambiguous or disguised. Males employ diversionary purpose perhaps less frequently but when they do it often involves a sinister purpose, such as clandestine or unlawful endeavour. Examples are espionage or a criminal walking down a street ostensibly for a leisurely stroll but actually looking for an opportunity to burgle.

> Females oblige males to be dishonest in order to obtain sex. It follows that the more powerful the female, the more dishonest the male must be.

Breaking

Here *breaking* is terminating a transaction, an important manoeuvre. The female may walk away or, if stationary, simply say 'Goodbye.' Which person initiates the break is highly significant. An excessive, intolerable level of societal neurosis leads to *premature breaking* by both males and females even in routine and incidental encounters.

Effect of excessive neurosis

Alternatively, in the circumstances of an approach, the female will sometimes gleefully abandon the male before any resolution is reached. Outwardly she may be seeking to excite the male's interest by inviting him to pursue her, but its usual motivation is to provide her with enjoyment. Females find avoiding sex pleasurable: raising the cost of sex is a major expression of female sexuality.

Females enjoy avoiding sex

Statements and dubious statements of unavailability. The first serious sexual gambit can be a female announcement of her unavailability for sex. She will say that she has a boyfriend, must be home by a certain time, or give some other reason why she is unavailable to him.

There are a number of possible male responses. A first rule for the male is that no matter how irrelevant the statement seems (he might be just being friendly), or disappointed he feels, or how big a pack of lies he is sure he has just been fed, he must not display annoyance. A male failing this test will visibly give up on the female and dismiss her, possibly to go in search of another target. The DSoU is used as a test of the male and to allow the female to establish control.

The strategy most likely to result in penetration of the female is to reassure her with a reply such as 'It's alright, I'm disappointed because I like you but we'll just talk if you like.' The female wants to be satisfied that the male is not interested in only one thing; references to an existing relationship or appointment might for practical purposes be ignored since there is usually no way of knowing whether the female is telling the truth or merely attempting to establish the male's integrity ('niceness') and thus suitability as a sexual partner. The possibility that the statement of unavailability is true must be borne in mind, but the strategy most likely to result in success for the male is to carry on regardless, since there is a strong likelihood that, if the reasons given by the female for her unavailability were actually true, the situation which is presently shared with her would not exist at all. A conversation at this level would simply not be taking place. The male response is optimally followed by a relaxation of manner to further assure the female, making her feel at ease.

Dubious statements of unavailability

The female tests the male

The statement of unavailability, a true assertion, is advanced to become the dubious statement of unavailability. The female uses the DSoU as a test to see how amenable the male remains when she is no longer a target, whether he is only interested in her for sex, and so forth. Usually the very fact that interactions have progressed thus far renders the DSoU implausible. This procedure is routinely employed by females in some countries.

Proposals and propositions

In this scheme a *proposal* is an invitation or suggestion to embark upon some venture and a *proposition* is a proposal specifically for physical sex. Some early conclusions were as follows:

1. Do not ask a question which might provoke a No response. The answer will almost invariably be No.
2. Control is lost immediately a proposal is made and a refusal is accepted. ('Shall we go for a walk?' 'No, I'd rather stay here.')
3. In order to maintain control a veiled or even direct proposal from a female should immediately be met with an alternative proposal.

The female propensity to reject approaches

Assuming a successful approach has been made, females cannot help but reject proposals, according to their master strategy of raising the cost of sex. The female disposition to refuse proposals poses a singular problem for the male, and he may compensate by making it exceptionally attractive, perhaps an invitation to an expensive meal or exclusive venue. In European societies it is left to the male to make all early proposals.

Achieving control is a formidable task

This game constitutes contention for control of the relationship, even before the male considers it to have started. One conclusion was that male control is lost as soon as the first proposal is rejected; however, delay in the execution of the proposal is acceptable.

The reality is that females are only controlled when they want to be: the male

> A proposal is made and assented to but a delay is obtained: 'I have to buy some slips (knickers) first.' This serves to prevaricate while reminding the male of his ultimate objective, providing him with incentive to tolerate the delay.

Male breeding competition. The following is a speculative list of categories of males who are or will become sexually inactive, and therefore non-reproductive, with an intensification of male breeding competition.

Genetic Martyrs (males at the low end of the bell curve, either physically or mentally).
Tramps and other males of indeterminate status.
Most drug addicts.
The physically ill and/or incapable.
The physically unattractive.
The mentally ill.
Exclusively homosexual males.
True paedophiles.
Males who only have sex with prostitutes (non-reproductive).
Males who are too proud.
Males who consider the rituals involved superficial and demeaning.
Males who cannot tolerate female control.
Males who do not respond to signals (object to being manipulated).
Neurotic males, or males who control their neurosis by taking slow deliberate actions.
Males who lack confidence.
Males who cannot cope with rejection.
Males too shy or self-conscious to make an approach.
Males who never meet females (e.g. in prison or at work).
The physically disfigured.
Males who fail to display feminine markers (e.g. scruffy, clothes in need of repair).
Males who smell.
Males who are too lazy.
Males who never have any money.
Males who are too honest.
Males who are impatient (want sex immediately).
Males who fear females (e.g. due to violence).
Males unskilled at persuasion.
Males unable to talk trivia.

must make the female want to accept his proposal. His sometimes forbidding task is to manipulate himself into a position where a proposal may be made without revealing his interest, or at least its true extent. The task is especially demanding if he is already smitten or in awe of her beauty.

Nasty games which bolster the female ego

Ordinarily the status of the female is proportional to the status of the male she can attract. At a certain threshold however, a crossover occurs. Once this threshold is exceeded the status of the female becomes proportional to the status of the male she can reject. This behaviour is typical of Base and Spoiled Female (BSF) and then a proposal may be encouraged expressly so she can deliver a rejection.

Synchronization and the cocoon effect

During the outing following the acceptance of a proposal the well-known effect of synchronization may be evident. The couple will start to speak at the same time, or reach for their drinks simultaneously. There is likely to be 'assortative mating' whereby pairs form having roughly equal physical attractiveness. Another recognised phenomenon is incidental touching, where the female marks the male with a brush of her hand or other seemingly casual touch. With the cocoon effect the couple can become completely immersed in each other and oblivious to their surroundings.

Disco dynamics

Conditions for female participation

In the West at least, any system of pairing must be to the advantage of the female or the female will not participate. Following this, the question was posed as to what features a nightclub offered to attract females. The location must appeal to her or she would not attend; if females did not attend, neither would the males.

Why nightclubs attract females

Firstly, there is loud music, which removes ambiguity of intention from males: he is unlikely to make the effort of shouting into a girl's ear if he were not interested in her, incidental comments being almost impossible. Secondly, alcohol is widely consumed, reducing inhibitions, and instinctive behaviour favours the female, the male's suit being rationality and logic. Alcohol is a poison and the male's ability to withstand impairment by it over several hours increases male competition and demonstrates his fitness. Thirdly there is dancing which, it is said, females equate to sex, and which allow her to make superficial judgments of male character by the overt body language displayed. Fourthly, a large number of people are present, with staff on hand should any inappropriate advances be made, and likely other males would come to her rescue were she to lose control.

This last is also true of shopping centres, an intensely female-friendly environment.

Manipulating the male

If a female is approached and she says 'I don't know you' what is really meant is 'I can't manipulate you.' Similarly 'It's got to be natural' means 'You may only approach if I signal, or some special situation arises.' The closest contemporary European females normally come to making an approach is 'Do you have a light?' The Jostle and Collision signals may also be employed. However, there is evidence that formerly it was the female who made approaches. In light of her superior verbal skills, her ability to self-efface and dexterity at manipulating relationships, this is perfectly feasible.

Demanding control. Do you have a light? (DYHAL?)

The evidence for this is the existence of *approach displacement* and its advanced associate, response displacement. Approach displacement is evident when a female, having seen a male she is attracted to, quickly and animatedly becomes engrossed in a conversation with her female friend. (This superjacent activity can be compared to that present during neurotic suspension.) Manifestly the engagement with her friend replaces an approach to the male.

Approach and response displacement

If this supposition is correct then response displacement is the more recent evolutionary development, and it is indeed more conspicuous than approach displacement. Response displacement typically takes place in a bar or café. A male addresses a female sitting near him at the bar, but the response is directed to a neutral third party, a person working behind the bar. Sometimes a long and engaged conversation will be held with a café worker or barman to avoid transacting with the nearby male, who may already be known to her or even a former intimate.

Avoiding engagement

Response displacement has been observed in overt form, when a girl put her hand in front of her mouth to prevent herself replying to a friendly greeting.

There seems to be a general female policy of manipulating the male into doing her work, as evinced by the modern phenomenon of men pushing prams and changing nappies. By 'her work' is meant activity at which she is naturally adept and innately superior; specifically in this instance, arranging social events and managing relationships.

The female manipulates the male into doing her work

The evolutionary origin of the policy may be uncertain but its benefit is not. By watching the male struggle with operations which she finds facile, she learns

A pram survey was undertaken in central Amsterdam on six consecutive Saturdays during 1992. Of the couples, in 142 instances the female partner pushed the pram, in 187 instances the male partner pushed the pram. That is, in the case of couples, more men were pushing prams than women.

Dr Timothy Perper spent 84 hours observing American singles bars and found that, in this environment, two-thirds of approaches were by females.

his strategies almost before he has learned them himself. Then when she wishes to prevail she can draw upon her natural ability and dominate.

Relational initiatives

This sequence ultimately falls down however. The female can become so passive, lazy and out of practice that she becomes inept at even those functions which fall within her natural domain.

Ultimately females become inept even at their natural functions

Effectively the female is ensuring that only those males who are willing and able to perform her functions will have offspring. Virtually every *relational initiative* must be taken by the male: writing a letter, making a telephone call, proposing a meeting and so on. An address or telephone number given to the female will be treated as a token and not used. The likelihood is that every move the male makes will be discussed with other females but, with few exceptions, he must take the initiative if progress is to be made.

Females' enthusiasm for involving third parties

Sharing a feature of IPoE, but with wider application, is *indirect invocation* which has as its primary purpose avoiding confrontations. It conforms to the general female policy of avoiding conflict, especially encounters which might involve physical force. Anne holds a grievance against Barry, but instead of confronting Barry directly she complains about it to Charlie. Indirect invocation accounts for the female readiness to involve police and other authorities in minor complaints or during domestic disputes.

The male ego requires control

The traditional female role is that she gives the male the illusion of control while in fact retaining it, and this can be established during the signalling, approach and proposal stages. As the male-female game advances however, the pretence wears unsustainably thin and it becomes obvious to the male that all control must be ceded to the female if he is to get what he wants. Males crave control, seeking to impose their will on their territory and the people and objects within it. In this situation the male may instinctively reject the female, abandoning the amenity she offers, solely because it is the only control left available to him.

A day at the airport. One day I badly wanted to get out of Amsterdam. I couldn't go away because of two submissions being made to journals so I went to Schipol airport for an afternoon out. On a large viewing balcony I saw the back of a blonde head, alone at a corner; she was leaning against the railing at the front. For a while she and I were the only people there, and I left to walk around another part of the airport and returned. Eventually I went up and started talking to her. She told me she was waiting for the airplane below to depart, carrying her boyfriend away for several months. She had bid him farewell in the departure lounge but its departure was delayed – she had already been waiting for around an hour. Since that time she had been staring fixedly at the aircraft, obviously dwelling on the sensations the situation evoked in her. I chatted, became intimate at one point and suggested she might give me her telephone number, but it was passed over. A few minutes later I made a further allusion to her number and almost under her breath she said that I should wait until her boyfriend's aircraft had departed. I left her to her emotional indulgence and went for another wander around. About half an hour later I returned and she was still there, but by this time she had become not so much a prospective consort as an object of curiosity.

It is a noteworthy fact, of interest not only to the physician but to the anthropologist as well, that an infallible remedy exists whereby the process of fading bloom, so manifest in old maids, can not only be arrested, but the already vanished bloom of youth can even be reinstated, partly at least, if not in its entire charm. Unfortunately our social conditions rarely permit its application. This remedy is a regular, orderly, sexual intercourse. We can often observe that when an elderly girl is still fortunate enough to attain matrimony, a marked change in her appearance takes place shortly after her marriage. Her shape obtains its former roundness, the roses return to her cheeks, and her eyes regain their former brightness. Marriage then is a real fountain of youth to the female sex. Thus nature has its fixed laws that inexorably demand obedience, and every unnatural mode of life, every attempt to adapt the organism to conditions of life that are not in keeping with the laws of nature, inevitably leaves marked traces of degeneration. This is true of both the animal and the human organism.

Dr. H. Ploss quoted in *Woman and Socialism* (1879)

12 Consolidation and Beyond

Romance, consolidation, consummation and the long-term

What does a female mean by 'romance' and how is it measured? Various sex effects are described, plus bonding mechanisms and the historical background of marriage.

The indulgence of romance, IoR, is a vague but nonetheless important mechanism females use to limit sex. Inherently difficult to define, it involves some intangible specialness which by its nature is difficult to repeat or routinely obtain. Mundane events carry low IoR while novel or unique events score high.

'How did you meet him?'

The foremost means by which females assess IoR is with the query 'How did you meet him?' The reply assigns a value to the relationship which, however, is not numerical. A relationship incurring low IoR is more likely to be ended by a female because her peers have determined it to be lacking in status. High IoR might occur with a meeting at an exotic location, at a wedding, or in any number of situations where meeting a new partner is unusual or uncommon. 'Love at first sight' has high IoR because it implies singularity. Marrying a childhood sweetheart carries high IoR, probably because it is so rare.

Routine or systematic processes carry low IoR

Low IoR will be associated with an encounter in a supermarket, where one of the parties might have been partner-hunting as if shopping for a can of beans, or any systematic process such as dating agencies and internet dating. Adolescent females neglect IoR because they have yet to acquire expectations of it. However with experience and maturity its existence and terms are appreciated and then females will sometimes lie to each other about the circumstances of meeting their partner if it carries low IoR.

Homosexuals and romance. Relationships in series

Indifference to IoR largely accounts for the high level of promiscuity often found among male homosexuals. For the female, besides limiting sex, IoR supports monogamy, particularly encouraging females who have experienced a series of relationships to settle down. Achieving a level of IoR greater than that formerly obtained becomes harder and harder. The female will inevitably become aware of this with each new alliance.

IoR must be capable of being discarded

A striking aspect of the IoR mechanism is that there must be some process by which IoR can be discarded. It was reasoned that such a process must exist before an actual example was observed. The female cannot tolerate any obligation to enter into a relationship because, like rape, it runs directly counter to her master strategy of raising the cost of sex.

The signal among male homosexuals in the centre of Brighton was to walk around the local supermarket carrying a baguette and a bag of sugar.

Suppose a female were to meet, purely by chance, a male who had long desired her in circumstances which carried high IoR. The meeting was entirely by coincidence, or under conditions that, had the male been a different one, she would be happy to report the circumstances to her contemporaries. However, the male is such that a relationship is unwanted.

Normally she would go to great lengths to avoid such a meeting, because she would rather preserve IoR for her indulgence in the future – throwing it away demeans it.

When IoR might be discarded

However in this scenario she has failed to avoid her admirer, maybe because the encounter has happened so quickly that she was unable to take evasive action. Possibly he has rescued her from some major or minor crisis, or there has been a chance meeting at some remote, even exotic location. Then she has only two choices: enter into an undesirable (to her) relationship with the male, or discard the IoR.

It seems that some females, apparently expressing the male trait of logical compartmentalization, can deliberately indulge in intense romantic sentiment, drawing pleasure from it. However the IoR can be discarded just as frivolously as soon as is convenient to her.

Indulging in emotion

Assessments of IoR are made in other circumstances besides relationships, but 'How did you meet him?' is when IoR is most distinct and thus most readily identified. Perhaps the ultimate IoR for the female is having two males physically fighting over her. Situations involving great risk, especially risk of sudden death, also carry high IoR.

Encouraging two males to fight

Consolidation

Consolidation is when an association is unambiguously raised to an intimate relationship; this normally establishes a handle state. There is deliberate physical contact called the 'first move,' typically the first kiss. The male may have invested a great deal of effort into getting the female into a position where consolidation can be attempted.

The 'first move'

Public weakening of consolidation markers. A man takes a woman out on a first date and shortly afterwards she recounts every detail of the evening on her social network page.

Achieving successful consolidation

Successful consolidation may require meetings at two different locations, with the attempt at consolidation being delayed until the second. This and the stages previously detailed chronicle a generalised *relationship inception sequence* (RIS). Soon after consolidation the male adaptive template may come into play. He thinks 'I didn't know she felt so delicious (soft, warm, etc.)' and decide he definitely wants to experience more of the same.

In accord with her strategy of raising the cost of sex, the female may raise the cost of consolidation. The consolidation attempt might be spurned and interpreted by the female merely as a statement of interest. This could be a stalling tactic intended to test the male's commitment to her and garner more control over the relationship.

Obliging the male to consolidate in public

She may refuse to accept proposals from the male which allow privacy, insisting on consolidation or a consolidation attempt being made in a public or semi-public place. (The couple's demeanour usually make it fairly plain what is going on, that the intimacy is actually consolidation.) Insistence may even be made that consolidation take place in view of some of the couple's associates, raising the prospect for the male of a public rebuff.

Or, in a different scenario, the female may attract a male in a bar, and encourage apparent consolidation there. Then she could use him as a trophy for the duration and dump him as soon as they are out of sight of spectators.

Mutating a handle to a marker

These situations are varying degrees of the *public weakening of consolidation markers*. If weakening of consolidation markers is commonplace this can lead to a situation in which one individual thinks that consolidation has been achieved but the other does not. Then one party believes that a handle state has been established while the other interprets the consolidation actions merely as markers.

Proclaiming enhancement

When, despite all the obstacles which can impede it, consolidation is successfully achieved, the female will be eager to tell her friends what she has accomplished. However she would be wise to not exult in her new status too obviously to the male, lest he begin to doubt the wisdom of his actions.

Just as the female can maintain a relationship without consolidation, she can maintain a matriarchy without it being apparent to males. Matriarchal consolidation might occur with male and female police pairs. The female overreacts to some trivial misdemeanour and the male officer adopts a retiring role in an attempt to redress the balance. Once this pattern is accepted however a matriarchal power structure is in effect, since a chain of automatic responses has often begun. Suppose an over-zealous female officer pursued a piffling offence, and anger at the overreaction led to an altercation.

Consummation

The standard bargain is that the male gives the female a relationship while the female gives the male physical sex. That is, the male gives the female her kind of sex while the female gives the male his kind of sex. This exchange is formalised in marriage, with its development as an institution perhaps reaching its zenith in Victorian times. Then the ideal was of complete celibacy beforehand with little or no prospect of divorce after.

The standard bargain between males and females. Women as major employers

Incidentally, during this era the wife's automatic promotion to household manager, responsible for the hiring and firing of domestic staff, meant that women were by far the largest group of employers.

Even in those days there was always a *demi-monde* (literally, half-world) of women with whom males gained sexual experience in more or less improper liaisons. Gentlemen of this period, especially in the colonies, separated women into 'A-girls' and 'B-girls.' The former were virginal marriage material while the latter could be enticed to provide sex under certain conditions, although undoubtedly rarely by modern standards. Pregnancy outside marriage brought great shame, was a common cause of female suicide and led to many rushed marriages. Masturbation was strongly discouraged, with cold showers and vigorous physical exercise being recommended to young men as an outlet for their ebullient sexual drives. Binding devices were employed at night-time for recalcitrant onanists. This ethos against masturbation very likely contributed to the substitution and sublimation which forged an empire. Even today professional athletes are recommended by their trainers to refrain from sex before competing.

Suppressing sexual drives

This brings us to the current phase of the sexual cycle, that 'Battle of the Sexes' with philandering or loyal males and coy or fast females. In contemporary Britain many young women engage in casual sex after binge-drinking, with inebriated, feminized young men pursuing them from pub to pub. City centres are now avoided by anyone outside this age group, as drink and frustration often translate to obnoxious behaviour. Sex provided quickly in casual relationships and without a normal RIS may still serve the female interest. They increase neurotic tension, because tension will surely increase if the male believes that sex could only be a few minutes or hours away. But with the huge variability of human sexuality there will always be exceptions.

The current state of affairs

For the majority, the not so young and the not so keen on drunken revelry, the main losers are probably women over 40 of whom 'other men have had the best of them.' The current popularity of internet dating is testimony to the problems mature women face finding a partner once they have passed their reproductive peak. A report in 2011 revealed that more than half of women under 50 have never married. A survey conducted around the same time found

Internet dating

The 'Battle of the Sexes' again

that single men were now more likely to want to settle down and start a family than women. It seems that the 'Battle of the Sexes' game is cycling before our eyes.

Reputation of dating agencies

According to reputation, dating agencies attract a disproportionate number of people who are greedy or flawed in some way. The greedy wish to flit from partner to partner, or nurture unrealistic hopes of becoming romantically attached to a handsome millionaire. It may be that this profile has not changed with the dating agency's modern incarnation, internet dating, there are simply more participants. Numerous tragicomic tales exist of the encounters which have followed introductions from dating websites, some being the theme of TV programmes and newspaper articles.

A Catholic view – who defines right and wrong?

In his book *Libido Dominandi*, E. Michael Jones argued that people are controlled by the skilled manipulation of their passions and that sexual freedom replaces political freedom. Jones, an American Catholic, claims that discarding conventional, religion-based morality allows the rich and powerful to impose their will on everyone else: 'Power becomes the only measure of right and wrong. Either might makes right, or we are bound by the terms of a moral order that is not of our making. There is no third alternative.'

A role of religion

Who, he says, makes the moral law if not God? Here again religion serves a role in setting moral standards of right and wrong, if not in stone, then at the most allowing only very gradual change. Moral values must not shift rapidly or they would command no respect and thus no mass adherence. Further, Jones writes,

> **'Whoever controls sexual behaviour controls the state. And he who controls the mores of women controls sexual behaviour. That is the first lesson of sexual politics. He who understands that law understands why pornography and sex education and abortion and the government funding of contraceptives are all non-negotiable conditions for the current regime. Without them, they could not rule.'**

Sex was not advertised

Jones might have added the constant promotion of sex via the mass media. Before the 1950s sexual images were completely absent in advertising; in news reporting, references to sex took the form of coded euphemism. Men were not constantly assailed by idealised female forms, and for the most part were unaware of what they were missing.

Cui bono – who benefits? Power of the mass media

Underlying Jones' argument is that any public treatment of sex benefits the female, because it raises the value of sex and thus transfers power to her. The rich use their wealth to dominate the media, a simple task when they own it, and the mass media is ineffably more influential than the government. While the population, especially the male population, is distracted by their recently awakened sexual appetites, and diverted in pursuit of what they have been led

A Dutch friend was watching television and seeing someone on the screen he exclaimed 'He's a *hoerenloper.*' He had been able to recognise him as a prostitute-goer by his manner, and said it was something he could often do.

to believe is their fair quota of sex, an oligarchy is able to further its agenda unimpeded.

A manly stance

While the female seeks information about the temperament, habits and reactions of her partner, with deep emotional communion with him as her goal, the male seeks information about how she feels. Males express sexuality by touching, exploration and ultimately impregnation. The male instinct is to reduce the cost of sex, and males conferring high status to it are readily manipulated. Sex is like air: it only becomes significant by its absence. By its scarcity, or constant evocation, its value is raised. The ability to control and subdue instincts is a male trait: it is not manly to keep one's brains below one's belt, and the male who does will be easily exploited. Various perils such as pregnancy, sexually transmitted disease or an unwanted entanglement should dispose the male to self-control when navigating a new partner.

What men want, and how feminized men fail

In a normal relationship a delay will occur before consummation, although long-term relationships sometimes follow from what ostensibly started as a one-night stand. The female may use the lure of sex to try and secure an extended relationship, relying on the adaptive template. Or she may attempt (consciously or less consciously) to become pregnant in order to secure a lock-in on the male. The male may be seeking to exploit copulation bonding, the biological process by which coitus, especially if prolonged and repeated, inspires an emotional attachment, particularly in the female to her partner. However, the more partners the female has had, the less effective copulation bonding will be. That aside, females generally bond only to who they like, while males bond on shared experience.

Securing a lock-in on the male. How males and females bond

Relationships are established during any human interaction, and it is impossible for physical sex to take place without a connection of some kind being formed. Either bonding occurs to some degree when coitus takes place, or it is suppressed. Prostitutes, who can routinely copulate a dozen or more times per day, seem to exhibit only mildly peculiar behaviour out of hours but the hardened attitude of their customers attest to the effects of attempting to divorce physical sex from a relationship. Indeed some males regularly return to the same prostitute as an inferior substitute for a normal attachment. Emotional

Sex inevitably involves a relationship. Effect of visiting prostitutes

alliances are a major source of human misery but becoming inured to them must surely be the least satisfactory remedy. Perhaps ideally, your first love should be your last.

Arousing the female's interest

Regardless of what some may consider the ideal, experienced commentators agree that immediately jumping into bed is generally not the best way to begin a relationship. The female will expect the male to probe toward this end and it may increase her interest considerably, and greatly improve his prospects, if he does not attempt consummation within a few hours or days of consolidation.

Disclosure and debasement

Revealing intimate details during sex, and why

Disclosure takes place when the female reveals intimate details, perhaps of her family, personal history or former relationships, shortly after sex takes place. Its purpose is to reinforce bonding, encouraging the male to remain to support her during gestation of the child which right then might be in the process of conception. Rarely, disclosure is dramatically expressed by the female breaking into tears and begging the male never to leave her. Here the female reveals her fear of being abandoned with child. This overt expression is like a girl demonstrating response displacement by clapping her hand over her mouth, to stop herself replying to a greeting. It is an undisguised manifestation of a process which is usually only seen in a less obvious form.

Advancing disclosure to comprise a trial

Disclosure is advanced to become *debasement*, taking place pre-coitus. Here the female makes revelations and shares intimacies before copulation. In this form it is used as a trial of the male before coitus takes place. Intimacies are revealed in similar manner to disclosure but in this case the revelations diminish the female. The essence of debasement is that the female debases herself, making herself a less worthy mate. Invariably though, by her revelations, she also debases others.

She may claim to have been raped or abused. Since coitus has not yet occurred, the dynamic is now that the more demeaning the revelations are, the more challenging they are to the male. If sex is likely to occur then the

> One young woman made some astonishing revelations shortly before or after sex. She said that she had lost her virginity after being invited to someone's flat and smoking a joint which had been laced with heroin. She had come round to find the man inside her. Another time she revealed that a former partner had once killed someone in a bungled attempt to get money for heroin, a murder that had never been solved.

False rape allegations. In the *Archives of Sexual Behavior* (1994) Kanin detailed the results of a 9-year study, undertaken in cooperation with police in a small American metropolis, of rape allegations. Of the total of 109 cases, 45 (41%) were false. These false allegations appeared to serve three major functions for the complainants: providing an alibi, seeking revenge, and obtaining sympathy and attention.

revelations may be exaggerated in proportion to that likelihood, since the purpose of the debasement is to test the male or arrest sex entirely. Hence the recounted events may be exaggerated or wholly imaginary. Both disclosure and debasement reflect the danger the female instinctively countenances of becoming pregnant and being abandoned.

A means to test the male or forestall sex

Before the clothes come off there may be discussion of her monthly cycle, ostensibly to determine the likelihood of pregnancy. Since menstruation is taboo in many cultures (thus likely in ours in the past), this could also be a subtle expression of debasement. Women have a distinct enthusiasm for flaunting sanitary products in front of men, doing so both personally and collectively. A notable example was a TV advertisement showing a woman storming into her boss's office and throwing a sanitary towel at him as he sat behind his desk.

Menstruation, and flaunting sanitary products

Two vital factors, with profound implications, are that despite modern techniques which make pregnancy and disease easy to prevent, female instincts continue to be applied to curtail sex. Then when it does take place females often fail to employ or insist on contraception, despite it being overwhelmingly in her interest to do so.

Two vital factors

Disguised ovulation

Mammals announce their fertile state to nearby males, typically by exuding a particular odour. The cat is a good example; the female domestic cat advertises its readiness to mate by its behaviour and scent, but ovulation is actually stimulated by copulation. Ova are released to meet the sperm. The lioness however raises the cost of sex, demanding fitness in the male by withholding ovulation until many copulations have taken place. The lion that is unable to summon enough stamina to trigger ovulation by multiple copulations fails to father offspring. Lions will also kill the cubs of rival males when taking over a pride of lionesses; the domestic cat will eat its young if food is scarce.

How the lioness raises the cost of sex

The disguised fertile state of the human female is extraordinary, with several possible origins. One obvious candidate is that it provides the female with

In a 2007 paper in *Evolution and Human Behavior* evolutionary psychologists Miller, Tybur and Jordan correlated ovulation with the amount of tips erotic dancers received. The sample group of 5,300 erotic dancers were divided into three: those who were ovulating, those who were menstruating, and those who were in-between. Each of the women did a 5-hour shift. On average, the ovulators made $325 in tips, the menstruators $185 and the others, $260.

increased control of sex, for by removing the male imperative for sex at a specific time she is able to ration the amenity to her advantage. Alternatively or additionally, the increased frequency of copulation strengthens bonding, leading to a more stable environment for rearing children. That such a basic female biological function is disguised should lead us to expect similarly profound adaptations in mental processes, evolved for similar ends.

Disguised oestrus in the human female

Nonetheless, the fertile state is not entirely hidden, for vestiges remain. Lap dancers have been shown to attract higher tips during ovulation and, as previously mentioned, adulterous females appear to time their liaisons to coincide with it. A Fertile signal exists, at least putatively: a female may appear more confident, stand out from other females and exhibit a spring in her step. The rapist who was able to detect ovulation in females would only have to copulate a few times in his lifetime to ensure the transmission of his genes and the persistence of his strategy.

Vestiges of oestrus – signalling ovulation. The 'rapist strategy'

Another phenomenon is menstrual synchrony whereby females living in close proximity tend after a while to menstruate together, apparently as a result of hormones secreted from the armpit. Many African villages maintain a special hut for menstruating women, who are regarded as unclean and untouchable during this time. The effect is evidently not strong enough to synchronize the entire female population of the village. Some potential origins of menstrual synchrony are: equalized competition for resources; shared risk of predation; among social animals, the sharing of care of offspring; and for a migratory species, uniform pace of migration. Menstrual synchrony appears to be the vestige of a breeding season.

Menstrual synchrony is a vestige of a mating season

The progression of disclosure to debasement exactly duplicates the development of the statement of unavailability, SoU, to the dubious version of the same, DSoU. Both progressions illustrate the micro-evolutionary nature of procedures: they are behaviours that dynamically adapt according to the opportunities and demands of the environment. According to this evolutionary hypothesis, debasement is advanced disclosure; the disclosure mechanism

The micro-evolutionary nature of procedures

has evolved to form a distinct procedure serving compatible, but nonetheless distinct, aims, encouraging bonding in the first instance and testing the male before copulation takes place in the second.

Religion and sex

Religious immortality. The crescendo of religious services

As sex becomes more notional, debasement does so too. A correspondence exists between religion and sex: religion is the ancient sublimation of sex, for both provide the individual with a kind of immortality. A religious ceremony involves mental preparation, a crescendo and a spiritual climax, followed by relative tranquillity. This is especially true of Pentecostal and Evangelical meetings with high emotional content.

Carl Rogers' disastrous involvement with a convent

Jones described in *Libido Dominandi* how the introduction by Carl Rogers of group counselling to nuns at the Immaculate Heart of Mary convent in Los Angeles led to its rapid demise. Rogers' attempt to achieve self-actualisation for the nuns led to a breakdown of formality, open expression of emotions (to each other, rather than to God) and intimacy, sometimes sexual, between the convent's members. Particularly it was noted that masturbation and prayer were mutually exclusive: their religious devotion was a part substitution, part sublimation of their sexual drives. When their emotions were unleashed and sexual activity took place, even in isolation, their religiosity dissipated.

'Giving witness' as debasement

A common practice during Evangelical religious meetings is 'giving witness,' during which a convert, usually a fairly recent one, describes the wicked life they lived before they found their Saviour. A dynamic similar to debasement applies: the more sinful the convert claims he was before, the more impressive, and sought after to appear at such meetings, he is. Exaggeration of former misdeeds plainly takes place. This phenomenon is proposed as a wider expression of debasement; a procedure, originating in sex, is again extended beyond the sexual realm.

False memory syndrome as debasement

Demonstrably false claims of abuse in childhood have been cited as examples of 'false memory syndrome.' Sex has become increasingly notional, being constantly evoked all around, yet physical enjoyment of it is relatively rare. Then as sex becomes increasingly abstract, debasement claims become further divorced from reality. One is reminded of Jung's proposal that people should have sex weekly in order to maintain their psychological health.

> *Have sex, stay sane.* A homosexual male nurse, working in a psychiatric ward in Brighton: 'Half the people in here, all they need is a good fuck.'

Beyond consolidation and consummation

Origins of the dowry and bridegroom traditions

Historically the female was regarded as a burden on the male. By his physical strength and practical ability, only the male was able to create wealth. This is the origin of the dowry, and its Western remnant is the convention that a bride's family pay for the wedding. Incidentally, Darwin wrote that the origin of the best man tradition was his role as the groom's accomplice in stealing a bride from a neighbouring village. This continues in Armenia to this day.

Spinsters and bottom drawers

The unwed maiden faced spinsterhood, usually having to live with her parents. She was regarded pityingly by her contemporaries, seen as lonely and incomplete. In recent history young women routinely kept a 'bottom drawer' of goods being saved for their married life. Her task then was to win a husband by making him believe that it was he who was winning a prize, while the reality, certainly economically, was the reverse. He would be subtly enticed with signals perceived only unconsciously, and her outward resistance served to increase her desirability to the male her target.

Male reproductive success relies on his ability to make an exception

Older, experienced men were aware of female entrapment and the consensus among them was to regard womankind as an adversary. This is an important point – that, aware of this consensus, male reproductive success relied on his ability to make an exception. This accounts for males' willingness to occasionally bend rules or admit exceptions, but firmly resist attempts to make the exception the norm. A targeted prospective husband might think, 'Yes, they all tell me that women are best avoided but this one is different and our relationship is special.'

How a husband might discipline his wife, and why

Until recently no special regard would be given by neighbours to the sounds of a nearby wife being beaten. There would be no intervention by the authorities unless the injuries were severe or the stick used was wider than a man's thumb: this is reputed to have been the original 'rule of thumb' (attributed to Sir Francis Buller). Under the principle of coverture, a husband was responsible for the debts his wife could run up in his name and her behaviour, including any criminal acts she committed. Of course, the husband might face social ostracism or violence from others if the punishment was thought to be unwarranted or excessive. Among the working class in the north of England until the 1930s and 40s it was common practice for a wife to have all her teeth extracted shortly after marriage to save her husband the cost of future dental visits.

Saving for years to marry

In earlier, more masculine times it was not unusual for older males to pair with young females. A man needed a tidy sum to marry, it being his obligation to provide the marital home and all its furnishings. Young couples often had to save for years before they could marry. Then, a man could be sued for 'breach of promise' for breaking off an engagement but a woman could not. In a very feminine society the situation is reversed, with mature women sometimes pairing with younger men, often using them as trophies, a perverse reversal of the evolutionary norm. Reproductive success relies on a youthful female, the age of the male being practically immaterial.

Trophy wives and toy boys

One attraction of marriage may be the unconscious hope that it freezes the relationship in its paragonic state. A common joke is that a man gets married hoping that his bride won't change, while a woman gets married hoping that her husband will. Both are inevitably disappointed. Stories circulate of modern marriages in which a fiancée has satisfied her partner's every sexual desire beforehand but has abruptly withdrawn herself the instant the marriage ceremony was completed. This of course is the exact opposite of what took place when pre-marital celibacy was the norm. These stories could be attributed to urban legend but an actual example is known.

Both are inevitably disappointed by marriage. Withdrawing sex after marriage

After the initial phases of a relationship, when the partner is no longer regarded as a paragon, many alliances persist out of habit. The relationship tends to continue as it did before unless something or someone disturbs it. Most relationships are terminated by females: the commonly accepted figure is 70% but this neglects an unknown proportion where the female has effectively manipulated the male into terminating, a sort of 'constructive dismissal.' For example the female could treat the male with such disdain that he ends the relationship to maintain his self-respect.

Most relationships are terminated by females

Without wishing to demean something which is precious and increasingly rare, love in the long-term probably owes much to the partners having used each other as a focus for their emotional gaze for so long that they simply cannot imagine another filling that role.

Force of habit

Just as the ultimate basis of sex difference is the abundance of sperm and the limited resource of the egg and its gestation, the essential dynamic of the sexes rests on the passivity of the female and her subjugation by the male during sex. By denying the male the ability to 'punish' her with sex and denuding him of control, the active and demanding female will often find that making her sexual appetite obvious will be counterproductive, especially in the long-term.

Sex as 'punishment'

> Gallup et al. in a 2003 paper 'The human penis as a semen displacement device' demonstrated that a penis with a glans and coronal ridge displaced more semen than a penis without these features. Displacement of semen took place when the model penis was inserted at least 75% of its length into an artificial vagina.

The Coolidge effect – The story goes that President and Mrs Coolidge were visiting a government farm in Kentucky and after arrival were taken off on separate tours. When Mrs Coolidge passed the chicken pens she paused to ask her guide how often the rooster could be expected to perform his duty. 'Dozens of times a day' was her guide's reply. She was most impressed by this and said, 'Please tell that to the President.' When the President was duly informed of the rooster's performance he was initially dumbfounded. Then a thought occurred to him. 'Was this with the same hen each time?' he inquired. 'Oh no, Mr President, a different one each time' was his host's reply. The President nodded slowly, smiled and said, 'Tell that to Mrs Coolidge!'

From Bermant, 1976 in Glenn Wilson's *The Great Sex Divide*

Sex effects

The Coolidge effect

Probably the dominant male sex effect is the Coolidge effect. According to this, sexual activity in many male animals is proportional to the number of partners. It seems never to have been confirmed in humans but has been demonstrated in rats, chickens, sheep and cattle.

Evidence in animals

A male rat will become exhausted by copulation with five female rats in oestrus, and ignore the females licking and nudging him to perform. Yet he will be suddenly restored to vigour when a sixth female is introduced. In sheep, by the time the ram copulates for the fifth time with the same sheep it takes him 16 minutes to finish, but with five different female sheep all are serviced within two minutes. A bull's sexual activity will wane after being paired with a single cow, but with the introduction of a second its interest is restored, not only vigorously engaging the new cow but with renewed interest in the first. If a series of novel cows are presented one at a time, his response to the tenth is nearly as vigorous as his response to the first.

Evidence of our prehistoric sexual habits. The penis as a pump

The shape of the human penis and the properties of semen provide us with important clues about prehistoric sexual practices. Little or nothing is known about our ancient sexual habits, and due to the isolation of communities they must have been extremely varied. However the evidence of our bodies strongly suggests that females were enjoyed by several males in succession. The shape of the glans makes it an effective pump, scooping out up to 91% of previously deposited semen. Some species have spines or barbs on their penises to accomplish the same thing. The sensitivity the human male experiences shortly after climax is to prevent him from displacing his own deposit.

The size of the human testes, or rather their proportion relative to total body weight, is yet more proof of the prehistoric sharing of women. Among animals, the more males that are likely to have impregnated a female, the larger the testes are. The male that produces more sperm has a higher chance of siring offspring by beating other males' sperm to the egg, by the sheer quantity of his ejaculate. In gorillas, where a single dominant male has a harem of females, the testes are 0.03% of his body weight. In chimpanzees, where multiple males service a female in season, the figure is 0.3%. Humans lie between these values at 0.08%. It has also been proposed that the sperm of separate deposits compete with each other in so-called sperm wars. About 30% of the sperm in each ejaculate is defective, and their role could be to impede the sperm of other males. While no proof of this theory has been found, it seems implausible that these 'crippled little soldiers' serve no purpose.

Size of the testes in various primates. 'Sperm wars'

Seminal fluid, the fluid that carries the sperm, contains the anti-depressants dopamine, oxytocin and vasopressin, as well as the sex hormones testosterone and oestrogen. These substances produce a sense of contentment and even elation in the female, and this doubtless contributes to copulation bonding. A healthy woman can easily have sex every three days, which would mean the constant presence of seminal matter being absorbed through her reproductive tract. Given that women historically had sex more often than they do nowadays, we might wonder what the aggregate effect on society might be of millions of women not getting the sex they had hitherto.

The cause of being 'shag happy.' Cumulative effect of women being deprived of sex

The main female mechanism relating to physical sex is probably *insatiation*, whereby the more sex a woman gets, the more she wants. This is encapsulated in the saying 'The only thing harder than turning a woman on is turning her off again.' On another level, the sexually-sated male is generally content but for the female her status increases according to the number of admirers she has, and for this there is no limit.

The insatiability of the female

Another female effect, which has never been formally confirmed, is *partner reidentification*. In this, a female with a long-term monogamous partner imagines she is having sex with another. A common theme of problem pages a few decades ago was queries from wives concerned that they could not stop themselves imagining one of the male idols of the day – the actor currently playing James Bond perhaps – while they were having sex with their husband. Wilson confirmed that many women do not enjoy sex, and partner reidentification would serve to combat boredom with the same male partner.

A proposed effect of 'partner reidentification'

Millions of years have passed giving opportunity for mutations to occur, so we could even argue that if a trait conferring reproductive advantage can exist, it will. Partner reidentification, by increasing the frequency of sex and thus the number of progeny, would certainly enhance reproductive success.

If it can exist, it will

13 Outstanding Procedures

Spoiling, vicarious generosity and transduction

A female receiving an unwelcome approach from a male can impose diminishment on him. Like a dog, she can bite. The nature of that bite was a mystery until transduction was identified. Some other procedures are detailed, most of which have not been mentioned hitherto.

Spoiling is removing a component from an object, thereby to devalue it. Both things and people may be spoiled.

Definition of spoiling, and the original model

Archetypal spoiling is a trick used at public auctions. While viewing the lots a person who wants a particular item removes an essential part and puts it in his pocket. Then the item is devalued, reducing the amount the other bidders are prepared to pay for it. He has reduced the item's desirability to others and is likely to obtain it himself at less cost.

The spoiled object is unlikely to be restored

If his gambit fails, and despite his ploy another bidder secures it, the spoiler is unlikely to give the removed part to the winning bidder. To do so would be to admit what he has done, increase the item's perceived value by revealing his desire for it, and increase its actual value by making it complete again. The item has been spoiled, perhaps irrevocably.

Spoiling in the sexual realm

A female emitting a false or erroneous signal to a male is a simple example of female spoiling. In this instance the element being removed is the male's ability to respond to that particular signal. Once he has determined its true nature he is unlikely to respond to that signal again. He is also less likely to trust to signals generally. A male employing the Klingon strategy might spoil his rivals' chances of winning his paragon by his presence or remarks. Similarly, a spurned female who has failed to secure a male she desires might employ various spoiling tactics to prevent other females securing a relationship with him. In some contexts spoiling is as an advanced, possessive form of marking.

Spoiling by disrupting associations

Homosexuals dressing up in police and firemen's uniforms are spoiling, by weakening the associations these uniforms have with masculinity, authority and orthodoxy. Similarly 'anti-racists' adopting skinhead styles are spoiling by disrupting the association between that mode of dress and the wearer's political beliefs.

Eavesdropping on a conversation

A more subtle form of spoiling involves eavesdropping on a conversation, which is regarded as impolite in many cultures. Commonly, people within earshot turn off their attention to a conversation which is unlikely to be confidential, given that it is taking place in a public setting, but which clearly does not concern them. An eavesdropper could suddenly interject something

Spoiling by Joe Orton and Kenneth Halliwell. Orton and Halliwell achieved notoriety in the 1960s removing otherwise innocuous books from an Islington library, altering them, then surreptitiously replacing them on the shelves. Dust covers were altered and flyleaf text added, usually on the pair's favourite themes of murder, homosexuality and incest.

The text typewritten onto the flyleaf of *Clouds of Witness* by Dorothy L. Sayers ended: 'This is one of the most enthralling stories ever written by Miss Sayers. It is the only one in which the murder weapon is concealed, not for reasons of fear but for the sake of decency! READ THIS BEHIND CLOSED DOORS! And have a good shit while you are reading!'

In 1962 they were discovered and police found 72 stolen books and 1,653 plates removed from art books which had been used to decorate the bedsit Orton and Halliwell shared. They were sentenced to 6 months in prison. In 1967, in the same bedsit, Halliwell murdered Orton then committed suicide.

into the conversation, surprising the others. This would be a simple form of spoiling; the thing being removed is the assumption of privacy. Individuals who are intimate, such as close friends, family members or lovers, might share a distinctive greeting or farewell, and imitating it in their hearing would also be a form of spoiling.

Imitating a distinctive address

'Spoiling a child' is a vague term but nonetheless valid in this context. Some of the elements which might be removed are moderate expectations (of treats or life), capacity for self-control and the expectation of punishment for wrongdoing. Some paedophiles, who must surely be the worst kind, exult in the knowledge that their activity is permanently ruining the child, by removing their sexual innocence and trust in the wider world. Premature sexualization of children by the mass media and instilling irrational fear of paedophiles are other forms of spoiling, by the same measure.

Exulting in spoiling a child

Some cultures are retarded by an inherent tendency to spoil. An individual showing exceptional ability or inventiveness in such a society may provoke suspicion and resentment, and this is expressed by accusations of sorcery or superiority. He may be vilified, banished or even killed. The collective instinct to spoil has removed him, or his ability to contribute, from society. By spoiling the society inflicts backwardness on itself.

Spoiling by accusations of witchcraft or superiority

The most basic expression of spoiling is smearing excrement and this is *primordial spoiling.* Animals do this to mark or adapt their habitat but it is sometimes seen in the mentally ill and aged persons suffering from dementia. This is the primitive instinct to spoil, freed of inhibition. The component being removed is cleanliness. When burglars leave faeces behind, as sometimes

Primordial spoiling

occurs, their marking of the premises has regressed to primordial spoiling. Probably the normal catharsis of primordial spoiling in contemporary Western society is soiling a clean lavatory pan.

Leaving a mess

Vicarious generosity

Giving away, often enthusiastically, something which is not one's to give is *vicarious generosity*. This is the procedure being effected when people are generous with other people's things.

The proposed origin of vicarious generosity

In the tribe or settlement which is our evolutionary model, the female was vulnerable to violence and abuse and could even face eviction by the male. It was he, and he alone, who produced the wealth that sustained the family or extended family group. In order to reduce her vulnerability the female would curry favour among her neighbours with gifts of produce or materials which, inevitably, were the product of another's labour.

Gaining goodwill with the fruit of another's labour

The gifts served as a store of goodwill, inviting reciprocation in times of hardship but also to provide her with sympathetic treatment and an escape route for herself should a dispute arise with her husband. She might displease her caveman owner, or the powerful brute who held absolute sway over the household. If she were to be ejected from the communal dwelling and left to fend for herself in that hostile environment, for example into the depths of winter or to face hungry wild animals, she could perish. With a store of goodwill she is likely to be taken in by her neighbours. Vicarious generosity appears to be feminine in nature, with this putative evolutionary origin.

Sharing music and software, foreign aid, and transferring authority to a foreign power

One contemporary example of vicarious generosity is the avid sharing of copied music and software – the donors would surely not be so eager to distribute copies if they had invested considerable time and effort producing it themselves. Another example is when governments give large sums in foreign aid, using tax revenue earned by others (and usually contrary to the wishes of the majority). Selling or allowing to be sold a country's infrastructure to foreign speculators, or a government giving jurisdiction to a foreign power, authority which it does not possess but merely holds in trust, is another example of vicarious generosity.

Delivering a rejection on another's behalf

Another form of vicariousness, unambiguously female this time, is *vicarious rejection*. This is when a female, occasionally an older relative, delivers a rejection to a potential suitor in place of the target. However it is most commonly encountered when one of two females are approached; then the non-target, ostensibly acting to protect the target but eager to deliver a rejection herself, and further motivated by having been passed over, will deliver a verbal rejection on the target's behalf or impel the target to break.

Risk disencumberment

A female trait is to fear the worst. She will foresee the worst possible outcome and often attempt to shift the risk she perceives onto someone else.

In a feminine environment a request is made for help carrying boxes. It could be a group of feminine men, or with a supervisor who has spent his whole career 'watching his back'; indeed this could be the only thing at which he excels. The assistance will only be provided if it is agreed that the helpers will not be held responsible if one of the boxes is dropped. A guarantee must be given that the helpers will not face the consequences of any mishap before assistance is given.

Shifting risk onto someone else

This is the policy of *risk disencumberment*. In a formal setting a contract will be produced attempting to disclaim liability for every possible outcome. The current obsession with health and safety, stifling many activities, is a product of female fears and her response to them. These regulations have become so pervasive that they touch every aspect of working life.

Foreseeing every risk

The discovery of transduction. In a crowded Amsterdam discotheque I made the mistake of taking up an empty place next to a large, unattractive Dutch girl of about 19, on the benches around the dance floor. As often happens however, the error turned out to be enlightening.

I sipped my beer and paid no attention, but after her first glance sideways, then another and another, I began to get that signalled feeling. She was talking to one of a party sitting nearby, a docile, wimpy-looking male. Her manner was also gross: '*Wat*?' she kept repeating sharply, when something was said which she had not heard above the music.

Some minutes later the male spoke to me. After only six or eight words she joined in and involved me in conversation. Then I was drawn in, and the more I told the more she wanted to know, making me uncomfortable, so I broke on the pretext of getting more beer.

Mercifully the empty space had been taken when I returned and I sat a small distance away. However she was looking in my direction, smug and pleased by her involvement with me; her movements had become livelier and more pronounced, almost bouncy.

Again there was that feeling of having fought a battle and lost. I became sure that it was something inflicted on me, generated within but triggered externally. In this case there could be no doubt – I had not done, gone or entered into battle; I had merely been polite. She had drawn something from me and been enhanced and it could only have been at my expense.

Insurance is a form of risk disencumberment, where an insurance company is paid to carry risk. However double risk disencumberment might take place when buried terms in the contract allow the insurance company to reject a claim. In one case in Yorkshire, an insurance company refused to settle a claim for flood damage after an unexceptional storm on the grounds that it was an 'Act of God.' The insurance company disencumbered itself by reflecting its risk back onto the policy holder.

An insurance company reflects back the risk

Or, in reinsurance, the insurance company which ostensibly carries the risk is actually only a reseller, disencumbering itself of liability by passing it further up a chain. This is a common, if usually undisclosed, practice. Even Lloyds, the long-established international shipping insurer and supposed apex of the insurance business, disencumbers itself by its use of 'names,' private individuals who ultimately carry its risk.

Passing the risk up a chain

Transduction

One of the most significant discoveries in Procedural Analysis was the mechanism of *transduction*, the major medium in the game of emotional manipulation. Neurosis is said to be induced, but when false feelings are inspired it is called transduction. Transduction is ubiquitous but seems never to have been formally acknowledged as a distinct process. The importance and prevalence of the mechanism certainly justifies the introduction of a new term. Transduction can be either positive or negative, and examples of positive transduction will be given first of all.

Inducing false feelings

In positive transduction a person is falsely enhanced. In a restaurant, the attitude and manners of the waiting staff inspire genteel behaviour in the diners, who often assume airs and graces they normally would not. The staff's task is to make the customers enjoy their visit, perhaps making them feel that they are part of higher society and more refined or sophisticated than they really are. This of course is all part of the pleasure of going out for a meal. The restaurant's objective is to encourage the diners to return.

False enhancement of restaurant diners

A comparable process takes place on an airplane, where the cabin crew treat the passengers graciously and with friendly formality to inspire correct behaviour in them. The aircraft contains a large number of tightly packed passengers in a potentially dangerous situation, and only one passenger failing to inhibit their nervousness could spread panic. The cabin crew encourage formal and reserved behaviour to minimize the likelihood of such an outburst.

Inhibiting panic attacks on an airplane

The best example of positive transduction however might be the casino doorman. His job is to greet each customer by name, making each one feel like a regular customer, even if that customer has only visited once before. The customer is made to feel like a big shot, a 'high-roller.' On having this feeling

The casino doorman

inspired in him he acts to conform to it, and in his role (or with his temporary self-image) as an important figure, known to all, he surely doesn't want to be seen gambling paltry sums like fivers and tenners. Thus he is encouraged to gamble with higher stakes, to the profit of the establishment.

Making a punter gamble more

Most transduction is undoubtedly negative however; it imposes diminishment. This is the origin and main application of the procedure, because its most common application is to induce false guilt. Feelings of guilt, whether valid or not, are capable of confusing and incapacitating an opponent, especially one that was nurturing feelings of anger and close to striking out.

Negative transduction

A fairly mundane instance of negative transduction, but which gives an insight into how profitable it can be, occurs when a person is made to feel that they are being a nuisance or somehow being unreasonable when seeking the return of a loaned item. Really the onus is on the borrower to return someone else's property, generously loaned to them, without having to be badgered for it. Perhaps the borrower is disgruntled that their attempt to mutate the handle to a marker – in effect, steal the item – has not been successful. It is easy to imagine a lender who is sensitive to transduction assuming that there is validity to the feeling he experiences and, not wanting to make a fuss, he gives up trying to reclaim it. By doing so he hands *de facto* ownership of the item to the borrower.

Converting a loan to a gift using transduction

The transduction mechanism accords with many other female behaviours which follow from the male's greater physical strength and aggression, providing the female with a defence against it. Females have inherent, biologically derived superior verbal skills, coined their *eloquence advantage*. This is employed as an adjunct to transduction to confuse and disorient the male with distorted, exaggerated or unfounded accusations of blame. We use fact and logic to determine whether the emotion we experience is false; the second-stage response to transduction is anger.

Females' eloquence advantage

Another commonplace female defence mechanism is frequent smiling, fostering familiarity and creating a cosy atmosphere, raising the cost of disturbance of it. Objects and people are rendered non-threatening by the use of diminutive terms such as *doggy* instead of *dog*, *daddy* instead of *dad* (or *father*), *bloke* or *lad* instead of *man*. First name terms are encouraged, even on first acquaintance, for the same reason. Use of the telephone is favoured by females not only because of her love of talking but also because it allows relationships to be maintained without any possibility of physical sex or aggression. Incidents will routinely be discussed with several females by *divulgence and referral*, whereby they discuss events and refer to older or more experienced females. By its passage through them or others a minor incident or utterance may be embellished and exaggerated out of all proportion. Thus it is amplified as a weapon for use against the male.

Adopting diminutive terms to make people and things seem less threatening. Referring to other people

Once I met a bog-eyed medical student, who wanted to be a surgeon, at the Amsterdam flat of my friend, a male medical student. The young Dutchwoman and I retired, at her invitation, to a nearby bar to continue our conversation. We were talking about sex differences and the conversation came round to female orgasms. 'I like orgasms, I want them' she said and after a couple of beers the thought had not unnaturally occurred to me that I wouldn't object to giving her a hand with some. I told her, rather matter of factly, that I would like to make love to her. She declined, telling me that her boyfriend was returning the next day. Sometime later I kissed her on the cheeks and we went our separate ways. The parting was completely amicable.

A day or two afterwards she telephoned my friend and caused such a fuss that it almost caused a permanent rift between us. I didn't have a clue whether my crime was to have made an unambiguous remark, to have accepted her decline too readily, or failing to share in her eager anticipation of the orgasms she was to have when her boyfriend returned.

Repulsing unbidden approaches. Inspiring passion

Transduction is often used to repulse unbidden approaches, and as an adjunct to rejections generally. The male may be left with a vague sense of having acted improperly or having failed to live up to expectations. It is often evident in leaving behaviour, when a male is left with a similar sense of disquiet.

Alternatively, if the male is susceptible, his attraction may be elevated to passion with provocative or endearing postures.

'Our cosy circle'

Manipulating the male by promise of inclusion

A male manipulated into acting for a female can display a distinct zeal, as if the fact that he is acting for another completely authorises his actions. When a female wishes to manipulate an unfamiliar male into doing something for her she can often achieve her objective by creating a false sense of intimacy. The male is made to feel that he is being drawn into *our cosy circle* – that he is, or will be, promoted to a favoured position in her circle, conferring various unspecified privileges, especially if he satisfies her wish. This same sense of intimacy is used to strengthen a pair bond, or create a sense of togetherness among a group. OCC is sometimes expressed literally by a group standing or sitting in a circle. However central to the OCC mechanism, giving it its unmistakably feminine stamp, is that it is defined by those it excludes.

The earlier example of a female maintaining a circle of hopeful suitors is just one example, although perhaps the definitive one, of promoting a false expectation of receiving a payoff in the future. A false hope or prospect is transduced. In this case the false emotion being inspired is optimism.

False expectations

Females can even give the appearance of having a duty to transduce. A small clique of females are settled at a place, perhaps in a pub or club, when a particular male enters. Some grievance or dispute exists between him and one of the females. Then the group will, with a display of apparent reluctance, gather up their belongings and depart. By no stretch are they obliged to leave, but they give the impression of having to do so.

Giving the appearance of having a duty to transduce

Accusations of 'racism' and 'sexism' are pure transduction, for these terms were defined solely to taint. The free and uninhibited interchange of ideas, including discussion of racial and sexual differences, is a prerequisite for a

Accusations of 'racism' and 'sexism'

Never satisfied, or the barking psychiatrist – Young Swedish women now demand that their men use the lavatory in a strictly sedentary posture – partly, I am told, for reasons of hygiene, but, more crucially, because a man standing up to urinate is deemed to be triumphing in his masculinity and, by extension, degrading women. I am not taking the pissoir, dear and trusting reader; this is for real. To micturate from the standing position is now viewed among the more progressive Swedes as the height of vulgarity and possibly suggestive of violence.

'All my friends demand that their husbands or boyfriends sit down,' says Jessica, from Uppsala. 'I think it shows respect for the women who clean,' adds the 31-year-old biologist. 'My brother, for example, would not dream of standing up. Among the young, leftish intelligentsia there is also a view that to stand is a nasty macho gesture.'

Her English husband has refused to be cowed, she admits, because 'it infringes his manly rights.' Reward for his heroic stand? Full-time cleaning duties.

Yola, a 25-year-old trainee psychiatrist, is yet more strident. She dumped a boyfriend, in part, for refusing to comply. His replacement is better trained. 'What can I do?' implores Ingvar, the new boyfriend, and one can see his dilemma: Yola is painfully pretty. As she says, 'They either want me and they do what I say, or they can go.'

'The way they go to the toilet is just another example of why men are so bad. They watch football, they have not good manners. Women have had enough.'

Jasper Gerard, 'Absolutely Potty,' *The Spectator*, 22 April 2000

psychologically healthy, mature and truly democratic society. An important part of the game of Disguised Defection is to erode the discrimination of the opponent, because this disrupts his ability to recognise defection.

Creative transduction

Advanced transduction to create benefit

Facilitating the policy of transduction, actually an advancement of it, is the procedure called *creative transduction*: generating or inventing a problem for the purpose of blaming someone else. A trivial example would be a female giving evasive and non-committal replies on the telephone, then accusing the male of harassment when he persists, wanting nothing but a conclusive answer. More seriously, she might goad a male until he threatened or struck her, at which point she calls the police with an accusation of domestic violence, using the crisis she provoked to have him forcibly removed.

Women are never satisfied. Divorce in the 1920s

Being a long-term monogamous relationship, with a lock-in, marriage satisfies virtually every female instinct yet often she is still not satisfied with it. Women are never satisfied; likely this insatiability has contributed to our rapid evolutionary development. Now there is practically a state of anarchy in relations between the sexes: a large number never marry and of those that do, many divorce.

One snapshot in time can be quoted from the 1920s. Then it was considered chivalrous for a husband to arrange to be discovered in a hotel room with a woman not his wife, who was brought in specially for the purpose. Being found alone with another woman in such circumstances was regarded as proof of adultery, and this charade was performed by a husband to grant his wife an easy and respectable divorce. Current female dissatisfaction with relationships largely derive from the ethos they have themselves fostered.

Creating the problem of over-population

Arguably the dire environmental condition of the earth, with many species facing extinction, is an example of creative transduction whereby females create problems and then blame males. Masculine industry and technology are blamed for their polluting effects but the true cause of the current environmental crisis is over-population. If the world's population were a tenth of its current level, as it was as recently as 1750, then the global effect of our presence would be insignificant. Our living standards would also be vastly improved.

Fake hate crimes

Pure examples of creative transduction

A phenomenon which demonstrates creative transduction in pure, unadulterated form is fake hate crimes. In these, crimes are later discovered to have been perpetrated by the supposed victims. Scores of these have been documented, notably by Laird Wilcox. Initial reports are given great prominence in the media but on discovery of the perpetrator the reportage tends to be rather more muted. A few which have taken place since Wilcox's 1995 compilation are listed.

Non-white police officers in London received messages saying 'Not wanted. Keep the police force white. Leave now or else.' The sender was Gurpal Virdi, a Sikh police sergeant, who had been denied promotion. ('Sikh seeks sneaky solution' *Guardian*, 4 March 2000.)

Kerri Dunn, a psychology professor at Claremont McKenna College, claimed that her car was vandalised and painted with 'racist, anti-Semitic and sexist epithets' on 9 March 2004 while she was preparing 'a lecture for a forum on racism.' Shortly afterwards two thousand students and faculty rallied to protest against 'hate crime.' Dunn, who had said she was considering converting from Catholicism to Judaism, was sentenced to a year's imprisonment for filing a false police report and attempted insurance fraud. (*LA Times*, 18 March 2004; AP, 15 December 2004.)

During local elections in Ajoie, Switzerland, in October 2006 'racist' flyers were found pasted on walls targeting mixed-race socialist candidate Yannick Erard. This brought suspicion on the conservative opposition party who favoured immigration control, and Erard won the election. Police found one of Mr Erard's fingerprints on the back of a flyer and he admitted pasting them up himself. (Radio and TV reports, 8 January, 10 January and 21 February 2007.)

Signs were vandalised with the word 'Nazis' and painted with swastikas at the Baltimore Hebrew Congregation and Beth Tfiloh Community School in Pikesville, Maryland. Three Jewish teenagers, Matthew Ian Saunders, Daniel Alexander Diaz and an unnamed 17-year-old were later found to be responsible. (WBAL-TV News, 6 October 2008.)

Quinn Matney, a homosexual student at the University of North Carolina, claimed to have been attacked with a scalding hot piece of metal and told 'Here's a taste of hell, you fucking fag' on 4 April 2011. The report was later admitted to be false. On 11 June 2011 another homosexual, Ryan Grant Watson, a University of Iowa graduate student, made a similar false claim involving an attack and anti-homosexual abuse. Both men were charged with submitting false police reports.

Sharmeka Moffitt, a 20-year-old black woman in Louisiana, claimed in October 2012 to have been set on fire by three men who also scrawled the initials KKK on her car in toothpaste. She had burns over more than half of her body and was in a critical condition. The incident was considered a possible hate crime until it emerged a day later that the wounds were self-inflicted.

The paradox that many practitioners of transduction are also susceptible to it

Populations vary greatly in their ability to transduce and their susceptibility to it. Paradoxically it seems that groups who are adept at transduction are themselves susceptible to it. One would think that those who practice transduction would be aware of the mechanism and hence resistant to it. The paradox is resolved however with the proposal that two populations exist: those that are unaware that their enhancement or diminishment of others is false, and those who are conscious that it is.

The former group believe what they are saying, and are simply applying a view or opinion which others have given legitimacy. Their transduction will be unconscious if their world-view is absorbed from others or they have a tenuous grasp on reality.

The latter group, who are aware that the feelings they induce are false, is more culpable.

Challenge signals and overt challenges. Challenges are expressions of defiance and can take subtle as well as overt forms. When young lovers are at play, the girl will put her nose in the air and adopt a posture of mock disdain, inviting a physical response from her boyfriend. A woman may ostentatiously lean back on a chair while operating a computer, or arrogantly lean against a photocopy machine. The presence of a male is required for such a signal to be emitted, but in the presence of a perceptive one the display will be short-lived. Challenge signals are a means by which power can be continually tested and incremented when a response is not forthcoming.

Overt challenges are impelling: they demand a response. They require attention, and secure a relationship by the involvement they demand. Challenges call for a limit to be imposed, pleading for the boundaries of acceptable behaviour to be made explicit; it may be an instinctive request for subjugation. Overt challenges take the form of confrontations with authority and subversive acts; they are ambiguous in intention if not in form. A good example of an overt challenge is knocking off a policeman's helmet – in former times, in the right circumstances, this could have been regarded simple high jinks.

Dispersive procedures

The class of behaviours called *dispersive procedures* serve to diffuse normal male responses such as anger and dismay. Their obvious manifestation in everyday British life is light-hearted jests, when someone makes a trivial request and the reply is No. Another common dispersive procedure is suggesting payment for something which is normally free.

Jests which test

A female working behind a bar is asked for a glass of water by a male. Initially the request is refused, superficially as a joke. However this enables her to gauge his reaction and test her ability to refuse in earnest. The dispersive procedure is a precursor to a definite refusal being made, and in the absence of appropriate male responses it eventually will be. Under conditions of strong feminine influence such refusals will made with irritating frequency and sometimes in complete seriousness.

When a pleasantry ceases to be one. Dispersive procedures more generally

Governments sometimes informally leak a prospective policy to the media to test reaction to it; this is another example of a dispersive procedure. A policy might be proposed, to great objection, but after measuring or exhausting the opposition a milder version can be successfully introduced. Alternatively if the opposition is formidable the policy may be abandoned.

The Psychic Assault

1. The psychic assault is essentially a political manoeuvre. The female manipulates the male into a position where she could have sex but refrains from doing so.
2. She maintains the male in a state of arousal or false expectation.
3. She scores points to satisfy and bolster her ego.
4. She evokes images of granting sexual favours to another (the more perverse her selection, for this purpose, the better) but grants them to the male or males in her audience either rarely or never.
5. She quits from a male suddenly or prematurely, because she prefers to assault rather than engage in a proper relationship.
6. She grants and withdraws sexual favours to a male with whom she is involved in a relationship without logic or reason.

In the State of Texas until 1974 it was legal for a husband to kill his wife and her lover if he found the two having intercourse.

Females always go too far

The Challenge signal is another form of dispersive procedure. The female continually tests her power and ultimately elicits subjugation by overplaying her hand. Applying supra-maximization, she cannot resist taking the maximum possible payoff. Females always go too far.

The psychic assault

Confounding the male. The origin of the name 'bikini'

The psychic or mental assault, colloquially the 'mindfuck,' serves to spite and confound the male. The confused and disoriented male is easier to manipulate. This behaviour can be so disturbing to fundamental male instincts as to be the sexual-political equivalent of the nuclear bomb. (The bikini was so named because of its 'explosive effect' on males, nuclear tests being conducted around that time at Bikini Atoll.)

Psychological instead of physical torture

When soldiers were captured in former battles against Afghans and American Indians, the prisoners were turned over to their women to be slowly tortured to death. The women enjoyed their work and excelled at it. The psychic assault may be its Western equivalent, applied not physically but psychologically. It has profound mental effects on males, potentially contributing to the incidence of spree and serial killers. The psychic assault is a display of power, and also constitutes a challenge.

Addiction to women

The psychic assault could explain the addictive attachment a male can acquire to a lap-dancer. The male might instinctively regard the assault as a trial. The trial is a regular staple of popular romantic narrative – in fairy tales the knight must slay a fearsome dragon to win the hand of the beautiful princess. The male might interpret his adversity as an endurance through which he must pass to achieve his goal.

Could this be the model for other forms of addiction? National lotteries also maintain their customers in a state of false expectation. Although rationally everyone knows that their chances of winning are minute, the disappointment in people's demeanour when they check their tickets to find they have not won is plain to see.

Giving females a voice and allowing them to express their views on contemporary social problems is like asking the Devil for advice on how to cure sin. The weight of human misery and downright trouble, not to mention evolutionary damage, caused by allowing a small segment of the population, the fortunate, attractive, reproductive females, free rein of their instincts is enormous. So much of the social cruelty which is routinely being inflicted, and the burden of guilt arising from it, would be prevented if more normal relations between the sexes could be achieved.

The changes brought about through the women's movement may have decreased women's happiness. The increased opportunity to succeed in many dimensions may have led to an increased likelihood of believing that one's life is not measuring up. Similarly, women may now compare their lives to a broader group, including men, and find their lives more likely to come up short in this assessment. Or women may simply find the complexity and increased pressure in their modern lives to have come at the cost of happiness.

'The Paradox of Declining Female Happiness,' *American Economic Journal: Economic Policy*, 2009

14 Concluding Matters

Consequences and conclusions

More important than power is what is done with it, and a weak person given power becomes not strong but strongly weak. Influence and the denial of patrimony are discussed, with a few conclusions.

We should take care not to confuse *normal* with *usual* – for it is perfectly feasible that abnormal behaviour be routine. Some like to claim that there is no such thing as normal – 'What's normal anyway?' – but this is being disingenuous. Petty criminals habitually burgle and steal, which is abnormal behaviour. Nor has it in most cases anything to do with mental illness. Many abnormal behaviours of lesser degree exist which are not specifically proscribed. While normality obviously incorporates a range of behaviour, Procedural Analysis, especially by its breakdown of signals, markers, tokens and handles, can objectively determine what is normal and abnormal in everyday social interaction.

What is usual is not necessarily normal

Elevated female influence results in greater emphasis being placed on emotion. Females have not historically inhibited their own and each others' instincts; the male performed that role, and without his influence irrational fear will flourish. The more latitude the female is allowed, the more her capricious instincts will be expressed, the more she will project her nature onto the male and the more insecure of his intentions she will become. A reinforcing cycle of fear is established.

The more latitude the female is allowed...

Then any proposal will be construed as a token for sex; she will actually become incapable of giving a correct telephone number or address. She will start to give her address or telephone number then cross it out, claiming that she cannot remember it. Or she may try and change it, realise her predicament and then dictate it. In any event the final details will be incorrect.

Anything can be interpreted as a token

When males see females unreservedly following their instincts they want to do the same. Indeed the absence of inhibition by females has a pervasive effect on males, making control of their own impulses an increasingly arduous burden. Males will also find it difficult not to show their emotions, putting them at a disadvantage in their interactions with females. Of course a male who followed his instincts to the same extent would quickly find himself imprisoned.

Effect of female disinhibition

Females projecting their capricious nature onto males largely accounts for their trepidation of guns and other weapons. The female becomes so divorced from cold, rational self-mastery that she can only imagine the weapon being used. Less than a century ago national figures, including Hitler, were able to stand and wave during motorised processions along crowded streets at a time when civilian gun ownership was commonplace. That was a more masculine era, but it would be unthinkable today – now even the Pope rides behind bullet-proof glass.

The former, masculine attitude to weapons

Peer group loading

The degree to which people are influenced by an event depends very much on its source. For example, you the reader could be attacked by an Albanian, a friend of yours could be attacked and tell you about it, or you could read of someone being attacked by an Albanian in a newspaper. Each incident would likely make a person wary of Albanians, but to very different degrees.

Different types of influence

It is proposed that three levels exist, and these levels are fundamentally different for males and females. Two sexes, three levels makes six classes of influence, which are weighted (loaded) by different amounts. The scheme is referred to as *peer group loading*, PGL.

Three levels for each sex

MALE	FEMALE
Individual	Personal
Peer	Relational
Societal	Community

Females almost always reduce things to the personal. An observation by a male is likely to be interpreted by her as being specific to him in some way. Her instrinsic bias is toward matters of personality and personal experience and the extent to which this outlook can be applied is limited. In contrast, with his ability to objectively isolate themes, the male can regard the individual, and thus himself, in the abstract.

Females always relate in personal terms

Indeed it seems that our 'sense of self' is really an illusion, the product of an evolutionary short-cut. Without this illusion we would need a separate organ overseeing the brain, and that would need a higher organ overseeing that, and so on.

His capacity for abstraction gives the male comprehension of societal dynamics and the conflicting and complementary forces within it. The female emphasis on personality and her natural inclination toward familial concerns severely limit her appreciation of national affairs.

National affairs are a male province

In another expression of DSoD the female will fiercely insist on the uniqueness of her personality, stressing her personal likes and dislikes, while being strikingly, sometimes astonishingly, conformist.

It is difficult to identify a female instinct that does not derive from mate-selection or child-rearing. Her instincts are consistent with her evolutionary role, and increasing the cost of sex is the instinct that underlies all others. Many of these instincts are anachronistic, especially if we consider the extent to which contraception and scientific advances can reduce the cost of sex. Females insist on instinctive behaviour, demanding anachronistic behaviour from males.

Female instincts are anachronistic

Male instincts are generally valid. Without doubt, expressions of male sentiment can be unintelligent, embarrassingly crude and sometimes plain wrong, but in the aggregate they are reliable. Because of their relevance to wider society, male instincts deserve precedence.

Male instincts deserve precedence

There are plenty of exceptions, though most times their infrequency merely confirms the general rule. The exceptional female who prevails in a masculine setting illustrates how seldom this can be achieved. A few females express male traits, a greater number can competently imitate males. More often the environment will have been grossly modified to allow her to thrive.

Any middle course is seen as safe

Female avoidance of risk means that radical solutions to society's problems will be abhorred, even when radical measures are necessary. Notwithstanding, feminized societies are unstable, hence shifts in public opinion can take place relatively quickly. One proposal was of Super-Masculine and Super-Feminine States:

1. The Super-Masculine State dominates;
2. The Super-Feminine State becomes extinct.

Invalidity of instinct: The train driver. When someone jumps or falls in front of a train, for example on the London Underground, a large proportion of drivers have to change jobs or take early retirement. They cannot help feeling somehow responsible. Until 1855, on the invention of the steam railway, no-one had ever travelled faster than a galloping horse. The basis of the train driver's guilt is that he is a man running or riding across a field, and as he travels he sees a walker, but does not change direction to avoid him. The high level of guilt on killing a walker is consistent with the low likelihood of a fatality when moving at what would, for most of our evolutionary history, have been natural speed. In evolutionary terms the train driver is a runner or rider; now however, he is controlling a machine which goes only backwards and forwards and takes hundreds of metres to stop. His instincts have not caught up with technology.

Women and politics

A weak person given power becomes not strong, but strongly weak. Machiavelli is the great master of power politics and an analogy in his style would be of a weak and indecisive king. An enemy is gathering at the border. His generals clamour for a pre-emptive attack, but the king uses his power to overrule them and nothing happens. Soon the moment to strike is lost and the army invades, toppling the prevaricating king.

A weak person given power. Inevitable domination by a more masculine opponent

Such is the situation with a feminine population – over-sensitive, critical of itself, tolerant of its enemies and doomed to domination by a more masculine one.

The modern phenomena of relatively youthful, physically attractive political leaders, having a large segment of the electorate still undecided a few weeks before an election, and bloated bureaucracies, are all symptoms of feminization. It has been claimed that due to the female vote balding politicians of any stripe are unelectable. The last bald prime minister was Churchill (1951) and no bald American president has been elected since Eisenhower (1953). An interesting comparison may be made with the practice of some American Indian tribes, who would elect a chief solely on the length of his hair.

Fickle electorates. Balding political leaders

One rare study found a direct link between female influence and size of government. There was a consistent pattern of dramatically increased American State spending shortly after women started voting. In some cases expenditure more than tripled.

Female voting leads to big government

To the extent that modern society is male-dominated, male power is only allowed insofar as it is to females' benefit. Thus an army or police force is

Did women's suffrage change the size and scope of government? This was the question asked in a 1999 study by Lott and Kenny published in *The Journal of Political Economy*. The answer was a resounding Yes.

Although the 19th amendment to the US Constitution giving women the vote was approved in 1920, the states implemented it at different times. Women got the vote in four states even before 1900, in eight states between 1910 and 1914, and in 17 states in 1917-19. This staggered introduction enabled the influence of economic change and events such as the First World War to be excluded.

'Although a number of women took advantage of their new right to vote immediately, it took several decades for turnout to fully adjust. We find the growth in female voter turnout to be positively associated with the expansion of government.'

masculine, by its hierarchical structure, ability to exercise force and power to punish, but it can be, and is, directed by politicians to further feminine goals.

Consequences

Most males work to benefit females

A not insignificant matter is female longevity. Men die several years sooner than women on average, so usually a wife inherits her husband's wealth. This is a routine, wholesale transfer of wealth from males to females. Traditionally legacies were left to male heirs.

Accounting for the ferocity of civil wars

Darwin observed that 'the competition is always the most severe between the most closely allied species.' Similar species compete for the same resources, and that competition will intensify when resources become scarce. This law accounts for the acrimony of disputes between neighbours and the notorious ferocity of civil wars. Veale argued in his flawed classic *Advance to Barbarism* that the Second World War was effectively a civil war between European rivals. The DSoD theory is pertinent here and again, paramount to any consideration of strategy is the choice of adversary.

Males' contribution is dismissed. A dysgenic society

Denial of patrimony is now taking place on a massive scale. Marker transformation and similar manipulations allow females to exploit male-derived amenities unthinkingly. A feminine media constantly evokes the 'men and women' of our armed forces and the 'men and women' who did historic deeds. Our masculine heritage, including millennia of inventive effort and battles fought at great personal cost, is denied and dismissed. By any objective measure women's historical legacy is practically zero.

The reality today is that women's contribution to progress is minor and the advances they have achieved owe their genesis to systems and technology developed by males. In its aggregate, feminine influence is profoundly dysgenic. As a consequence Western societies are not evolving but regressing.

Instincts are the source of emotion and emotion is the ultimate engine of behaviour. What is happiness but the contented satisfaction of our basic desires? But, as has been described, emotions can be manipulated. Given the existence, if not the prevalence, of false emotions we would be wise to confront our many problems, and particularly to identify their origin, with rational minds and cool heads.

Bibliography

Adam's Curse, A Future Without Men, Bryan Sykes, Bantam Press (London) 2003.

Advance to Barbarism: The Development of Total Warfare From Sarajevo to Hiroshima, F.J.P. Veale, Mitre Press (London) 1968.

All About Women: What Big Sister Doesn't Want You to Know, 2nd ed., Simon Sheppard, Heretical Press (Carshalton, Surrey) 2015.

The Book of General Ignorance: A Quite Interesting Book, John Lloyd and John Mitchinson, Faber (London) 2008.

Brainsex: The Real Difference Between Men and Women, Ann Moir and David Jessel, Mandarin (London) 1989.

Cannibals and Kings: The Origins of Cultures, Marvin Harris, Random House (NY) 1977.

Crying Wolf: Hate Crime Hoaxes in America, Laird Wilcox, Editorial Research Service (Olathe, Kansas) 1995.

Decline and Fall of the Freudian Empire, H. J. Eysenck, Viking 1985.

The Descent of Man and Selection in Relation to Sex, 2nd ed., Charles Darwin, John Murray (London) 1901.

Divorced Dads: Shattering the Myths, Sanford L. Braver and Diane O'Connell, Penguin Putnam (NY) 1998.

Evolution and the Theory of Games, John Maynard Smith, Cambridge University Press 1982.

The Evolution of Desire: Strategies of Human Mating, David M. Buss, Basic Books (NY) 2003.

Flipnosis: The Art of Split-Second Persuasion, Kevin Dutton, William Heinemann (London) 2010.

The Great Sex Divide, Glenn Wilson, Peter Owen (London) 1989; Scott-Townsend (Washington D.C.) 1992.

A History of the Modern World: From 1917 to the 1980s, Paul Johnson, Weidenfeld & Nicolson (London) 1983.

Introductory Psychology, Tony Malim and Ann Birch, Macmillan 1998.

Jewish History, Jewish Religion: The Weight of Three Thousand Years, Israel Shahak, Pluto Press (London) 1994.

Libido Dominandi: Sexual Liberation and Political Control, E. Michael Jones, St. Augustine's Press (South Bend, Indiana) 2005.

The Manipulated Man, Esther Vilar, Abelard-Schuman 1972; Pinter & Martin (London) 2008.

The Miseducation of Women, James Tooley, Continuum (London) 2002.

Modesty in Dress, James Laver, Heinemann (London) 1969.

The Naked Woman: A Study of the Female Body, Desmond Morris, Jonathan Cape (London) 2004.

Prisoner's Dilemma, William Poundstone, Doubleday (NY) 1992.

The Selfish Gene, Richard Dawkins, Oxford University Press 1976.

The Tyranny of Ambiguity: An Account of the Development of a System of Human Behaviour Analysis called Procedural Analysis, 2nd ed., Simon Sheppard, Heretical Press (Carshalton, Surrey) 2013.

The Woman Racket: The New Science Explaining How the Sexes Relate at Work, at Play and in Society, Steve Moxon, Imprint Academic (Exeter) 2008.

Woman and Socialism, August Bebel, Socialist Literature Company (New York) 1910.

Index